Women and Working Lives

Divisions and Change

Edited by

Sara Arber
Senior Lecturer in Sociology
University of Surrey

and

Nigel Gilbert
Professor and Head of Department of Sociology
University of Surrey

First edition 1992
Reprinted 1994

Published by
THE MACMILLAN PRESS LTD
Houndmills, Basingstoke, Hampshire RG21 2XS
and London
Companies and representatives
throughout the world

ISBN 0–333–56534–7 hardcover
ISBN 0–333–61814–9 paperback

A catalogue record for this book is available
from the British Library.

Copy-edited and typeset by Povey–Edmondson
Okehampton and Rochdale, England

Printed in Great Britain by
Antony Rowe Ltd
Chippenham, Wiltshire

EXPLORATIONS IN SOCIOLOGY

**Published by Macmillan*

Series Standing Order

If you you would like to receive future titles in this series as they are published, you can make use of our standing order facility. To place a standing order please contact your bookseller or, in case of difficulty, write to us at the address below with your name and address and the name of the series. Please state with which title you wish to begin your standing order. (If you live outside the UK we may not have the rights for your area, in which case we will forward your order to the published concerned.)

Standing Order Service, Macmillan Distribution Ltd, Houndmills, Basingstoke, Hampshire, RG21 2XS, England

Contents

Part II Breaking Male Definitions of Work

List of Tables and Figures

Tables

List of Tables and Figures

Figure

Preface

The chapters in this book are based on presentations at the British Sociological Association Annual Conference held at the University of Surrey in April 1990 on the theme of *Social Divisions and Social Change*. The conference was organised by Sara Arber, Nigel Gilbert, Roger Burrows and Catherine Marsh. Two of the chapters in the book were from a conference panel session organised by Julia Brannen. Three other volumes of conference papers are published simultaneously: *Consumption and Class: Divisions and Change* (edited by Roger Burrows and Catherine Marsh), *Fordism and Flexibility: Divisions and Change* (edited by Nigel Gilbert, Roger Burrows and Anna Pollert), and *Families and Households: Divisions and Change* (edited by Catherine Marsh and Sara Arber).

We should like to thank all those who gave papers, the organisers of the panel sessions and those others who contributed to the success of the conference. In particular, we would like to thank the contributors to this volume, and Anne Dix and Sheila Tremlett of the British Sociological Association for all their encouragement and support. The Department of Employment is gratefully acknowledged for permission to reproduce Figure 5.1, and for permitting the publication of Chapter 6 which is based on research which it funded.

SARA ARBER
NIGEL GILBERT

Notes on the Contributors

Sheila Allen is Professor of Sociology at the University of Bradford. She has researched and written extensively in areas of work, employment, gender and race and ethnic relations. Her recent books include: *Homeworking: Myths and Realities*, 1987 (with C. Wolkowitz); *Gender Divisions Re-visited*, 1990 (ed. with D. Leonard); *Race and Social Policy*, 1988 (with M. Macey). She is a past President of the BSA.

Sara Arber is a Senior Lecturer in Sociology at the University of Surrey. She is co-author of *Doing Secondary Analysis*, 1988, and *Gender and Later Life*, 1992. She has published widely on inequalities in women's health, social stratification, informal care and gender issues in later life.

Julia Brannen is Senior Research Lecturer at the Thomas Coram Research Unit, Institute of Education, University of London, and has done extensive work on families and households. She is co-editor of *Give and Take in Families*, 1987, and co-author of *Marriages in Trouble*, 1982, *New Mothers at Work*, 1988, and *Managing Mothers*, 1991.

Kay Richards Broschart is Professor of Sociology at Hollins College, Roanoke, Virginia, USA. Her current research focuses on the history of women in the social sciences. She is author of articles on women in the professions, the family and adult development.

Richard Brown is Professor of Sociology at the University of Durham. He was President of the BSA, 1983–5, and the first editor of the BSA journal, *Work, Employment and Society*, 1986–9. Co-author of *The Sociology of Industry*, 4th edition, 1981, and editor of *U.K. Society: Work, Urbanism and Inequality*, 1984. He has also written many papers on work and employment.

Shirley Dex is Senior Lecturer in Economics at the University of Keele. She has published a number of books on women's employment: *The Sexual Division of Work*, 1985, *British and American Women at Work*, 1986 (with L. B. Shaw), *Women's Occupational Mobility*, 1987, and *Women's Attitudes towards Work*, 1988.

Jean Duncombe is a Senior Research Officer for the British Household Panel Study, University of Essex, working on a qualititative project concerning inter and intra-household allocations of financial resources. She is co-author of *Scheming for Youth*, 1989 (with D. Lee, D. Marsden and P. Rickman). Her current research interest is in the allocation of emotional resources.

Nigel Gilbert is Professor of Sociology at the University of Surrey. His recent books include *Opening Pandora's Box: a Sociological Analysis of Scientific Discourse*, 1984 and *Computers and Conversation*, 1990. He has written many papers on social stratification, the sociology of science and cognitive science.

Gillian Leighton is a feminist and mother. She previously taught at Anglian Higher Education College, Cambridge, and currently teaches in Ipswich and lectures part-time for the Open University and the University of Maryland. Her research interests are the sociology of work, gender relations, the family and marriage.

Madeleine Leonard is a Lecturer at Queen's University, Belfast. She has recently completed a PhD thesis which examines informal work strategies in a Belfast working-class community.

Fiona Poland is Development Officer at the Research Exchange, University of Manchester, and has worked in applied survey and ethnographic social research for over 10 years. Her publications explore ways of developing useful and accessible research methods in relation to informal care and community issues. She is nearing the completion of her PhD.

Ian Procter is Lecturer in Sociology at the University of Warwick, and a member of the ESRC/CNRS sponsored research team on Unemployment and Attitudes to Work in Britain and France. He is author of *Service Sector Workers in a Manufacturing City*, 1988.

Peter Ratcliffe is Lecturer in Sociology at the University of Warwick, and a member of the ESRC/CNRS sponsored research team on Unemployment and Attitudes to Work in Britain and France. He is author of *Racism and Reaction*, 1981, and has written in the areas of race, ethnicity, research methods and housing.

Jacqueline Scott is Director of Research, ESRC Research Centre on Micro-social Change in Britain, University of Essex. She is author of recent articles on generations and collective memories; conflicting beliefs about abortion; gender differences in parental stress; and response effects. Her current research is on the impact of socio-economic change on family life.

Carole Truman is Lecturer in Social Policy, Manchester Metropolitan University. She has researched and written on many aspects of women's work and employment including flexible work, new technology, women returners, equal opportunities and the experience of self-employed women.

Patricia Walters is Senior Lecturer in Sociology at the University of Salford. She is joint author of *Women and Top Jobs 1969–1979*, 1981. She has researched women's employment in Britain and France focusing on the impact of state policies, and is currently working on a comparison of feminisation of the legal profession in France and Britain.

1 Re-assessing Women's Working Lives: An Introductory Essay

Sara Arber and Nigel Gilbert

The nature and extent of women's participation in waged work is intimately connected with their unpaid domestic labour as mothers and housewives. Two primary concerns orient this collection of papers from the 1990 British Sociological Association conference: first, to examine alternative explanations for the persistence of gender inequality in the labour market, focusing on the ideology of motherhood, the domestic division of labour and the impact of gendered social policies. Second, to question the meaning of work, suggesting that a simple dichotomy between waged work and unpaid domestic labour is inadequate to describe the contemporary situation of women. Between waged work and unpaid domestic labour are various forms of self-employment, petty enterprise and exchanges used by women to generate resources. These strategies are both constrained and enabled by women's domestic lives and their networks of personal and social relationships.

A subtheme of this collection is divisions among women. Women's working lives are fundamentally influenced by the composition of their family and their stage in the life course. Unlike the 1930s when the key marker was marriage (see Chapter 2), today it is the birth of the first child which signals a major change in waged work and domestic labour. Parental status divides women and for this reason many of the chapters focus solely on mothers. Such a focus can lead to the assumption that childcare is the only constraint on women's occupational achievement, neglecting more broadly based gender ideologies and the discriminatory practices of employers.

Another key division is class. The important differences between women are not those suggested by the conventional measures of husbands' class, but stem from women's own positions in the labour market. Women in professional occupations are more similar to their

1

male co-workers in terms of occupational achievement and earnings than women in lower level clerical, service and manual occupations are to their male counterparts (Crompton and Sanderson, 1990). State and employment policy changes may be producing greater class divisions among women with children. In the UK, highly educated women in the professions and management are supported by maternity legislation and employer's child care facilities which help them to combine full-time employment and motherhood (see Chapters 4 and 7). Provisions which are advantageous to high-earning women bring little gain for the vast majority of mothers who, in Britain at least, generally interrupt their waged work during the early years of child-rearing.

A strength of this collection is that all the chapters draw on recent empirical data to address the disadvantaged position of women in the labour market and to uncover hitherto neglected aspects of women's working lives. A wide range of methodologies is used including large-scale surveys (Chapters 3 and 6), oral histories (Chapter 2), in-depth interviews (Chapters 9 and 10) and ethnography (Chapter 12). Four chapters present cross-national data: Scott and Duncombe analyse whether national ideologies about women's role can explain the divergent nature of women's employment participation in the USA and UK; Walters and Dex, and Procter and Ratcliffe compare France and Britain to assess how far government policies and national ideologies of motherhood explain the different pattern of women's labour force participation and occupational achievement in these two societies; and Broschart takes the USSR as a case study of a society which has a long history of legal sex equality in employment and where women form a majority of the labour force, yet substantial horizontal and vertical sex-segregation remains.

Contributors in the first part of the book address a range of explanations for women's disadvantaged position in the labour market and lack of occupational achievement. In the second part, contributors question the adequacy of male definitions of work for women, showing that women use a range of strategies, intimately connected with their domestic lives, to produce resources. Before outlining these themes, an overview of the key characteristics of women's participation in the labour market in the next section will provide a factual backcloth to the specific studies in each chapter.

WOMEN'S LABOUR MARKET PARTICIPATION AND OCCUPATIONAL ACHIEVEMENT

Women's position in the labour market may be described in terms of five key characteristics:

(1) Women's labour market participation has increased markedly since 1960 in all Western countries. Women make up over 40 per cent of the labour force in Britain, the USA and in France (chapters by Walters and Dex, and Scott and Duncombe), and 51 per cent in the USSR (chapter by Broschart).

(2) The recent growth in women's employment in the UK has primarily been an increase in part-time work by married women; 46 per cent of all employed women and 53 per cent of employed married women work part-time (our analysis of 1985–86 General Household Survey). This contrasts with France and the USA where a similar proportion of married women are in paid employment but few work part-time. Chapters 3, 5 and 6 examine explanations for these cross-national differences, including the impact of policies in Britain which make it financially advantageous for employers to hire part-time labour (i.e. demand-led factors) and the lack of adequate child care provision which constrains women to seek work during school hours (supply-led factors influenced by state policies). In Britain, but not in France, part-time compared to full-time employment reduces women's occupational achievement.

(3) Being a parent has a major impact on labour force participation for women, but little effect for men. Only 9 per cent of women with children under five work full-time in the UK, and 23 per cent work part-time (Table 1.1). A fifth of women with school age children work full-time, but a much larger proportion, 44 per cent, work part-time. Table 1.1 shows that the major determinant of UK labour force participation is the age of the youngest child and participation depends only slightly on the woman's own age. Nearly a third of women with children over age 16 in the household work full-time and over a third work part-time. The highest level of participation, 77 per cent, is among women in their forties with older children. For women who have no children (in the household) there is a strong age trend; full-time work decreases with age and part-time work increases with age. (The majority of women over age 40 have had children who have left the parental home.)

Table 1.1   Percentage of women working full-time and part-time by age and age of youngest child, in 1985–6

	20–29	30–39	40–49	50–59	All
Under 5 years					
% Full-time	8	10	8	—	9
% Part-time	20	26	25	—	23
N =	(1312)	(1145)	(84)		(2541)
5–16 years					
% Full-time	17	21	23	19	21
% Part-time	34	46	44	35	44
N =	(211)	(1922)	(1236)	(198)	(3567)
16+ years					
% Full-time	—	46	35	23	30
% Part-time	—	28	43	32	37
N =	(1)	(124)	(980)	(938)	(2043)
No children in household					
% Full-time	74	68	48	29	56
% Part-time	8	12	25	26	16
N =	(2200)	(694)	(639)	(1668)	(5201)
All women					
% Full-time	47	27	32	26	34
% Part-time	14	33	39	29	28
N =	(3724)	(3885)	(2939)	(2804)	(13352)

Source: General Household Survey, 1985–6 (authors' analysis).

The way in which childbearing in Britain is associated with leaving the labour market, taking on part-time employment and returning to lower status and lower paid occupations (occupational downgrading) has been well documented (Martin and Roberts, 1984; Dex, 1987). These negative effects of childrearing are more pronounced in Britain than in France. For example, in Britain only 3 per cent of mothers remain continuously employed, compared to France, where 32 per cent of mothers do so (see chapter by Walters and Dex).

(4)   Horizontal sex-segregation, in which the labour market is divided into typically women's jobs and typically men's jobs, has been prevalent throughout history (Hakim, 1979; Bradley, 1989).

During the Second World War, women entered traditionally male industries such as shipbuilding and munitions, but even within these industries they were recruited to perform different tasks than men (Chapter 2). Horizontal sex segregation is marked even in societies such as the USSR which has had a long history of legal equality for women (Chapter 8). The evidence suggests that horizontal sex segregation is closely linked to inequalities in status, rewards and promotion opportunities. Typically female jobs command lower wages than typically male jobs (Arber, Dale and Gilbert, 1986).

Table 1.2 Women and social class. (a) Proportion of women workers in each class, (b) proportion of part-time workers in each class, (c) median weekly full-time earnings for men and women. Britain, 1985–6

Social class	(a) % women	(b) % part-time	(c) Median full-time weekly earnings Men (£)	Women (£)
Non-manual				
Higher professionals	12%	3%	244	191
Employers and managers	24%	5%	227	152
Lower professionals	61%	24%	197	155
Junior non-manual	75%	33%	167	106
Manual				
Skilled manual	14%	8%	153	92
Semi-skilled and personal service	58%	36%	131	89
Unskilled manual	62%	59%	121	84
All	44%	21%	168	110
N =	(21 588)	(21 588)	(9637)	(4358)

Source: General Household Survey, 1985–6 (authors' analysis).

Within both the non-manual and manual labour markets, the proportions of women and of part-time workers decrease as status and income increase, see Table 1.2. Only 12 per cent of higher professionals and 14 per cent of skilled manual workers are women, compared with 75 per cent of lower level non-manual workers and 62 per cent of unskilled manual workers. Only 3 per cent of higher professionals work part-time compared with nearly three-fifths of unskilled manual workers. Overall, women working full-time earn less than two-thirds the weekly earnings of men (Table 1.2(c)). The earnings gap between men and women narrows among higher professionals, and employers and managers, but is larger for clerical workers and those in skilled manual occupations.

(5) Vertical sex segregation, in which one gender is more likely to be restricted to the lower rungs of an occupational group than the other, is a major source of occupational disadvantage for women in all industrialised societies. Even in the USSR, despite women comprising over three-quarters of the medical profession, under half of all top leadership positions are held by women (Chapter 8), and in other areas of the Soviet economy, such as business and industry, vertical sex segregation is much greater than in the health and education professions.

The above five characteristics of women's labour force position are interlinked and together serve to constrain women's occupational achievement and reduce their income from paid employment. The economic differential between women and men continues to be very substantial. A comparison between the wages of men and all working women (Tables 1.2(c) and 1.3(a)) shows that working women receive much lower weekly wages than men in each class. This is both because of women's lower full-time wages and the high proportion who work part-time. Women's disadvantaged labour market position impacts on their financial well-being in later life, especially through their lesser ability to accrue occupational pension entitlements (Ginn and Arber, 1991; Arber and Ginn, forthcoming).

One way in which women might achieve economic parity with men is to work full-time during the early child-rearing years. Under a tenth currently do so in the UK, but this reaches nearly a quarter among women who are higher professionals, and employers and managers. Table 1.3(b) shows that women with pre-school children have higher weekly earnings in each socio-economic group than other women. Such women need these high earnings in order to finance childcare. Despite their relative economic power, Brannen's chapter demonstrates that mothers with a full-time labour market commitment do not represent a vanguard in terms of their domestic power or equality

Table 1.3 Weekly earnings of women by social class (in pounds), (a) for full-time and part-time workers (b) by age of youngest child for full-time workers. Britain, 1985–6

	(a)			(b) Full-time workers		
Social class	Full-time	Part-time	All	Under 5	5–16	No children/ Aged over 16
Non-manual						
Higher professionals	191	121	171	*	*	185
Employers and managers	152	75	111	155	126	157
Lower professionals	155	72	111	164	157	154
Junior non-manual	106	39	88	115	107	105
Manual						
Skilled manual	92	31	88	92	90	92
Semi-skilled and personal service	89	35	66	105	91	87
Unskilled manual	84	26	44	*	*	85
All	110	38	78	127	113	109
N =	(4538)	(3763)	(8301)	(194)	(668)	(3676)

* Base number less than 20
Source: General Household Survey, 1985–6 (authors' analysis).

in their marital relationship. A number of other chapters focus on the constraints faced by mothers in maintaining their position in the labour market (Chapters 5 and 6).

High levels of labour force participation are not a panacea for women. Waged work may be a precondition for women's economic power, but is not a sufficient condition. Just because women work for wages does not necessarily improve their status or position in the family (Tilly and Scott, 1987). Without a change in the domestic division of labour and with women constrained to low-status, low-paid, often part-time jobs, waged work may have little liberating effect for women. It may simply increase their burden and severely curtail or eliminate any 'unobligated time'. We have little knowledge of the circumstances under which women's paid work changes their power in the family or their domestic roles. Nevertheless, Leighton's chapter shows that employed women whose middle class husbands are unemployed do have economic and domestic power. Their own labour force position has a determining influence on their husbands' subsequent labour market status.

IDEOLOGY AND SOCIAL POLICIES

The chapters in the first part of the book examine the reasons for the persistence of gender inequalities in waged work and the ways in which the web of disadvantage might be broken. Cross-national studies are particularly valuable for this purpose. Three sets of explanations are explored in detail: first, the ideology of women's place being in the home, the ideology of motherhood and the domestic division of labour; second, gendered social policies, which aim to facilitate women's labour force participation; and third, general social policies which are not specifically geared to women, but have an impact on women's labour market position, such as the provision of pre-school education, publicly funded childcare, and the structures of taxation and benefits.

The historical importance of the ideology of women's place is emphasised by Brown. He examines the effects of married women's employment during the Second World War on participation rates after the war, and the consequences of women's employment in what are conventionally regarded as 'men's' occupations, such as shipbuilding, for longer-term changes in patterns of occupational segregation. He argues that these changes did not challenge the gendered division of labour. The women were from shipbuilding communities and accepted their communities' definitions of men's and women's work and the legitimacy of men returning to these jobs after the war. However, the experience of married women's employment had longer-term consequences in fuelling the post-war expansion of women's paid employment.

Scott and Duncombe's chapter starts from the observation that there are gender differences in patterns of employment in the UK and USA, with a higher proportion of mothers in the USA continuing to work full-time. They examine how far these patterns relate to differences in gender-role attitudes between the two countries. Their analysis of large-scale survey data shows that Americans are less likely than the British to assert that women's employment has a detrimental effect on family life, but that in both countries women are still defined as primarily responsible for family care. There is a need for substantial changes in beliefs about gender roles before there is likely to be equality in the domestic and employment spheres. General state policies may be more important than gender role attitudes in explaining these cross-national differences in employment: in Britain, there are state regulated financial incentives for employers to engage part-time labour, whereas in the USA, employer benefits, such as health insurance, are only available to full-time employees, and the ability to offset child care costs against tax encourages mothers to continue to work full-time.

A key group in any discussion of British women's employment is the small proportion of women who return to work full-time following the birth of their first child. Brannen's study examines the popular assumption that where both parents have an equal full-time commitment to paid employment there will be greater equality between parents within both the employment and domestic spheres. This assumption is wrong on several counts. Brannen examines inequalities in domestic roles, marriage and parenting, focusing on the pervasiveness of dominant ideologies about motherhood and the centrality of the mother–child relationship. Women's labour market roles conflict with official discourses, reinforced by powerful agencies and institutions, about 'breadwinners' and 'proper mothers'. Brannen shows how women resolve these contradictions, not by redefining the domestic division of labour in the home, but by a process of accommodation to existing inequalities in domestic roles. Thus, the ideologies of motherhood and marriage remain powerful forces inhibiting change.

A much higher proportion of women with children work continuously in full-time employment in France than in Britain, where the norm is for women to leave employment following the birth of their first child and often subsequently resume part-time employment in a lower status occupation. These cross-national differences have generated substantial research to explain them and to examine their consequences for women's occupational achievement.

Procter and Ratcliffe examine two explanations for the differences between Britain and France. First, French culture is more supportive of women's employment than British culture. This explanation receives only limited support, since there is no evidence that the domestic division of labour is more equitable in France than in Britain and only minor differences are found in attitudes towards working mothers in the two countries. Their second explanation relates to child care. In Britain there is no public support for child care through taxation or the social security system and only minimal publicly funded provision. This contrasts with France where there are both substantial tax allowances for child care and social security provisions to facilitate payment of childminders and employed carers within the child's home, as well as publicly funded nurseries and universal pre-school education from age three upwards. Procter and Ratcliffe conclude that these general social policies and fiscal arrangements facilitate women's continuous full-time labour market participation in France despite the absence of a broader culture to legitimate it.

Walters and Dex use large-scale survey data to examine women's employment in the two societies, finding that French mothers' greater career continuity has positive consequences for their occupational achievement. This contrasts with the disadvantageous consequences of British mothers' more intermittent pattern of working. They conclude that general social policies, such as the provision of nursery education and the structure of taxation rates, are not gender-neutral in their effects. These policies influence mothers' employment continuity and are as important as intentionally gendered social policies that aim to address mothers' labour force participation, such as maternity leave and childcare provision specifically for working mothers.

Truman takes up the theme of gendered social policies in her examination of the UK government's concern that women are a 'wasted economic resource'. She challenges the assumptions which underlie this characterisation and casts doubt on the idea that initiatives by employers will improve the occupational attainment of women. These initiatives are designed to help female employees combine a career with domestic responsibilities. The schemes examined include workplace nurseries, flexible working and job shares, working from home, and re-entry and retainer schemes. All have in common the assumption that women are dependent on men and that women do and should bear the brunt of the responsibility for organising child care and the home. They do not challenge the gendered division of labour in the home and so perpetuate the view that employed women should continue to do a double shift of paid employment and unpaid domestic labour. In addition, the schemes magnify class divisions among women. They are designed for the benefit of employers who wish to retain their most valued, highly trained and highly paid female employees. There is no suggestion by employers or the government that such schemes should be expanded to embrace all women workers.

The final chapter in this part provides a powerful case study of the way in which even a high level of women's labour force participation and formal legal equality for women is insufficient to promote actual equality in either the employment or the domestic sphere. Broschart examines the Soviet Union, where women have had a long history of equal employment rights and there has been an unprecedented pattern of full employment for women. At the same time the state has introduced gendered social policies which have served to maintain and extend the gendered division of domestic labour. The inequitable role obligations of Soviet women are reinforced by protective labour laws and by the lower average pay scales assigned to women's work within an economy with substantial horizontal sex segregation. Protective legislation was enacted to help ease women's dual employment and family burdens, but Broschart shows that one of its effects has been to inhibit women's economic advancement, particularly in terms of vertical occupational mobility. Soviet women assume a heavy and inequitable share of the work of maintaining the family and household and thus, although they officially hold the same constitutional rights as men, they do not enjoy equal status or comparable rewards in the labour market. The ideology of women's place is thus strongly related to women's economic position in the Soviet Union as well as in Western countries.

BREAKING MALE DEFINITIONS OF WORK

The second part of the book examines conventional male derived definitions of paid work. These chapters spring from a feminist concern to open up new areas of investigation and redefine existing issues. It is noteworthy that three of the four chapters are qualitative studies which treat women's lives in a holistic way and probe in depth at everyday experiences and relationships.

These chapters are characterised by a perspective which sees women as active and autonomous, creators of their own working lives. Despite being constrained by their domestic obligations, they use aspects of their domestic roles, personal and work relationships to 'make out'. In these chapters, waged work, informal waged work and petty enterprise are all considered as intimately tied to women's domestic lives and personal relationships. A theme running through these accounts is the way in which material resources facilitate women's engagement in a range of forms of work, with the corollary that the distribution of resources divides women.

Existing sociological research on the wives of unemployed men (Morris, 1985a, 1990; McKee and Bell, 1985) has focused on the wives of working-class men. Leighton's chapter redresses this imbalance by examining the wives of unemployed professional and managerial men living in South East England. She demonstrates that whether a wife is in paid employment influences the timing and nature of her husband's return to the labour market, the way money is organised within the household, the domestic division of labour and marital relations. Her findings cast doubt on conventional class analysis which sees women's economic position as derivative of their husbands'.

Leonard's sample of wives of unemployed working-class men in Belfast represents the other end of the socio-economic spectrum. Because of UK social security regulations, these women were unable to work in the formal economy without their husband's benefit being substantially reduced. This contrasts with Leighton's sample, in which many of the wives continued in formal paid employment because their power in the labour market was such that their earnings were higher than their households' potential benefit entitlement. Because of the disincentive effect of the social security regulations for low paid working wives, the women in Leonard's sample adopted the solution of informal wage labour in order to cope with their family's financial needs.

Leonard reminds us that while unemployed husbands do indeed constrain women's opportunities for formal employment, women may become economically active in other ways. The Belfast wives were employed informally ('off the books') as contract cleaners by employers who operated in the formal economy; such employers have been encouraged by UK government policies of privatisation and subcontracting to minimise their labour costs in this way. On the one hand, the women could be seen as being exploited by employers, but on the other they were adopting their own labour market solutions to meeting their family's needs, while combining work with their traditional housewife role. This chapter demonstrates the ways in which women's work, even in this highly disadvantaged section of the labour market, can provide strong supportive networks between friends, neighbours and relatives, for example when they work for the same contract cleaner.

Britain in the 1980s was said to be an 'enterprise culture', with a strong emphasis on self-employment and small businesses. Academic research activity has reflected this emphasis. However, with a few notable exceptions, most research has failed to consider the gender of the small business owner as an important issue. Existing research is confined either to a genderless model of small business and self-employment, or focuses primarily on male entrepreneurs. Allen and Truman argue that it is not possible to superimpose women's experiences of running a small business or of being in self-employment on to existing models. Instead, women's self-employment and small business activity must be analysed in terms of their disadvantaged position in the formal labour market and their primary role in unpaid domestic labour. Allen and Truman argue that there is a need to employ feminist perspectives to demystify apparently male-oriented entrepreneurial skills. They also suggest that the growing body of work on how paid and unpaid work interact has made little or no impact on research on the relationship between small businesses and the domestic sphere, in respect of both women and men.

In the final chapter, Poland uses ethnography to explore what being self-employed means to women and how self-employment fits into women's everyday lives. She analyses aspects of enterprise which are close to home and constitutive of everyday life. The working-class women she describes are engaged in various types of informal selling that generate income for the women concerned, although this activity would not be counted in conventional surveys of self-employment or labour force participation. Informal selling is an activity which builds on women's responsibility for managing time and relationships. Women use aspects of sociability as a resource in initiating and closing sales, but their scope to develop these further into more sustained self-employment is limited by lack of access to other resources, such as mobility. Most of the women were employed in the formal labour market at least part-time, and in many instances undertook petty selling in their workplaces without management's knowledge. Poland illustrates how women's official and unofficial work is linked, and the role of social ties in structuring informal market exchanges.

Part I

Women's Labour Market Position: Ideology and Social Policies

2 World War, Women's Work and the Gender Division of Paid Labour

Richard K. Brown

The question of the scale and nature of the effects of war on society has long been debated by historians (Marwick, 1968, 1974; Calder, 1971). One issue which features prominently in most discussions of the question is how far wartime experiences can be regarded as having significant consequences for the position of women. In the Second World War the mobilisation of 'womanpower' was very thorough-going and extensive. This gives rise to the question of what effects women's wartime employment had on subsequent patterns of paid work. Two main aspects of this question will be considered in this chapter. Did the employment of many women, especially married women, who had previously been economically inactive, whether through choice or constraint, have consequences for participation rates after the war? Did their employment in what were convention-ally regarded as 'men's' occupations lead to any longer-term changes in patterns of occupational segregation?

The evidence which will be brought to bear on these questions comes from two small-scale studies carried out in the North East of England since 1983. Each involved interviewing women who had been em-ployed in war work between 1939 and 1945. Forty-five women who had worked in the shipbuilding industry on Tyneside and Wearside were interviewed in 1983–4; 70 women who had been employed in the Royal Ordnance Factory at Aycliffe in County Durham, set up during the war for the filling of ammunition, were interviewed in 1988–9. Neither sample can be regarded as in any way representative; they are only a few of the survivors of the workforces employed at the time (forty or more years earlier). They had responded to requests for volunteers to talk about their wartime experiences.

In the case of both industries women volunteered or were con-scripted to undertake entirely unfamiliar work. In shipbuilding the jobs they did were traditionally seen as 'men's work' and the fact that women performed such work successfully in wartime at least implicitly

17

questioned conventional patterns of occupational segregation. The filling of ammunition had customarily been women's work even before the outbreak of war, and the wartime need for it disappeared very quickly as the war ended. The main question in relation to the munitions workers therefore is how far and in what ways did the wartime experience affect levels of economic activity and attitudes to employment of women (and especially married women) after 1945.

As developments since 1945 have illustrated, it is important to keep these questions of changing levels of economic activity and changes in patterns of occupational segregation separate from each other. They do not necessarily co-vary. The period since 1945 has been notable for a steady and continuous increase in the rate of married women's employment. On the other hand, although there is currently consider-able controversy about patterns of occupational segregation (Hakim, 1979; Siltanen, 1990; Walby and Bagguley, 1990), there is no doubt that considerable sex segregation remains. Furthermore, as Walby (1986) and Bradley (1989) have both argued, it is important to consider the ways in which industry specific factors can lead to varying patterns of segregation in different industries.

Oral history interviews cannot, of course, provide a decisive answer to either question, even when they are considered in conjunction with material from other sources. What they do provide is some indication of how those directly involved experienced and reacted to these wartime upheavals. This may go some considerable way to showing how it was that war caused social change or, equally important, in some respects failed to do so. Before considering this evidence in more detail it will be helpful to outline the overall pattern with regard to women's employment during the Second World War and to consider some of the comments others have made about these issues.

WOMEN'S EMPLOYMENT 1939-45

From a situation where there were 13 million men in employment (and more than a million unemployed) in 1939 but fewer than half a million in the armed forces, conscription and the direction of labour increased the numbers of men in the armed forces to more than 4 million by the end of the war. In the process unemployment was virtually eliminated, but the number of men in civilian employment also fell to just over 10 million. About half a million women joined the armed forces, but their civilian employment grew from under 5 million in 1939 to 6 million at its peak in 1943 (Department of Employment, 1971, p. 218, Table 116). Women had constituted just under 30 per cent of the employed population in 1931; by 1943 this had risen to 38.8 per cent (Summerfield, 1989, p. 196). As a result, despite the loss of 2 to 3 million men to the armed forces between 1939 and 1945, the total in civilian employment remained close to its pre-war level until the final two years of the war, and then only fell to a level 1 million lower than before the war.

These overall figures conceal very considerable internal restructuring. Between 1939 and 1943 (the peak year for the mobilisation of women) the number of women in the working population grew by just over two million, an increase of 42.4 per cent; in the same period the number of women employed in the 'metal industries' (which included engineering and shipbuilding) grew from 433 000 to 1.6 million, an increase of 277.6 per cent (Parker, 1957: Table 26, facing p. 210). Many of the women employed in the wartime industries had previously been in employment; the Wartime Social Survey reported that 71 per cent of the women aged 18 to 59 employed in industry in 1943 had been in employment when the war started. In many cases this employment had been in engineering or other manufacturing industries, but 28 per cent had been 'distributive workers, waitresses, etc.', 19 per cent 'labourers and domestics' and 6 per cent in the 'professional, administrative and clerical category' (Thomas, 1944, quoted in Summerfield, 1989, p. 30).

The age and marital status profile of the female labour force also changed. Whereas only 16 per cent of employed women were married in 1931, 43 per cent were in 1943. Reflecting this change, the proportion of women employees aged 24 and under fell from 41 per cent in 1931 to 27 per cent in 1943, whilst the proportion aged 25 to 44 rose from 43 per cent to 57 per cent over the same period (Summerfield, 1989, p. 196, see also pp. 117–18). A more detailed breakdown shows that whilst male employment in shipbuilding (+33%) and in engineering (+13%) grew over the wartime period even though the civilian male workforce declined, the proportionate increase in the number of women employed in these industries was very much greater: from 3000 to 22 000 in the case of shipbuilding and from 102 000 to 434 000 in engineering (Department of Employment, 1971, pp. 213, 215).

Interpretations of the significance of the wartime mobilisation of women workers differ significantly. Summerfield suggests that men and '(feminist) mythology' have, mistakenly, interpreted the wartime experience as bringing greater equality for women, even if the 'encouragement to work' and 'the expansion of collective facilities' were reversed after the end of the war (1989, pp. 185, 190); and Bradley argues that it is 'necessary to challenge the 'optimistic scenario' that 'the war was a liberating experience for women' (1989, p. 47). In contrast to these reported views both these authors argue that the wartime restructuring of employment was much less of a challenge to the gender division of labour than it might seem to be, and led to specific and limited changes.

Summerfield's core argument is that the mobilisation of woman-power took place within a framework of assumptions which perpetuated and even reinforced conventional notions of women's place. The mobilisation gave priority to women's responsibilities for child care and the running of the household. Collective provision for child care (in day nurseries) or of meals (in factory canteens, and British Restaurants) was limited; and neither the government nor employers and retailers would take action which might alleviate the problems of shopping for many women who were also working long hours in industry. Even the growth in part-time work during the war reinforced the 'centrality of women to the home' because it was seen as necessary to allow women to meet 'the needs of men, children and others who could not or would not look after themselves' (1989, p. 146).

Summerfield points out that women 'were admitted [to men's jobs]. . .under agreements which were operated to control and contain the change'. Employers insisted that women could only receive a male rate if they did 'men's work' unaided, and

> trade unionists demanded that women dilutees should be temporary and that the work they had done should be restored to men after the war. . .women were first and foremost the wives, mothers and dependants of men and women did not therefore have the same rights of remuneration for or access to work as men (1989, p. 179).

Summerfield concludes her study by arguing that 'the implementation of official policy during the war did little to alter but rather reinforced the unequal position of women in society' (1989, p. 185). Similarly Bradley points out how wartime experience highlighted the artificial and socially constructed nature of the sexual division of labour and showed how rapidly change could occur under the influence of 'national will' and government power; and laments the 'pertinacity' of men's 'negative views of women's competence' (1989, pp. 47–8).

The mobilisation of women during the war had far less effect on occupational segregation by sex than might have been expected in the light of common-sense understandings of the ways in which women took over 'men's work'. Partly this was due to the controls and constraints Summerfield identifies, but partly also to the fact that work was often 'reorganised' to accommodate women (and justify paying them on women's rather than men's rates) (Bradley, 1989, pp. 47–8). Walby suggests that the outcomes could vary significantly in different industries depending on 'the complex interaction of a number of factors' including 'the extent to which particular groups can mobilize the state' (1986, p. 201).

Walby also points out, however, that the war did affect women's access to employment, and thus their participation in paid work, in two ways: by the removal of the marriage bar and the institutionalisation of part-time work (1986, p. 188). The importance of the first of these changes receives endorsement from Marwick, who refers to it as 'an irreversible trend' (1974, p. 160).

It is important therefore to distinguish between the effects of the wartime experiences of women's employment on the gender division of paid labour, which were not great, and their effects on women's participation in paid work. (A third important question of interest is equal pay (Summerfield, 1989, pp. 174–9).) The war does appear to have initiated a change in women's (and especially married women's) participation rates which continued after the war. The proportion of the female labour force who were married remained at 43 per cent in 1951, the figure it had reached in 1943 (Summerfield, 1989, p. 196); and the proportion of married women in employment, which was only 10.4 per cent in 1931, had more than doubled to 22.5 per cent in 1951 (Census, 1951, p. 131), since when, of course, it has continued to rise. Much of this employment was and has continued to be in part-time work, and this development too may owe something to the wartime experience.

SHIPBUILDING

The North East of England has been one of the major shipbuilding centres in Britain ever since the nineteenth century. In 1938 39 per cent of the tonnage launched in the United Kingdom, and 13.1 per cent of the world's tonnage, was constructed in the region. Over 72 000 men were employed in the industry in Northumberland and Durham in 1931 (and 58 000 in 1951) in each case more than a fifth of the employment in shipbuilding and ship repair in the country as a whole. Locally the proportion of men employed in the industry was very high; for example, over a quarter of all male employees in Sunderland were employed in (or unemployed from) shipbuilding, ship repair and marine engineering in 1931 and nearly 18 per cent in shipbuilding and ship repair in 1951 (Census, 1931; Cousins and Brown, 1970).

The construction and fitting out of a ship requires the completion of a large number of distinct tasks. These have traditionally been carried out by skilled men, who have served apprenticeships, assisted by semi- and unskilled helpers and labourers, and organised in powerful trade unions which have sought to retain exclusive rights for their members to carry out certain work. Given the fluctuations in the demand for ships it is scarcely surprising that workers have vigorously defended their own particular areas of work and resisted threats of dilution – the introduction of less skilled workers to do skilled men's work. With few exceptions (e.g. the First World War) women were not and had not been employed on manual production work in shipbuilding and ship repair.

The introduction of women into shipbuilding occurred more slowly than in many other essential industries. The first national agreements about dilution were signed by employers and unions in 1940, to be followed by other agreements as the war continued (Inman, 1957, pp. 128–9). In the first two years of the war needs for labour were met from the considerable pool of the unemployed (Inman, 1957, p. 93) and then by drawing on workers who had left the industry in the inter-war period. It was not until 1942 that women became a substantial source of labour in the industry. From 1900 workers (0.9 per cent of the labour force) in December 1941 the number of women employed rose to 9000 (3.8%) in December 1942 and 13 000 (5.7%) in December 1943 (Inman, 1957, p. 91; pp. 142–3; pp. 137–8).

In addition to drawing on other sources of labour part of the reason for the slow introduction of women into shipbuilding was the resistance from both employers and men. There were technical obstacles (the need to provide facilities and training) but Inman (1957, p. 127) suggests that 'the basic obstacles to dilution in the shipyards were psychological, and the technical obstacles too often provided not a challenge but an excuse'. Something of the flavour of some employers' attitudes can be gained from the following quotation:

> In September 1939 the shipbuilders put on record the view, which was said to represent the consensus of opinion at the end of the First World War,

that women could only be employed usefully in the yards in so far as they could be segregated within four walls and provided with a separate entrance. It would serve no useful purpose to employ them in open shops or in the ships for, apart from their unsuitability for the work, any increased output obtained by their introduction would be more than offset by loss of output from the men already employed. (Inman, 1957, p. 127, fn. 2)

The Ministry of Labour and National Service recognised the need to overcome this prejudice and in 1943 produced a brochure which was sent to 'all concerned in the shipbuilding industry' to inform them of 'new ideas and new ways in which women can be employed in shipbuilding'. Particular attention was given to women's ability to excel at welding ('the average woman takes to welding as readily as she takes to knitting, once she has overcome any initial nervousness due to the sparks'), at electrical work and at painting, as well as at the 'less skilled though equally essential' work of cleaning ship. Government Training Centres were described as able to provide the necessary training (Ministry of Labour, 1943). These occupations were the ones most frequently found among our respondents.

One of the most notable characteristics of the women who worked in the shipyards in the North East during the Second World War was that they were local. Those we interviewed all came from the shipbuilding communities of Wearside or Tyneside. None of them could recall women coming from other parts of the country to work in the yards. In most cases they had close relatives who worked, or had worked, in the industry; in some cases relatives were important in the woman obtaining a job in the industry.

Not only did many of the women have relatives in the yards, but they were likely both to be known to other workers as well, and to know a good deal about the industry themselves even if they had never previously been inside a shipyard. This had a number of important corollaries. Respondents who had been in their teens or twenties during the war commented that many of the women they worked with had been older; these older women were unlikely to have been compelled to undertake war work, but could do so (and many had financial reasons for wanting to do so) because the work was so close to home. Those who had children could generally call on relatives, especially mothers, to help with child care.

Secondly, the women adjusted to their jobs and to conditions of work in the yards more quickly and easily because neither was completely unfamiliar. The reaction by the overwhelming majority of the women to the experience of working in shipbuilding was highly

positive (Ennis and Roberts, 1987), though of course, those we
interviewed were those who had remained in the industry and enjoyed
the experience enough to want to recall it forty years later. In spite of
their awareness of the very real dangers and difficulties of the jobs they
had to do, the women found working in shipbuilding and repair
something they looked back on with pleasure and enjoyment.

> I have always said they were the happiest years of my life. Mind the job that
> I'm in now – I've been a waitress for years, and I take a pride in it and I
> enjoy it, but . . . – there wasn't the challenge that there was then. You were
> given a need and you gave your all to it, and that was it.

For the women, as with male workers, part of the attraction of
working in a shipyard was the degree of autonomy and a freedom from
close supervision which was much greater than would typically be
experienced in a factory. Another attraction was the nature of the
product, something unique which grew before the workers' eyes and to
which their own contribution was obvious, and in many cases
important. This aspect of work in the industry was heightened by
the important events of launching the completed hull of the ship and
commissioning when fitting out or repairs had been completed.

> the first job that I had, they were laying a keel of a ship, and I was welding;
> and I worked with this [shipwright], like a squad of us, right up until we
> were finished the ship; and it was lovely starting off from the bottom, laying
> the keel, and then it had built up, the sides of the ship and then once the
> shell was up . . . you started working on the little cabins, all the different
> holds and everything . . . I loved the job I was doing; I liked the people I
> worked with, and I wasn't afraid of heights or anything like that – no, not
> then.

Thirdly, the women's overall highly favourable account of their
work in shipbuilding was paralleled by, and indeed perhaps partly due
to, an account of relations with male shipbuilding workers which was
equally positive. Though there were occasional stories of individual
harassment, and some accounts of male hostility to the presence of
women in the yards at all, the main impression given is a very positive
one. Certainly the fears expressed by the employers at the start of the
war proved completely unfounded. Indeed, male workers and particularly older men were reported as being 'protective'. A major influence
on this generally harmonious picture was the fact that the women who
worked in shipbuilding were not strangers; they were frequently the
relatives of male shipbuilding workers, and in all cases neighbours
from the same communities from which the men themselves came.

It is clear then that women were able to adapt to the demands of working in shipbuilding, and that it proved a largely positive experience for them. What is somewhat less clear is how far their employment under wartime conditions represented a real challenge to the long established, rigid, and (in normal circumstances) vigorously defended male monopoly of manual work in the industry. That women worked on manual jobs in shipbuilding at all represents some sort of challenge to the gender division of labour, but there were some features of the experience, as it was recounted in interviews, which made that challenge less than it might have been.

In two important respects the women shared very much the same conditions of work as the men. They worked the same hours, including overtime; and they shared the same basic conditions. These varied a good deal according to job and location: workers in the shops or fitting out a ship would at least be under cover, though it could be very cold, but those on the berths or working on the outside of a ship would be exposed to the elements and could have to contend with heights or confined spaces. Women, however, did have their own 'rest rooms' and in some yards were allowed to leave the job five minutes earlier than the men so as to avoid being caught in the stampede as the men left the yard at midday or at the end of the shift.

Most women employed in shipbuilding were not doing skilled work and received very little or no training. They did not, therefore, challenge the exclusively male control of the skilled work which the majority of manual workers in shipbuilding undertook. In those areas where women were given training, notably as welders (a relatively new job) and electricians, this lasted a few weeks or months rather than the five years of a skilled man's apprenticeship. Nevertheless in some individual cases it appears that a woman worker might gain skills which matched those of the men.

I don't want to sound big headed, but I was rather proficient at my job [welding], and I remember this fellow coming out, and I was going towards my work, and it was a rudder stem. . . And this fellow came over and he says 'That isn't your job, that's mine'. I said 'Oh no, I've been told to do it'. 'I tell you that it's mine – there's no woman allowed to do that sort of thing.' So I just looked, and I thought, oh well honey, you're 6ft. 2ins., or whatever, and I'm not going to argue. So I merely walked over to our foreman and I said 'Would you tell me what I have to do'. And he said 'Yes, that's your job'. So I said 'Well, you tell this gentleman that it is my job, and that I'm capable of doing it, and just let him know this' you see. And he was furious. . . and he was the only one that ever really quibbled.

Otherwise I mean... truly I do believe that any woman, if they are interested, can hold down a job like that with no problem.

The same woman was responsible for training men who had been invalided out of the forces and who had entered the shipyards to try to acquire a skill which would give them a job post-war. She and a number of other women were helped by labourers who were (generally rather elderly) men, a reversal of the 'normal' male/female relationship in the yards.

In contrast to such signs of women gaining access to formerly male skills and tasks, there were a number of features of their situation in the industry which indicated that they remained inferior to the men. Most obviously, with few if any exceptions, women were paid less than men even for the same tasks. According to the agreement with the unions women should be paid 'the full time rate and bonus of the displaced male employee where the woman is able to perform the whole of the duties of the displaced male employee without extra assistance or supervision', and this clause applied to skilled and to semi- and un-skilled work. In most cases it could be claimed that there were some things which women could not, or at least did not, do. Indeed, the protective attitude of male workers might be interpreted rather differently in the light of this clause – and its implications for the future.

A considerable number of those interviewed commented on the way men would help with or take over heavy work, though such help or protection was not universal. One woman's husband, for example, said about her job as a labourer: 'That was one of the heaviest jobs there is in the yard, you know, even now for a man, stage making'; but such a comment was relatively infrequent.

Thus women's employment in shipbuilding and repair during the war cannot be regarded as constituting a major threat to the traditional gender division of labour in that industry, at least in the North East. This was so despite the fact that women demonstrated that they were able to do much of the work, and that their presence in the yards had none of the dire consequences which some had predicted. There were too few of them, and mostly they were only able to undertake what was defined as non-skilled work – or parts of the job of a skilled man. In addition, by accident or design their employment in the yards had several features which emphasised its differences from the 'normal' pattern of men's employment. There were, however, more important reasons why the whole wartime experience made no real long-term impact on patterns of employment in the industry.

The women's positive account of working in shipbuilding was accompanied by expressions of regret that they had had to leave their jobs in the industry at the end of the war. In many cases the reason was pregnancy and subsequent family commitments. In some cases the traditionalist male assumption that a wife should not work outside the home was influential.

> 'Can I ask you how you came to leave the yard?'
> 'To get married. . . . I didn't want to leave, mind. I could have continued on working and that, but Sydney said he wasn't having his wife working in the same department as him. He's old fashioned.'

Most widespread of all, however, was the assumption that the women's jobs in shipbuilding were only 'for the duration', and that the men would want and need them on returning from the forces. 'We just accepted that when we went in, you know, we'd be there until the end of the war.'

One of the main reasons why the women's experience of working in shipbuilding was so positive was that they came from shipbuilding communities, were familiar, at least in a general way, with what working in the industry involved and were known to the men with whom they were working. Equally, however, this meant that they accepted the expectations and definitions of men's and women's work, and men's and women's roles, which were customary in those communities at the time. Their entry into a previously exclusively male world during wartime was made easier by their lifelong involvement in the communities which had grown up around the yards; this same involvement led to an acceptance of the fact that they would and should leave the yards when men were once again available to do the work. This was not a situation in which a sustained challenge to the existing gender division of labour in the industry could be expected.

Of course, even if some of the women had questioned why they should not continue in their wartime occupations there were many other barriers, as one of them found out when she tried, and failed, to obtain further training as an electrician.

Though women's wartime employment in shipbuilding did not challenge the gender division of labour, it may have had an effect, possibly long-term, on women's subsequent participation in the labour market. One of our respondents certainly thought so but her view may be optimistic, given the constraints on women's opportunities for employment, especially in areas like the North East. Our evidence from interviews is far from complete but it suggests that although most of the women undertook paid work at later stages in their lives, it was mostly in the service sector, and in the sorts of jobs which are conventional 'women's work'.

MUNITIONS

The Royal Ordnance Factory at Aycliffe, County Durham, started production in the Spring of 1941. Its establishment as a filling factory was part of the plan greatly to increase capacity for the manufacture of ammunition of all kinds that had been initiated before the start of the Second World War. The growth in the number employed in filling factories in Great Britain was phenomenal, from 8000 in September, 1939 to 160 000 between March and August, 1942. This was the peak figure and numbers declined to 92 000 in March 1945 and 40 700 in September of that year (Hornby, 1958, pp. 91–107; Inman, 1957, pp. 178–86). ROF Aycliffe consisted of about 1000 buildings on an area of 867 acres (Philipson, 1988, pp. 16, 120). Production was carried out in eight groups or departments, divided on the basis of product and/or process, and manufacturing detonators and fuses, bullets, shells, bombs and smoke bombs. As a filling factory Aycliffe received cases and explosives from engineering and explosives factories respectively and undertook the filling, assembly and testing of the final ammunition. In addition, there was a considerable range of ancillary services as well as the central administration.

At its peak the factory employed some 17 000 people, working on three shifts. Whereas women comprised 70 per cent of the labour force in filling factories in the country as a whole, they were about 85 per cent of the labour force at Aycliffe (Inman, 1957, p. 281). Women were the great majority of the manual workforce; the male manual workers, mostly too old or unfit for active service, did maintenance and transport work. In contrast, the more senior management, supervision and technical staff were predominantly male, though there were women labour officers, and women in supervisory and clerical posts.

Production at the factory had ceased by the end of 1945, the run down of the labour force being extremely rapid; the site was quickly taken over for a trading estate, where 6000 workers were employed as early as August 1946. The foundation and development of the new town of Newton Aycliffe followed shortly afterwards (Bowden, 1970; Philipson, 1988).

A major attraction of the Aycliffe site was the availability of a large potential labour force within daily travelling distance of the factory. The factory recruited from within a radius of 25 miles including the Teesside conurbation, Darlington, South West Durham, Durham City and its surrounding villages, and the East Durham coalfield. Workers were brought to the factory by train and bus, and had journeys of up to two hours each way in addition to their eight or nine hour shifts. In contrast to many other munitions factories, there was no hostel accommodation associated with the Aycliffe factory, though a few workers lodged in Darlington (six miles away); nor was there a day nursery for children.

Employment opportunities for women were relatively scarce in the whole area from which the factory sought to recruit, but particularly so in the mining villages. Indeed, the organisation of mining in the Durham coalfield was dependent on considerable inputs of (unpaid) female labour to provide meals, wash clothes and generally meet the needs of those working in the pits (Austrin and Beynon, n.d., p. 35). The woman Chief Labour Officer at Aycliffe commented in her interview:

> when we came up to Aycliffe we didn't want a hostel because there were so many women who could travel in and as you know they put on transport for them. The pit villages, the women . . . there'd been no employment for women; the men worked 'wet' and their clothes had to be washed every time. There were no washing machines so it all had to be done by hand. So, not only could the girls not go out but they had to work at that sort of thing for the men.

The majority of the women interviewed had been single when they started work at the factory and in this respect they were atypical of those working at Aycliffe about whom Inman (1957, p. 281) commented:

> some sixty per cent of these women were married, many with young children to care for. The average age of the women in this factory was thirty four years but well in excess of 1000 were over fifty years of age.

The majority had also had some experience of employment before volunteering or being sent to Aycliffe. Very little of this employment was in factories and most of it involved conventional 'women's work' in shops and offices and, for quite a number, domestic work in people's homes. For almost all those who went to work there the factory represented a quite new sort of experience. Reactions to it differed: 'a marvellous place, a really marvellous place' '. . . even on a nice day it still looked what a prison would look like, and when it was wet and the wind was howling – dreadful!'; but few could fail to be impressed by its size and complexity.

A great variety of work was carried out in the factory. The basic manufacturing processes, which differed considerably in detail depending on the type of ammunition, involved weighing and mixing explosives, making detonators, filling bullets, bombs and shells, and packing them into belts, boxes or other containers. These processes were carefully monitored by overlookers and supervisors, and further inspected by a formally separate group responsible to the Chief Inspector of Armaments. In addition women were employed as clerical workers, dealing with pay, records and so on, in the stores, a tailoring shop, the canteens and the medical centre, on testing, as drivers and as (semi-skilled) fitters.

Much of the work for operatives was repetitive, constituting only part of the whole process; women commented that they 'never actually did anything right through' and 'you were never shown the process from beginning to end'. Workers were, however, moved from section to section as production needs changed, and a number of those interviewed had been promoted to more responsible positions. Most workers reported receiving very little training, the initial induction being followed by being shown how to do the job, and then being left to get on with it. Some had had longer periods of training in the factory, or at least closely monitored working, and some had been sent elsewhere for more specialised instruction.

A major issue for the factory, and a constant matter for comment in interviews, was the question of safety and accidents. Many of the processes were inherently dangerous, and for most workers there was an elaborate and strict routine before entering their place of work, crossing from the 'dirty side' to the 'clean side' (inside) of the factory:

> first you took your food into the back side of the canteen and then any cigarettes or lighters, as I say, had to be left in the contraband, and you walked up some steps and the man would say to you . . . you had to say 'all clear' – you had to say that yourself. Then you walked in and these women would sort of frisk you again. Then you took your clothes off and put them into a sort of duffle bag with your number on and . . . I'll tell you what else we were issued with – a small bag on a tape and that hung round your neck. They preferred people to put a wedding ring, or any rings, in or money. You

weren't encouraged to take a lot of money, but that hung round your neck and right under your clothes.

. . . and then you crossed over a little wooden barrier on to the 'clean' side where you had to put your magazine clothing on which was white. . . and great clodhopper shoes – they were made from some special material I imagine – that you also had in your own kit bag on the 'clean' side, and then you weren't allowed to cross over again until you took all those off.

Despite such precautions, and what sounds like fairly intensive supervision, there were accidents, both explosions causing death and serious injury and mechanical accidents causing damage to limbs, particularly fingers. In addition some of the substances with which the women had to work caused illnesses of various kinds – nausea, eye irritations, dermatitis, chest complaints and so on. The most notorious was probably 'the dreaded yellow powder':

then we were moved to Group 2 and the dreaded yellow powder. A girl was lucky if she didn't get the 'rash' on this powder. The face swelled and became red and blotchy. Luckily I escaped it, but oh, to see one's face turning yellow. The palms of one's hands became brown. It was OK at work but it was awful outside when going to dances and pictures. One felt like a leper. For all people knew that you were doing war work you felt inferior because of this colour.

Given the variety of jobs which women did in the Aycliffe factory it is impossible to generalise about them. Equally it is difficult to generalise on the basis of our interviews about the women's reactions to their experience of working there. A few hated it: 'If I had my life over I wouldn't go back; it was something I would never do again – no'. A few found it a very positive experience: 'I couldn't say I had an unhappy moment really – it was really good'. Perhaps the dominant overall comment, however, was that it was 'a job that had to be done'. . . 'you just had to make the best of it'.

In general, though there were exceptions, the actual tasks which had to be performed were not much liked – 'that tedious little job'. The most frequently mentioned positive aspects of the experience of working at Aycliffe were the level of pay and the companionship of the other women travelling to the factory every day and working there. The wages were considerably higher than most of those interviewed had received before the war, and in some cases more than husbands earned. The importance of pay, of social relations at work, and of the particular job on which one was employed are reflected in the following, fairly enthusiastic, response:

The wages there were £5, £6 and £7 on the shifts you know, 7, 8 and 9 hours that you worked, which was really good, yes. I really enjoyed that. But most of all it was the women . . . we were all sort of the same, all our husbands and sweethearts away. We used to read each other's letters, tell each other secrets and everything, and it was really nice; and we sort of knew the children of the mothers that were married. We liked all that sort of thing, and we sang all day and everything . . . sort of altogetherness. There was the big table that you worked on, it was really nice. And we were on the cordite and I think we were rather lucky because the women that were on the powder, as you know, went yellow and everything, and they looked really bad, but the cordite was quite reasonable. I once had a turn on the bullets and I was terrified. When you used to fill those up – they went behind the glass case and the thing came down to press them, and if they were overfull they exploded. I used to . . . like waiting for the balloon to go off, and I hated that. I wasn't on that very long, it was mostly the cordite.

For the younger ones at the factory working there meant very little free time, but some of them commented on how much worse it was for older women with family responsibilities. Documents in the Public Record Office indicate that levels of absenteeism at Aycliffe were particularly high for women (20 per cent on the weekday morning shifts in September and October 1943, and nearly 39 per cent on Saturday mornings); whilst this may be an indication of the level of morale in the factory, it more probably reflects the effects of such a long working day, when travelling time is included, for women with heavy domestic duties as well.

Most of the women's work at Aycliffe represented no challenge to the conventional division of labour in factory employment. The work was dangerous, but in most other respects it was the sort of work which women have normally done – repetitive and not 'skilled'. Though there were some opportunities for women to secure promotion to more responsible positions, the factory hierarchy was also conventional with men occupying most of the positions of authority or technical expertise. On the other hand, in the context of County Durham in the 1940s employment in the factory did represent something new, both in that there was relatively little other factory employment for women in the region and in that many women had not worked outside the home after marriage except in cases of dire necessity.

On the basis of the interviews and the other evidence currently available to us it is difficult to be certain about the long-term effects of the experience of working at Aycliffe for women in the region. Of those who were interviewed a number left the labour market when the factory closed, or even earlier than that, because they were married and had children. As one woman put it 'I didn't work any more after because my husband came home and I did my own production'. Others worked, but in the same sort of range of occupations (except for private domestic service) as they had undertaken before the war.

On the other hand one or two of those interviewed used their experience of responsible work in the factory to go on to supervisory posts elsewhere after the war. There has been a growth in women's, and especially married women's, employment in the North East, as elsewhere in the country, and some of this has been factory employment. In Peterlee new town, for example, built in order to house miners in the East Durham coalfield, deliberate and relatively successful efforts were made in the 1950s and 1960s to secure employment for women on the town's trading estates (Philipson, 1988, pp. 125–33; pp. 199–202). Some of these changes in patterns of employment would have occurred anyway, as they did elsewhere in the country. However, greater economic independence for women may well have been hastened by the confidence individual women gained from their experience of working in the munitions factory. Certainly those who were interviewed, and several hundred others who attended a reunion in May 1989, left us in no doubt that their employment at ROF Aycliffe had been an important episode in their lives.

CONCLUSIONS

The munitions factory did not represent a major challenge to the conventional division of labour in manufacturing industry. With few exceptions women were doing the sorts of work they customarily did, and men performed the work which was heavier, more skilled, or involved the exercise of authority. It seems likely, though the evidence currently available is insufficient to support this point conclusively, that employment in the filling factory, with the unusual demands it made on the women directed or 'choosing' to work there, contributed to the changes which took place between the 1930s and the early 1950s in women's and especially married women's participation rates. As such it paralleled many other similar situations brought about by the wartime mobilisation of women's labour.

The case of women's employment in shipbuilding is rather different, but the numbers involved were very much smaller. The women who worked in shipbuilding during the war possibly experienced less of a change in their situation than employment at Aycliffe represented for at least some of the women working there. On the other hand these women were doing 'men's work' under the same conditions and for the same hours as the men working alongside them. Indeed, in some areas of relatively skilled work, welding being the most notable example, women demonstrated a particular aptitude for their tasks. Such a development had the potential to be a real challenge to the gender division of labour.

That it did not become so is partly due to some features of the wartime situation which tended to define women's position as not really fully equivalent to men's; for example, that they did not do some of the heaviest work, or work in some of the worst conditions. More important, however, the fact that the women came from shipbuilding communities, which made their induction into and experience of work in the yards so much easier than it might otherwise have been, also meant that they accepted those communities' definitions of what was appropriately and legitimately men's and women's work. Jobs in shipbuilding were men's jobs, and men coming back from the war would expect to return to them. In such circumstances, even though the women found working in shipbuilding such a very positive experience, it is scarcely surprising that shipbuilding reverted to being an exclusively male domain.

Two final points. This examination of women's wartime employment in shipbuilding and in the munitions industry provides further support for the argument (adopted by Walby and Bradley, for example) that studies of women's employment need to be undertaken on an industrially and/or occupationally differentiated basis. It also demonstrates once again the need to consider both the household and community and the work situation when examining change, or the absence of change, in the gender division of paid labour.

Notes

The shipbuilding project was initiated by Frank Ennis and Ian Roberts. I am grateful to the Nuffield Foundation for a grant (No. Soc/181(1112)) to cover interviewing and transcription expenses. The interviews were carried out by Frank Ennis and Ian Roberts between September 1983 and July 1984.

The munitions project was initiated by Frank Ennis and Lotte Shankland. Thanks are due for financial and other support to the Nuffield Foundation (Grant No. 181(1672)), Durham Community Arts Association and the

Department of Sociology and Social Policy, University of Durham. The interviews were carried out by Lotte Shankland, Gill Walker, John Dent, Jane Brown and Ann Scott between May 1988 and January 1989. Lotte Shankland and Jane Brown have undertaken a considerable amount of analysis of the munition workers' interviews. Ann Scott transcribed all the interviews for both projects, and did much else besides.

This chapter would not have been possible without all this work by my colleagues, which I would like to acknowledge with very many thanks. It would also not have been possible without the cooperation of those who agreed to be interviewed, and we are all grateful to them for their help. None of those named above can be held responsible for this account of the research.

3 Gender-role Attitudes in Britain and the USA

Jacqueline Scott and Jean Duncombe

In Britain there have been increasing incentives for married women to work or to return to work partly because a reduction in the number of school leavers has left a gap to be filled in the labour market (Truman, this volume). Yet social pressures in recent years may be working in the opposite direction, as the rhetoric of politicians emphasises the virtues of traditional roles in family life, and as the media insists that motherhood is once again 'fashionable' (e.g. *Guardian*, 8 March 1990). Social and employment policies have an important effect on women's labour market choices, as Walters and Dex demonstrate (this volume). However, whether British women take up any new employment opportunities may depend at least as much on attitudes, especially on those attitudes to do with women's place in paid work and family life (Fogarty *et al.*, 1971; Brannen, 1987; Gordon, 1990).

In America too, there is a renewed interest in gender-role attitudes, with the development of feminist concerns in the social sciences (Condor, 1986; Mason, Czajka and Arber, 1976), which have seen change in gender-role attitudes as both a goal of the women's movement and a possible cause of its rise (Chafetz, 1989). There has been a tendency on both sides of the Atlantic to suggest that women's increasing labour market participation and associated shifts in gender-role attitudes are linked with changes that are little short of revolutionary in women's roles and family life.

However, there are important differences between the British and American employment patterns of women, and this paper sets out to explore how far these are related to differences in gender-role attitudes in the two countries. The primary factor influencing gender-role changes is undoubtedly the marked increase of married women, including mothers, entering the labour market. It is likely that large scale shifts of attitudes would produce the climate for further socio-political changes concerning women's roles. On the other hand, unless gender-role attitudes become more egalitarian, inequalities, both in the structure of labour market opportunities and rewards, and in the division of labour within the home, will persist.

Against the prevailing optimism we argue that the characterization of changes in gender-role attitudes in Britain as revolutionary is highly exaggerated because it fails to recognise the contradictions associated with normative beliefs about women's familial and employment roles. Also, the support for working wives and mothers may have been overestimated because researchers have almost invariably failed to distinguish between full and part-time work; and thus have failed to explore or even to recognise the possibility of deep-seated objections to mothers who sacrifice family responsibilities by working full-time.

WOMEN'S CHANGING PARTICIPATION IN THE UNITED STATES AND BRITISH LABOUR MARKETS

In the USA, women's labour force participation has grown continuously since 1870 (Lopata *et al.*, 1986, p. 54), with a sharper increase from the 1950s onwards, to 39 per cent in the 1960s and 56 per cent in 1988 (Morris, 1990). Early employment growth was concentrated among single women but, during the past 35 years, there has been a striking increase in married women's participation. In the UK there have been broadly similar changes, with women making up 34 per cent of the labour force by 1948 and 43 per cent in 1984 (Dex, 1985; Morris, 1990), of whom 64 per cent were married (OPCS, 1989).

There are, however, significant differences between the two countries in the employment patterns of mothers. In the USA, since 1966, mothers of young children have been returning to work earlier and have become an increasingly large proportion of the work-force. As a result, in 1970, 24 per cent of married women with children one year or younger were in the labour force, while by 1985 the figure had risen to almost half (Morris, 1990). In contrast, British women apparently experience greater constraints (Morris, 1990), and the largest increase in Britain has been among women aged 35 to 54, that is, those without young children (Dex, 1985, p. 4). Furthermore, British married women are far more likely to be in part-time employment. Cross-national comparisons have to be made with care because in Britain the official statistical cut-off point for part-time employment is 30 hours a week, whereas in the USA it is 35 hours. However, at 42 per cent in 1981, the proportion of British women who work part-time is almost double that of American women (Morris, 1990).

There are many possible explanations for the differences in the working patterns in the two countries. For example, in the USA, child care can be offset against federal tax and health benefits are rarely available outside full-time employment; whereas hitherto in Britain there have been state-regulated financial incentives to employers to engage part-time workers. However, we are not concerned to explain the different employment practices of the two countries but rather how these relate to cross-national differences in gender-role attitudes.

'TRADITIONAL' AND 'EGALITARIAN' ATTITUDES TOWARDS THE FAMILY AND GENDER-ROLES

Implicitly or explicitly, writers on gender-roles tend to draw upon contrasting traditional versus egalitarian (or liberal) models and ideologies of the family. It is suggested that the pace of change is set by the more educated or middle class families, but the working class will follow. At their most optimistic, commentators suggest that men are becoming more liberal in relation to gender-roles, and family life is becoming more egalitarian (Rapoport and Rapoport, 1976, 1978; Berger and Berger, 1983; Young and Willmott, 1973; Fletcher, 1966). It is claimed that we have moved a long way towards the position where the 'new man' is radically different from his father and no longer expects his wife to stay at home and do the cooking (*Guardian*, 1990). Instead, he shares the domestic chores and child care equally with his wife who is now entitled and even urged to go out to work to gain her fulfilment and independence. But is such an optimistic scenario justified?

There is certainly room to doubt the extent to which gender-role behaviour has changed. Evetts (1988) found that although most women claim to have the support and encouragement of their husbands, very few husbands were able or willing to give any practical assistance in coping with child care tasks. It is more a case of men helping out (Brannen, 1987) and this help, according to Boulton (1983), may mean little more than an increase in men's interest and enjoyment of their children. Describing a small-scale piece of research in South Wales and the North East, Morris (1990) concludes that given the well-established pattern of female responsibility for domestic and child care tasks, a woman's paid work must take account of her domestic obligations, or those obligations must accommodate her employment.

Most gender-role attitude research has used the traditional versus egalitarian distinction. In the United States, researchers have argued that real changes in gender-role attitudes have followed the large-scale entry of married women and mothers into the labour market (Oppenheimer, 1982, pp. 28–31). The attitude shift with regard to the employment of married women has certainly been dramatic: a 1937 poll showed 82 per cent of the population *against* the employment of a married woman if her husband was capable of supporting her; while a 1972 poll found 68 per cent in *favour* of married women working (Cherlin and Walters, 1981). Harris identifies the clash which results when attitudes towards women's traditional domestic responsibilities do not shift in the same way as do attitudes towards women's labour force participation. He argues that women were

> being asked to work at two places at once: to work for half a man's pay on the job and no pay at all off the job, and to remain submissive and obedient to sexist husbands who no longer supported them. And so it was women who had most to gain and least to lose by kicking at the hollow pillars of the temple of marriage and childbirth (Harris, 1981, pp. 94–5).

It does seem that women have increasingly felt that they were getting a raw deal. Researchers have claimed that, in America, women have shown a marked shift towards more egalitarian gender-role attitudes since the 1960s. For example, using data from five sample surveys taken between 1964 and 1974, Mason, Czajka, and Arber (1976) conclude that there had been considerable movement among women towards more egalitarian role definitions. They found that

> while the traditional sex division of labor within the family continues to receive more support than do inequalities in the labor market rights of the sexes, attitudes about family roles have changed as much over the past decade as have those about work roles (1976, p. 593).

Especially important was the marked drop in the proportion of women who believed maternal employment is harmful to the child. There was some suggestion in the American press that there was a backlash against feminism in the 1980s with women becoming increasingly disaffected with the attempt to be super-women juggling full-time work careers and family life (e.g. *Newsweek*, 1986). However, using data from the General Social Survey in 1975 and 1985, Mason and Yu-Hsia Lu (1988) conclude that the profeminist change in attitudes continued through to the 1980s and an increasing number of Americans in all socio-demographic subgroups of the population, including men, rejected the traditional conception of women's familial role.

In Britain, there are no trend data to monitor changes in gender-role attitudes since the 1960s. In 1980, however, the Women and Employment survey asked about different views on the women's role, and some items have been replicated in the British Social Attitudes Surveys in 1984, 1987 and 1990. Reviewing the changes, Scott (1991) concludes that although acceptance of women's employment appears to be steady and high, in contrast only a small (and reducing) minority thinks that a woman working is beneficial both to a woman and her family. Witherspoon (1988) suggests that this may reflect a greater awareness of the real role-conflicts involved in juggling family responsibilities and employment demands.

Unfortunately, for the most part, attitudinal data in both countries fail to distinguish between approval for women working full or part time. As Brannen pointed out 'If you ask about full-time employment, it is likely to provoke more extreme reactions' (1987, p. 37). Moreover, even where analysis does distinguish the separate spheres of work, housework and child-care, usually writers tend to conclude by making optimistic claims for more egalitarian attitudes on the basis of attitudes towards work alone (full or part-time unspecified). In overlooking any differences between attitudes in the separate domains, authors therefore tend to reinforce the myths of the new man and the symmetrical family, which other data, especially concerning responsibilities for children, might challenge.

HYPOTHESES

The main purpose of this chapter is to compare gender-role attitudes in Britain and the USA and discuss the practical and policy implications of our findings. Our first hypothesis is that Americans will be more egalitarian in their gender-role attitudes than the British, because in America the extent of full-time employment of married women may have effectively undermined traditional gender-role beliefs; whereas in Britain part-time work provides a means whereby traditional family role division can be retained even though women go out to work.

Our second hypothesis is that gender-role attitudes will reflect the complexity of beliefs about women's paid work and familial roles. The usual characterization of gender-role attitudes as being egalitarian or traditional implies a unidimensional scale. At the one extreme are views that favour a traditional role division of labour – a male breadwinner and female housewife/mother. At the other extreme are the pro-feminist or egalitarian views that espouse more symmetrical gender-roles. This portrayal has been rightly criticised as being over-simplistic and crude (Condor, 1986). In our analysis we disaggregate gender-role measures because we believe that people may hold both traditional and egalitarian views, depending on what aspect of gender-role is being considered.

Our third hypothesis is that men and women will differ in gender-role attitudes, with women being more egalitarian than men. This is simply because it is in women's interest to change the status quo whereby women often carry the burden of two full-time jobs. Unfortunately many of the gender-role studies to date have focused only on women's gender-role attitudes, as if the ideology that defined women's role had nothing to do with men. Yet clearly women's changing role has enormous implications for the role of men, and men's attitudes are likely to reflect their own self-interest. Economic necessity will make men support women going out to work, but not lessen their belief in women's familial responsibilities. In particular we expect men to be far more likely than women to believe that maternal employment is harmful to children.

Our fourth hypothesis is that women who are in the labour market will be considerably more egalitarian in their views than women who are full-time home-makers. As Luker (1984) and Gerson (1985) point out, home-makers face a real threat to their identity in a society where women's status is becoming less tied to their husband's occupation and more tied to their own occupational achievements. Consequently home-makers may condemn women who undertake multiple roles as spouse, mother, and worker. With cross-sectional data we cannot tell whether the less 'traditionalist' women are more likely to go out to work, or whether employment undermines traditional gender-role beliefs. It seems most likely that the two processes operate in tandem. We will, however, be able to examine whether the gender-role attitudes of women differ between part-time and full-time workers, although again the direction of causality cannot be disentangled.

DATA AND METHODS

The data come from the British and American components of the International Social Survey Programme (ISSP) which mounts comparable cross-national surveys in 11 nations. In 1988 the module was on

Women and the Family, although in Britain, the data was collected in 1989. The American Survey was carried out in conjunction with the General Social Survey administered by the National Opinion Research Center in Chicago. The British survey was carried out by Social and Community Planning Research (SCPR). The ISSP module is a self-completion supplement, used in conjunction with a face-to-face interview of a multi-stage national representative sample of adults aged over 18 from the electoral register. The response rate was 66 per cent for the American sample and 70 per cent for the British study.

Dependent variables. The composite measure of gender-role attitudes is based on a nine item index which has an estimated internal consistency reliability coefficient (Cronbach's Alpha) of 0.80 for British data and 0.77 for American data. The exact question wording of each item is presented in Table 3.1. A factor analysis pointed to three different aspects of the gender-role index: role-conflict, role-segregation, and role-combination. (The British data yield the clearest factor loadings; however a separate analysis on the American data points to essentially the same three factors.) The first four items shown in Table 3.1 question whether there is a conflict between a woman's job and the needs of her family, and in particular the needs of her children. Thus, this first factor represents an assessment of the practical conflicts that may arise when women combine employment and familial roles, whereas the other two factors are more concerned with the principles of gender-role division. The three role-segregation items gauge attitudes towards the traditional division of labour between men and women; and the final two role-combination items tap beliefs about the benefits of women combining both family responsibilities and paid employment. On this basis, in addition to the single attitude items, we consider the three gender-role indexes: conflicts, segregation, and combination, along with the composite index of all nine gender-role attitude items. We also consider a related set of measures that tap beliefs about the family circumstances under which a woman should work full or part-time.

Independent variables. For our measure of the employment status of women we restrict analysis to home-makers and those in current employment, excluding women who work less than 10 hours a week. We further distinguish between part-time and full-time employment. In Britain, as we noted in the introduction, part-time work is less than 30 hours a week and in America it is less than 35 hours.

BRITISH AND AMERICAN GENDER-ROLE ATTITUDES

The pattern of gender-role attitudes is quite different in the United States and in Britain and, as can be seen in Table 3.1, there are significant differences on all but two items. The table shows the percentage of those who 'agree strongly' or just 'agree' versus those who 'neither agree nor disagree', 'disagree', or 'disagree strongly'. (For specified items, the direction is reversed and the percentage shown is those who disagree.) For this and all other tables in this chapter, those who cannot choose or do not answer are excluded. Americans hold more egalitarian attitudes concerning multiple role-conflicts than the British, with the British more likely to assert that family life in general and particularly pre-school children suffer if the mother is working.

The pattern, however, is quite different if we examine the role-segregation items that measure attitudes towards the traditional division of labour between men and women, and role-combination beliefs about women combining family responsibility and paid employment. Here, Americans are more traditional in their attitudes than the British. Interestingly, among Americans, there is far greater endorsement of the traditional position that asserts that what women really want is a home and children, and that being a housewife is just as fulfilling as working for pay. There is a tendency in the gender-role literature to envisage full-time work in terms of a fulfilling career. But this, of course, is not true. The majority of jobs that women occupy offer little fulfilment or autonomy in the work place. Thus, although Americans are more likely than the British to deny that work does family life harm, they are less likely than the British to assume that work is a blessing for the woman. This does not mean that in Britain women's employment outside the home is regarded as a panacea. Both Americans and the British resoundingly reject the notion that a woman and her family will all be happier if she goes out to work. Only 17 per cent of Americans and 19 per cent of the British view work as a source of family happiness. Approximately half the population of both countries agree that both the husband and wife should contribute to the family income. However, the British are far more likely to equate work and female independence. Among the British 63 per cent agree that 'having a job is the best way for a woman to be an independent person', compared with only 44 per cent of Americans.

A glance at the different levels of endorsement of the individual gender-role items implies that most respondents do not take a consistently egalitarian or traditional stance with respect to these

Table 3.1   Percentage endorsing egalitarian positions in Britain and the United States* (all adults aged 18 or over)

	Britain	*USA*
Role-conflict		
A working mother can establish just as warm and secure a relationship with her children as a mother who does not work (% agree)	59%	66%
All in all, family life suffers when the woman has a full-time job (% disagree)	41%	50%
A pre-school child is likely to suffer if his or her mother works (% disagree)	36%	44%
A woman and her family will all be happier if she goes out to work	19%	17% ns
Role-segregation		
A husband's job is to earn money; a wife's job is to look after the home and family (% disagree)	53%	51% ns
A job is all right, but what most women really want is a home and children (% disagree)	48%	39%
Being a housewife is just as fulfilling as working for pay (% disagree)	36%	23%
Role-combination		
Having a job is the best way for a woman to be an independent person (% agree)	63%	44%
Both the husband and wife should contribute to the household income (% agree)	54%	50%
Minimum base *N*	(1223)	(1340)

*All differences are statistically significant at $p < 0.05$ unless marked ns

measures. This can be illustrated more directly if we examine the results from a cross-tabulation of responses on two items: family life suffers when the woman has a full-time job, and a woman and her family will be happier if she works. It might appear that these two items are measuring almost the same thing and pressures of consistency would make people who agree that family life suffers if the woman works, also reject the notion that the woman and her family would be happier is she goes out to work. However, as Table 3.2 shows, the majority of people do not give either a consistently traditional or a consistently egalitarian response on both items, although in both Britain and the United States the traditional stance is far more common (27 per cent and 23 per cent, respectively) than the consistently egalitarian position (14 per cent and 11 per cent). What is more interesting, however, is the high percentage of respondents who deny that the full-time employment of women is detrimental to family life but who also remain sceptical about whether working wives make for family bliss. Following Witherspoon (1988) we call this group 'realists' because they appear to be conscious of the difficulties in combining the demands of both family and career. In Britain, more than a quarter (27 per cent) and in America two fifths (39 per cent) are 'realists', adopting a complex stance that denies that family life and women's employment are incompatible, while nevertheless acknowledging the strains in juggling work and family demands. (The 'other' category mainly consists of those who adopt a neutral position about the impact of women's employment on family life.)

Table 3.2   Consistency of responses to two items assessing whether women's employment is detrimental or beneficial to family life*
(row percentages)

	Egalitarian on both items	Traditional on both items	Realist	Other
Britain (N = 1255)	14%	27%	27%	32%
USA (N = 1325)	11%	23%	39%	27%

* Question wordings: (i) A woman and her family will all be happier if she goes out to work. (ii) All in all family life suffers when the woman has a full-time job.

It is already apparent that we can make no simple generalisation about whether Americans are, as we hypothesised, more egalitarian in their gender-role attitudes than the British. Moreover, it is clear that gender-role attitudes are far more complex than any overall summary egalitarianism versus traditional scale might imply. However, in order to test the extent of differences in the gender-role attitudes of the two countries, we will examine the differences in means for each of the three gender-role indexes suggested by our factor analysis (role-conflict, role-segregation, and role-combination), as well as our composite gender-role index of all nine items. The mean score is based on a response scale ranging from 1 to 5, where the higher the number the more egalitarian the response. As can be seen from the top row of Table 3.3, there is no overall difference in the combined gender-role attitude index of either country. However, it would be quite wrong to conclude that there is no cultural difference in attitudes. Rather, it is apparent that Americans are more egalitarian when the first four measures from Table 3.1 are combined to make the role-conflict index. But the British are more egalitarian on the next five measures that make up the role-segregation and role-combination indexes. This is an important point to emphasise because although there is no difference between the two countries when the gender-role attitude index is considered overall, the British are more egalitarian in their stance that *in principle* role-combination is beneficial and traditional role-segregation is less desirable. However, the British are more traditional than Americans in their concern that *in practice* working may clash with family life, and in particular the care of pre-school children.

Table 3.3   Differences in gender-role attitudes* between Britain and the United States

	Britain	*USA*	*T-ratio*
Sex role index	3.16	3.14	0.64 ns
Role-conflict	2.98	3.13	−4.29[†]
Role-segregation	3.15	3.01	4.03[†]
Role-combination	3.48	3.30	5.32[†]
Minimum $N =$	(1125)	(1206)	

* Mean scores based on a 5 point scale, high scores are more egalitarian.
[†] $p < 0.001$.

Our hypothesis that Americans would hold more egalitarian views than the British is not supported by the data. Americans are only more egalitarian when it comes to considering the potential role clash between work and family responsibilities. In part, this may reflect the different level of child care provision in the two countries. It may also reflect the fact that in Britain the expectation is that women with families will work part-time rather than full-time and that their working pattern will be subservient to their family responsibilities. In answer to a normative question asking about what a woman's working pattern should be in different circumstances, the British are more likely than Americans to insist that a mother should stay at home when their child is under school age. However, as Table 3.4 shows, once the child has reached school age, the overwhelming preference of the British is for women to work part-time (68 per cent). Americans are far more likely than the British to endorse full-time work both when there are pre-school children (10 per cent versus 2 per cent), and also when the children reach school-age (31 per cent versus 13 per cent). Only a very small minority in both Britain and America (11 per cent) feel that women with children over 5 should stay at home.

Table 3.4   Attitudes towards the different circumstances in which a woman should work (column percentages)

		Britain	USA
If children under school age?			
No, stay at home		64%	48%
Yes, work part-time		26%	30%
Yes, work full-time		2%	10%
Don't know		6%	10%
	N =	(1274)	(1380)
When her children have started school?			
No, stay at home		11%	11%
Yes, work part-time		68%	45%
Yes, work full-time		13%	31%
Don't know		7%	11%
	N =	(1274)	(1380)

Differences in Men and Women's Gender-role Attitudes

Our third hypothesis is that men would be more traditional in their gender-role attitudes than women, because, in general, men stand to lose more than women if the status quo is changed. As can be seen from Table 3.5, women are generally more egalitarian than men in both countries on the role-conflict items, they are less likely to perceive a detrimental impact of working wives and mothers on family life. In Britain, women are also more egalitarian with respect to the segregation items that concern the traditional gender division of tasks. In America men are marginally more likely than women to deny that being a housewife is as fulfilling as working for pay. This is in fact the only item, for either country, where men appear more egalitarian than women, although the difference is not statistically significant. The

Table 3.5   Differences in gender-role attitudes among men and women in Britain and the United States

| | % endorsing egalitarian response | | | |
| | *Britain* | | *USA* | |
	Men	*Women*	*Men*	*Women*
Role-conflict				
Warm relationship with child (% agree)	52%	65%	59%	70%
Family life suffers (% disagree)	38%	43%	48%	51% ns
Pre-school child suffers (% disagree)	29%	40%	37%	49%
Woman and family happier (% agree)	15%	23%	16%	18% ns
Role-segregation				
Wife's job is home and family (% disagree)	47%	58%	48%	54%
Women want home and children (% disagree)	42%	52%	36%	41% ns
Housewife as fulfilling (% disagree)	35%	36% ns	24%	22% ns
Role-combination				
Job best way to be independent (% agree)	60%	66% ns	42%	46% ns
Husband and wife contribute to income (% agree)	51%	57% ns	47%	52% ns
Minimum *N* =	(545)	(676)	(575)	(758)

* All differences are statistically significant at $p < 0.05$ unless marked ns.

gender difference is not significant in either country for the role-combination items, although the direction is consistent with our hypothesis that women are more egalitarian. Thus our hypothesis is for the most part confirmed: women are more egalitarian in their gender-role attitudes than men. In particular, women are less likely than men to regard a mother's employment as harmful to her children.

Gender-role Attitudes and Women's Employment Status

Our final hypothesis suggests that women who were employed would be more egalitarian in their gender-role attitudes than home-makers. For this analysis we use two dummy variables. The first contrasts employed women and full-time home-makers and for this variable the distribution is similar in both countries: 67 per cent of Americans and 63 per cent of British women are currently employed. The two countries, however, differ markedly for our second dummy variable that contrasts the percentage of women employed full-time versus part-time. In Britain 40 per cent of employed women work part-time, compared to only 24 per cent in the United States.

Our hypothesis that employed women are more egalitarian than women who are full-time home-makers is overwhelmingly confirmed. In both countries the difference between employed women and home-makers is highly significant on all items except one. (The figures for all employed women are not given in Table 3.6.) The one exception is that, in America, employed women and home-makers are equally likely to believe that both the husband and wife should contribute to the household income. On all other items, however, the difference is very large with as many as 25 percentage points difference between the two groups of women.

In Britain, there are differences between women who work full-time and women who work part-time, with full-time workers significantly more egalitarian on four of the nine items. Women who work full-time are far more likely than part-time workers to reject the notion that family life or pre-school age children suffer when the woman goes out to work; and they are more rejecting of the traditional segregation in gender-roles. In America, however, there is no significant difference between the gender-role attitudes of women who work full or part-time, although the direction is broadly consistent with the British data and with more cases these differences might become statistically significant.

Table 3.6   Differences in British and American women's gender-role
attitudes by employment status*

		Employed full-time	Employed part-time	Homemakers
Role-conflict				
Warm relationship with	Britain	78%	70% ns	55%
child (% agree)	USA	81%	76% ns	58%
Family life suffers	Britain	65%	39%	29%
(% disagree)	USA	66%	57% ns	33%
Pre-school child suffers	Britain	58%	42%	28%
(% disagree)	USA	63%	54% ns	37%
Woman and family happier	Britain	29%	32%	12%
(% agree)	USA	18%	25% ns	12%
Role-segregation				
Wife's job is home and family	Britain	86%	66%	40%
(% disagree)	USA	70%	64% ns	33%
Women want home and children	Britain	74%	59%	39%
(% disagree)	USA	54%	44% ns	29%
Housewife as fulfilling	Britain	47%	47% ns	22%
(% disagree)	USA	27%	30% ns	13%
Role-combination				
Job best way to be independent	Britain	72%	75%	56%
(% agree)	USA	49%	44% ns	39%
Husband and wife contribute	Britain	64%	64% ns	41%
to income (% agree)	USA	57%	50% ns	47% ns
Minimum *N* for Britain =		(175)	(119)	(195)
Minimum *N* for USA =		(295)	(94)	(197)

* All differences between homemakers and employed women (both full- and part-
time); and all differences between full- and part-time workers are significant at
$p < 0.05$ unless marked ns.

The differences among women in their gender-role attitudes has
important ramifications for interpreting the gender differences discussed above. If we compare the attitudes of women home-makers
with those of men, then home-makers turn out either to differ little, or
be even more traditional, than men. It is women who are in paid
employment who are far more egalitarian than men in their gender-
role attitudes. With cross-sectional data, it is impossible to resolve the

direction of causality between employment and gender-role attitudes. Longitudinal data are needed to determine whether women with less traditional attitudes are more likely to go out to work, or whether employment encourages egalitarian gender-role beliefs.

CONCLUSIONS

Our first hypothesis that Americans would be more egalitarian than the British in their gender-role attitudes is partially confirmed. Americans are more likely to assert that women can work without it having negative ramifications for children or family life in general. However, the British are more likely to take an egalitarian stance on attitudes towards traditional role-segregation and on the desirability of women combining both paid work and familial roles. It would be foolish to claim that we can explain this cross-national difference without further analysis. However, it is important to note that women's labour force participation may be less disruptive to traditional family roles in Britain, because so many women only work part-time. This preference for not allowing employment demands to interfere with family responsibilities is also seen in the fact that the British are more likely than Americans to assert that women with pre-school children should stay at home, and are less likely than Americans to support mothers of school-age children working full-time.

Our second hypothesis that gender-role attitudes can not be adequately captured by an overall traditional versus egalitarian gender-role index is undoubtedly true. We have been able to demonstrate that people's attitudes vary greatly according to what aspect of family life or work is being considered. Moreover, it is quite clear that people respond differently to different measures in a way that demonstrates that gender-role attitudes are quite complex. For example, we found a high proportion of respondents adamantly rejecting the notion that family life suffers if a woman takes on full-time work, while, at the same time, rejecting the assumption that families will be happier if the woman works. We believe that this reflects both support for women who choose to work and also a realistic appraisal of the difficulties of combining employment and family demands.

Our third hypothesis that women would be more egalitarian than men in their gender-role attitudes is substantially confirmed. In particular, men are more likely than women to assert that families and children suffer if the woman works. However, this does not stop men agreeing that both the husband and wife should contribute to the household income and acknowledging that housework is less fulfilling than working for pay. Thus our conclusion must be that the much trumpeted 'new man', who wishes a fully egalitarian gender-role division in family life, is not much in evidence in our data.

Finally, we do find evidence of a substantial difference in gender-role attitudes between home-makers and women who are employed in the labour force. Both in America and Britain, employed women are far more egalitarian in all aspects of gender-role attitudes than women who do not work for pay. Because we only have cross-sectional data we can not determine whether women with egalitarian gender-role attitudes are more likely to find employment, or whether employment promotes more liberal gender-role attitudes, but we suspect that both processes operate in tandem. In our data, we found a further but less spectacular difference between full and part-time workers. British women who work full time are more likely than part-time workers to reject the belief that women's employment is harmful to family life and are more likely to reject traditional gender role-segregation.

There has been a considerable amount of evidence to suggest that employment not only brings financial benefits but also has a positive benefit on mental health, especially in terms of self-esteem and sense of purpose (e.g. Gove, 1972; Sieber, 1974; Thoits, 1983). However, the literature suggests and most empirical studies confirm that working women are more likely to experience psychological distress than working men (e.g. Radloff, 1975). It is unlikely that women will reap the benefits of employment unless there are substantial changes in female labour market conditions and substantial shifts in normative beliefs about gender-roles. In particular, unless high quality child care and flexible work hours become widespread, working mothers will continue to experience role conflict in terms of guilt and anxiety about not being a full-time parent, especially when the children are young. Moreover, unless beliefs about gender-roles change, and women stop being defined as primarily responsible for family care, women who are in paid work will have to struggle to do a double shift of employment and family care while still fearing that their families will suffer.

Notes

The support of the Economic and Social Research Council (ESRC) is gratefully acknowledged. The work was part of the programme of the ESRC Research Centre on Micro-Social Change in Britain. We are also grateful to Nick Buck, Randy Banks and Lilian Zac for their assistance in processing and analysing the data, and to Howard Schuman and Shirley Dex for helpful comments on an earlier draft.

4 Money, Marriage and Motherhood: Dual Earner Households after Maternity Leave

Julia Brannen

This chapter considers a lifestyle which, with the demographic changes expected in the 1990s, promises to become increasingly significant. There will be a rising number of households in which the arrival of children signals, not the mothers' withdrawal from the labour market, the typical practice in Britain in the post-war years, but a continuing full-time commitment by both parents to full-time employment. Women who work full time when they have a young child may be expected to be in the vanguard of equality, not only in terms of their attitudes to and practices in employment, but also with respect to parenthood and marriage. In this chapter, the perspectives of women in this situation are analysed with respect to three central, interrelated issues: the significance women attach to their full-time earnings; their responses to the (still unequal) division of childcare and domestic labour in the household; and their social construction of the maternal role. These are issues which are integral to an assessment of the significance of the dual earner life style: about whether (or not) the lifestyle produces equality between men and women in the household and how far it leads to a redefinition of, or an accommodation to, existing gender roles.

An opportunity to explore these issues is afforded by a longitudinal study conducted at Thomas Coram Research Unit in the first half of the 1980s among two groups of women: those who intended to resume their full-time jobs under the maternity leave provisions and those who chose the so-called traditional option of withdrawal from the labour market. First, it is necessary to set these household and employment patterns in the British context.

THE BRITISH CONTEXT

Britain is a country of extremes for employed mothers: compared with the rest of Europe it has one of the highest employment rates for mothers of school-age children, yet one of the lowest rates for mothers of pre-school children (Brannen and Moss, 1988; Moss, 1988). While in the mid 1980s, 45 per cent of British women were in employment (11 per cent full-time and 34 per cent part-time) when they had a child of school age, only 29 per cent of those with pre-school children (8 per cent full-time and 21 per cent part-time) were in paid work (Moss, 1988). This latter figure contrasts sharply with countries such as Denmark and Sweden where around four fifths of mothers of children under two are in the labour market, though less so with Germany and the Netherlands with 32 per cent and 21 per cent respectively (Brannen and Moss, 1988).

In spite of a high divorce rate and the growth of single parenthood, most British women in the early 1980s resigned from the labour market around the time they gave birth. Among women having their first child at the end of the 1970s, only 17 per cent were in paid employment within six months of the birth (8 per cent full-time and 9 per cent part-time); overall a mere 3 per cent of mothers resumed employment within six months of any birth and remained in the labour market during the child-rearing years (Martin and Roberts, 1984). Such findings contrast markedly with the lifetime employment patterns of mothers in France (see Walters and Dex in this volume). Joshi (1987) estimated that, following childbearing, British mothers lost on average between four and nine years of employment, depending on how many children they had and the spacing of these children.

Paradoxically, although the growth of technology and consumerism have lifted some of the material burdens attached to being a mother, the tasks carried out by mothers in industrial societies have expanded rather than contracted as a result of a growing emphasis on the maternal role, especially with respect to the psychological development of children (Chodorow, 1978; Schutze, 1988). It is notable that, as British research shows, parental, i.e. maternal, desire for daycare is principally defined in terms of its educational and social benefits for children rather than the ways in which it benefits mothers in paid employment (Blatchford, Battle and Mays, 1982; Haystead, Howarth and Strachan, 1980). Such findings make sense in the context of the dominant culture which currently surrounds childhood and parenthood in Britain, namely the emphasis placed by professionals on the importance of children's development. Up to the pre-school age of three years, these ideas are mediated indirectly through the practices of mothers; once the child reaches three years the direct input of experts becomes acceptable, though the mother continues to be seen as the central emotional figure for the child.

At the same time, under the influence of the Women's Movement, the past twenty years have seen a growing awareness in Britain concerning inequalities between men and women, especially in terms of their relationship to the labour market. However, there is much less awareness of the position of mothers. With respect to policy, the 1970s saw the introduction of only minimal legislation concerning maternity rights. The Employment Protection Act (1975) gave mothers who had been with their employers for at least two years the right to their former employment (not the same job) after childbirth, to return within 29 weeks following the birth, together with a small amount of paid leave (18 weeks at 90 per cent of earnings). The Act required women to return to full-time employment. In contrast to other European countries, British maternity rights have been curtailed rather than expanded. Such rights do not question women's responsibility for child care. In other countries maternity leave is about the mother's and baby's recovery after the birth process; in Britain it has been confounded with parental leave which is intended to allow each parent to take care of the child in the early months. Only mothers are assumed to require such leave; fathers are not considered to have a role to play. (Similar assumptions are reported with respect to the US (Dowd, 1986).) Furthermore, the state in Britain has taken no steps to encourage and facilitate the setting up of child care facilities, with the exception of the removal of the tax on placements in workplace nurseries in 1990. The result is that there is virtually no provision, private or public, for the under twos (Brannen and Moss, 1988; Moss, 1988).

THE STUDY

Although this chapter is about the perspectives of the mothers who resumed employment after childbirth, one of the principal aims of the study was to investigate the effects of daycare on children. Three groups of children were included: those cared for by relatives, those cared for by childminders, and those cared for in nurseries, together with a fourth group who, at least initially, were to be cared for at home by their non-employed mothers. The study group was composed of 185 households in which the women intended to resume their former employment on a full-time basis following maternity leave. A further group of 70 women not intending to return was also included. Both groups were selected through large employers of women and maternity hospitals in the Greater London area. The mothers and children were first studied while the children's mothers were on maternity leave, that is, when the children were 4–5 months old. They were followed up on three subsequent occasions: when the children were 10–11 months (after the employed mothers' return to employment), and when the children reached 18 months and 36 months.

The households were selected on a number of criteria: that the child was the mother's first born; that the mother was living with the child's father when the child was born; that the mother was born in the United Kingdom or Ireland; and that the child would be, at least initially, in one of the types of care mentioned above. Another aim was to achieve an equal balance of women in higher status occupations (professional and managerial) and lower status jobs (clerical and manual workers.) The study more than adequately represented women in higher status jobs but substantially under-represented women in manual employment. This latter situation was in part a consequence of the sample area and our sampling strategy but was also due to the fact that women in manual work rarely qualify for maternity leave in Britain. When they do return to the labour market following childbirth, they tend to find new jobs.

The study employed the strategy of combining qualitative and quantitative approaches with respect to the fieldwork, analysis and writing up of the research. Data from the mothers were collected about themselves, their children and the children's fathers via tape recorded interviews. An in-depth interviewing technique was combined with a more structured approach in which specific questions were designed to give precise responses. The latter were coded and computed and used in conjunction with the transcribed qualitative material. Some of the qualitative material has proved to be a complement to the statistical material, while other parts raise major queries about the meaning of the statistical data. Such inconsistencies are in themselves a significant data source which aids rather than impedes interpretation (Hammersley and Atkinson, 1983, p. 199; Fielding and Fielding, 1986, p. 31; Bryman, 1988, p. 133). They proved particularly useful in making sense of these data.

THEORETICAL ISSUES

The fact of both parents having an equal full-time commitment to paid employment, uninterrupted by childrearing, is popularly assumed to lead to greater equality between parents within both the employment and domestic spheres. This assumption is examined and considered wrong on several counts. Within the employment sphere, equality is impeded by the ways in which gender ideologies are reproduced in the workplace (Beechey, 1987), a situation which has resulted in the continuing segregation of men's and women's jobs (Hakim, 1979), and discrepancies between men's and women's ability to earn a living wage (Siltanen, 1986).

Within the household which is the focus of this chapter, equal attachment to employment does not translate to equality in domestic gender roles. The first explanation for this relates to the ways in which the earnings of each partner are regarded and used. As others have noted (Jephcott *et al.*, 1962; Morris, 1990), the argument that women's earnings increase their power in the household is over simple since the effect may only be to reduce the demands on the man's wage and to free it for other kinds of expenditure. For example, the study provided evidence that men's money may be reserved for securing the longer-term or more basic needs of the household, while the woman's earnings may cater for more immediate or secondary priorities. Furthermore, as the work of Jan Pahl has indicated, an important determinant of access to and the distribution of household resources is the intra-household system of financial management (Pahl, 1989). The perception of the significance of men's and women's employment and earnings, especially in the household context, is therefore likely to be influenced by factors other than whether or not women decide to stay in employment after childbirth and, if they do decide to stay, whether both parents spend the same number of hours in the workplace.

A second explanation for why it seems unlikely that equal hours in the workplace translate to equality in the household, relates to expectations in marriage. If it is the case, as others have argued, that romantic love, communicative togetherness and emotional sharing are the salient ideals of modern marriage, rather than the search for and achievement of material equality (Burgoyne, 1987), then dual earner couples are likely to negotiate their 'work contracts' (inside and outside the household) on this basis rather than on the basis of conforming to a particular type of household employment pattern. In the construction of a new equality concerning the division of labour in the household, dual earner couples must forge new types of relationships together with a rhetoric in which equality is placed alongside, rather than covered up by, the current ideological baggage of a 'proper marriage' which turns on ideas about love and togetherness.

A third explanation as to why the dual earner lifestyle does not necessarily lead to a revolution in the private sphere relates to the gendered construction of parenthood and the powerful influences upon the construction of parenthood. Parental roles both shape and are shaped by the allocation of domestic and child care responsibilities and the ways in which men and women relate to one another in their partnerships. The behavioural and ideological practices of parents are also formed in a larger arena than simply the household. The growth of the army of experts, and the discourses concerning child care and childhood have required greater participation and new skills on the part of parents, notably mothers.

The discourses surrounding motherhood in the twentieth century have continued to emphasise the centrality of the mother–child relationship. From the 1950s, through the influence of Bowlby (1951), full-time maternal care was seen as essential in the prevention of emotional disorders in children. In addition, the latter part of the century has witnessed a new discourse which has demanded not merely the prevention of disorder in children but the maximisation of children's potential through the achievement of 'normal' development.

The main agent through which the norms of child development are to be achieved is the mother; moreover she is required not only to develop her child but also to take pleasure in doing it or the magic will not work (Urwin, 1985). As in the Bowlby discourse, the best conditions for this process are that the mother is full time, that is she is expected to devote all her time to her child's development. As mothers have often observed (privately), many full-time mothers fall far short of this goal, often letting their children get on with the process of growing up by themselves. This reality is however ignored by the official discourse.

Employed mothers are particularly vulnerable to official discourses on how to be 'proper' mothers since these discourses proscribe the 'leaving' of children. They are unlikely to be party to the private discourses of non-employed mothers particularly since, unlike mothers at home, they do not build up networks of other mothers after the birth (Brannen and Moss, 1990). In the absence of much informal contact with other mothers and fearing adverse effects from being absent from their children, employed mothers may seek to compensate their children for 'leaving' them and to allay their feelings of guilt by becoming ardent devotees of the 'child development industry'.

The ways in which women define money, motherhood and marriage are therefore unlikely to be mechanistically determined by the employment patterns which pertain to the household. They are definitions which lie at the heart of 'family life', a notion which is itself an ideological construction. They are permeated by a variety of ideologies which are reinforced by powerful agencies and institutions which extend beyond the labour market and the household. They relate to dominant ideologies concerning (a) male breadwinning – in particular, the idea that men are not expected to have breaks in their employment histories and, as a consequence, are the long-term providers for the household. They are contingent upon (b) ideas about love in marriage which tend to emphasise similarities within the couple and to cover up gender differences; and (c) ideas about the centrality and exclusivity of the mother–child relationship, ideas which have led to the prescriptive norm of full-time motherhood in the first years of children's lives.

Since these dominant ideologies are clearly somewhat at odds with a dual earner lifestyle in which both parents have an equal attachment to the labour market, a central task will be to explore how far women's definitions of their situations conform to and conflict with dominant ideologies. Secondly, if it is the case that these ideologies are reproduced in women's accounts, it is then necessary to throw some light upon the ways women deal with the disjunction between their employment behaviour on the one hand, and the ways in which they define their roles as earners, partners and mothers on the other. In other words, if the dual earner lifestyle does not undermine notions of a 'normal family life', how do women knit together ideological statements and practices which contradict one another? In short, my concern here is to examine the extent to which changes in public practices affect the ways in which ideologies are reinforced and played out in private relationships, among a group of families which deviate from the statistically and ideologically normative pattern.

WOMEN'S FULL-TIME EARNINGS – CORE OR PERIPHERAL INCOME?

In order to put the significance of full-timers' earnings into context, it may be helpful to indicate the employment patterns of these mothers and to compare them with the initially non-employed mothers over the course of the study. Of those who had a definite intention to return to work after maternity leave, 68 per cent were employed full time three years later, including 10 per cent who were still on maternity leave after a second birth. Those who definitely did not intend to resume work after maternity leave were unlikely to be employed three years later (76 per cent were not working). Those who were uncertain or who had already returned temporarily (9 per cent of the sample), were equally likely to be employed as non-employed, although if they were employed, most were in part-time jobs.

Women returning from maternity leave differ from non-returners in a number of ways. Returners, especially those who had a continuous full-time employment history throughout the study, were more likely to be older, to have higher qualifications (A level and above), to hold higher status occupations (Registrar General social classes 1 and 2), and to earn more than other groups. By the end of the three years, those with continuous full-time employment histories were less likely to have had a second child. Moreover women who resumed their jobs after a second child had only an evens chance of being in the labour market at the end of the study.

The issue of the way women defined their earnings was approached in a variety of ways and at different points in the study. Enquiries ranged from general open-ended questions about why women were returning to employment – financial reasons figured prominently here – to closed questions as to whether they contributed to particular items of household expenditure. An analysis of one set of responses produced one picture, while quite a different picture emerged from another part of the data. In some instances the data complement one another while, in other cases, there were contradictions.

A single question about whose money paid for the children's carers emerged as particularly significant when supplemented with spontaneous qualitative material in which women weighed up whether they could afford to work once they had paid the child care costs. Over four fifths paid for the daycare (primarily childminders and nurseries since many did not pay their relatives) out of their own earnings or out of joint earnings (through a joint bank account). Moreover, women saw these payments as their responsibility. As several women commented, since they saw themselves as having 'chosen' to go back to work, they therefore thought that they ought to pay for the child care. The definition of the decision to return to work as the mother's decision, rather than a household decision, is crucial here, even though the majority also gave financial reasons for returning (63 per cent of women in high status jobs and 72 per cent in low status jobs). Notably husbands' earnings were viewed without considering deductions for child care. Contingent upon employment as the mother's choice, women expected (and were expected) to bear the brunt of the costs of the dual earner lifestyle, including the running of a second car and paid domestic help.

The effects of mothers taking on the financial responsibility for child care and the dual earning lifestyle are twofold. First, they marginalise the value of women's earnings in the household *vis-à-vis* those of their husbands, both in real and symbolic terms.

> Half of my money gets paid out on childcare and the cleaner. [Why?] I think it's to do with the fact that I work that their cost is down to me. Because we've got a joint account in theory it doesn't matter. But I class it as coming out of my money. [What about your husband?] Yes, I suppose he does. Because he talks about 'As long as we're not spending more than half your salary it's probably worth it.' [Ms. Smith and her partner were high earners. Both were professionals working in the same large organisation.]

In many cases, husbands were said, as in the above example, to share the view that women's earnings were of secondary importance.

Second, the effect of women taking on the payment of the child care is a way of anticipating (and hence of coping with) withdrawal from the labour market especially if, for example, women had a second child. However, few women made this connection in the interviews. With two childcare placements to pay for, not to mention the additional domestic work involved, women may decide that it is not 'worth their while working' after a second birth. The culture of temporality surrounding mothers' employment underscores many women's accounts, even those of women who have no (immediate) intention of leaving the labour market, as in the following case.

> I've always said I will give up work when she starts school. I feel then I could do more of the things that I want to do... Just potter around without being disturbed... [Do you think you will give up?] I can't see us paying like a week's money to take her to school and pick her up. And then of course there's the summer holidays... I don't need a job that much – always providing we've got the money. [Ms. Ainsley, airline ground stewardess who uses a relative as a [paid] nanny.]

Questions about how much women earned show that, on average, their earnings represented a very substantial proportion of the household's total income (around 40 per cent). Closed questions about whether women contributed to particular items of household expenditure indicate that, in practice, women spent their money on the routine running of the household, notably the mortgage and the bills. Yet, at the same time, an examination of the ways in which women talk about their earnings is suggestive of ambiguity. Women not infrequently referred to their earnings as being for 'luxuries', 'extras', savings, and 'things we couldn't afford if I wasn't working'. The following quotation indicates some of this ambiguity.

> My money is important, yes. It's 50 per cent. We regard it as joint money.... But I mean because of the earnings of one of us, it means that we can save and we can enjoy spending on things.... [At the last interview, 18 months ago, you told me your earnings were mostly used as savings.] Yes, well, that's still my — . Well, I suppose it's my husband thinking 'I'm the one who's trying to cover everything in case you give up'. But I mean it's mainly joint money... It's mine that's providing the savings and care for [our son] and for my clothes [laughs]. I suppose sometimes if we have an extraordinary bill mine is the one who pays for it! [Ms. Jenson was a local government officer married to another local goverment officer. They were on the same grade and earned the same salary but worked for different authorities.]

There was little evidence that women's employment decisions were considered part of a household strategy as proposed by Pahl (1984). Moreover, men's and women's income retained a distinctive, separate significance, even though in practice they frequently formed an undifferentiated whole through a joint bank account.

Other questions (both closed and open) were designed to uncover women's longer-term employment goals. Employment did not seem to figure prominently in women's views of the future: the main benchmarks in their lives related to their children. No one mentioned the beneficial long-term consequences of a continuous employment record (Joshi, 1987), for example in the event of divorce or in connection with having an occupational pension in later life. Women's orientations centred on the short or medium term, not unsurprisingly given the overwhelming preoccupation with being a new mother, and they were significantly lacking in a long-term 'economic rationality'.

Questions were posed in order to encourage women to rank their jobs in relation to those of their husbands. In general most women said that when it came to the 'crunch' their husbands' jobs came first. One critical question, which was asked in the last round of the study to mothers who were still working when their children were three years old, required them to say which partner would be the one to give up employment should this become necessary. In the great majority of cases women said it would 'have to be' the mother. Justifications for this were as follows. First and foremost, husbands' jobs were said to assume more importance because they earned more or would do so in the long term. Second, employment was said to mean more to men than to women. Third, some women said that their marriages depended upon their husband being in employment because he would be happy only if he had a job. Conversely, husbands were seen as unlikely candidates for child care. It was noticeable that women put the matter this way round rather than the other, i.e. that they would prefer to be the ones to care for the child.

Attention to the content of what women said and what they failed to say – the absence of data as well as its presence – suggests that, even in that minority of cases where women gave their own jobs priority, they lacked a clearly and confidently articulated discourse with which to say why. The issue of absence of data can only be addressed if the respondent has some choice about what to talk about; women in the study were given ample opportunity to direct the course of the interview. The dominance of the ideology that men ought to be the main breadwinners appears to have effectively suppressed the emergence of a clear counter ideology.

A somewhat contradictory picture emerges, therefore, concerning the significance these full-time employed women attached to their earnings as a household resource. Despite their dual earner household employment pattern, the relative size of their earnings, and the use to which the earnings were put (on all major items of household expenditure), many viewed themselves as providers of peripheral rather than core income. In particular the ways in which women talked about their employment is suggestive of a culture of impermanence even though, as the longitudinal data reveal, many of them were anything but temporary members of the labour market.

WOMEN'S SATISFACTION WITH INEQUALITY ON THE DOMESTIC FRONT

In response to a single, normative question concerning gender roles, 84 per cent subscribed to the notion of equal shares in the division of child care and domestic responsibilities. Yet, in practice, fathers in less than 10 per cent of these dual earner households participated equally in either routine child care and the housework, or in such matters as the making and maintaining of the child care arrangements. Moreover, despite a clear normative commitment, employed mothers were noticeably uncritical of the failure of their husbands to share the workload.

The commitment to the ideal of equal sharing of the domestic workload was addressed by a single question, the responses to which were coded and quantified. This treatment of the issue may explain the simplistic, homogeneous picture which emerged. While the routine division of labour was explored by means of self-completion questionnaires and was analysed quantitatively, open-ended questions were posed with respect to decisions about child care, etc., and were analysed both quantitatively and qualitatively. Satisfaction with husbands' involvement was approached in two ways: firstly through responses to direct questions, computed and treated quantitatively on a four point rating scale, concerning women's overall satisfaction with husbands' contributions; and secondly through comments derived from a reading of the whole interview which were content analysed to obtain data about husbands' support around particular issues, as well as issues which emerged spontaneously.

The qualitative and quantitative data on women's satisfaction with their partners are somewhat at odds with one another, even though some 'contamination' between them may have taken place. The picture presented by the quantitative responses is one of a relative absence of dissatisfaction, which is surprising given the heavy work schedules borne by mothers and given their clear normative commitment to equality. For example, only 15 per cent of women were rated as being dissatisfied with husbands' support over the decision to return, and only 13 per cent over the making of the child care arrangements. Dissatisfaction was more prevalent in relation to routine domestic and child care tasks: 36 per cent were dissatisfied and 18 per cent gave a mixed response. The rest were coded satisfied or non-committal.

The material based on the qualitative analysis of the whole interviews in some instances contradicts the quantitative data, suggesting that women may be more dissatisfied than they professed to be. But what emerges most clearly are women's strategies for dealing with these dilemmas, namely the ways in which they justified the discrepancy between their equal involvement in paid employment and their inequitable share of domestic and child care work. In some cases, a less than equal contribution by husbands caused women to complain but only a little; others were uncomplaining. But both groups readily excused their husbands on the following grounds: their masculine gender, their high commitment to employment, their responsibility for 'breadwinning', and their lack of skill and expertise in caring and household work. Even those who voiced some criticism of their husbands rarely subjected them to overt or blanket criticism; for example, women restricted their complaints to specific activities and occasions. Alternatively, criticism was retracted and women blatantly contradicted themselves, as in the following quotation. Or the remark was balanced out with an approving one. Characteristically, women drew upon notions of 'fairness', sometimes falling over backwards to acknowledge signs of help.

> Although I've said he hasn't been very good, he has been very good. He's been very patient. It's unfair to say he doesn't do any.

Another strategy was to be 'thankful for small mercies' – to be grateful for any help that was proffered, however slight. No women directly challenged the assumption that they were the ones responsible for domestic matters, especially the child. The exemption of husbands from major criticism arises in the context of a variety of negotiated, normative assumptions concerning the conduct of gender roles. These assumptions were also renegotiated in the course of the research interview. During the interview women had to deal with the discrepancy between ideological and behavioural practices: a conservative ideology of gender roles and the realities of the dual earner lifestyle. In Britain the dominant ideology – that the man is the main breadwinner and that the woman should look after a young child full time and form the main, exclusive tie with the child – is evident and widespread in household practices, especially in the family formation phase of the life course. Such ideologies continue to hold sway even among this minority of non-traditional dual earner households.

Interviews are conducted according to normative assumptions concerning the disclosure of information and the conduct of interpersonal relationships. In the conduct of their marriages women expect and are expected to be loyal to their partners and not to let them down by revealing their deficiencies to others outside the marriage. This is not however to suggest that women were particularly protective of their marriages when confronted with the researchers' questions. Rather the issue is one of revelations concerning the marriage to any person, including the self. With respect to disclosure, wives are constrained by the normative emphasis upon happiness in marriage;

admitting to a less than happy marriage is uncomfortable and contradictory when an intact relationship is being outwardly presented to the world.

Women placed higher value on emotional sharing and togetherness in their relationships with their partners than they did on the practical division of labour in the household. It is notable that husbands were mentioned as confidants (at the first round of the study) – persons to whom women would turn to first in the event of a personal worry. Furthermore, partners were regarded far and away as the most supportive persons in women's first three years of being employed mothers. Eighty-five per cent mentioned their husbands as being among the three most important persons; 66 per cent mentioned their husbands first. Most of this support was not of a practical nature.

Expectations of emotional support from husbands resonate with ideologies of love and its centrality to Western ideas of modern marriage (Lawson, 1989). According to this formulation, marriage is defined at the level of feeling (love) and negotiated according to norms of altruism. The result is that difference and inequality, power and self interest are by definition excluded. As Phyllis Rose notes in writing about Victorian marriages:

> Perhaps this is what love is – the momentary or prolonged refusal to think of another person in terms of power. Like an enzyme which momentarily blocks a normal biological process, what we call love may inhibit the process of power negotiation – from which inhibition comes the illusion of equality so characteristic of lovers. (Rose, 1985, p. 16)

A careful examination of the nature of the actual support provided by partners reveals that, not infrequently, it was more potential than real. Many women found it hard to mention anything that their partners actually did. Rather they emphasised the importance of their partners 'just being there' or noted that they 'would' help in a crisis. Such support, albeit symbolic, was however real in its consequences and many women felt heavily reliant upon it. Paying homage to husbands' emotional support may therefore be seen as a strategy whereby attention is deflected away from underlying inequalities in men's and women's material situations. Instead it serves to bridge men's and women's very different experiences as marriage partners, parents and wage earners.

Attention to the subtleties of what women were saying, what they were not saying, and the ways in which certain issues were understated helped to make sense of the quantitative data concerning women's apparent satisfaction with inequality in the household, a finding which was initially rather puzzling. An understanding of the negotiation of the research interview is also suggestive of the way women dealt with potential conflict in their lives and the contradictions between ideologies and practice.

NORMATIVE MOTHERHOOD – THE SUPPRESSION OF EMPLOYMENT

In women's responses to open-ended, general questions about the experience of motherhood especially the pleasurable aspects, there were almost no references to women's status as employed mothers. Indeed, it would seem that these mothers largely constructed the rewards of motherhood according to features of 'normal', i.e. full-time motherhood. Given the social stigma attached to maternal employment when children are small, together with the guilt which most mothers in the study experienced at least occasionally, such socially acceptable responses are perhaps to be expected.

One of the main preoccupations was the importance of time with and for the child: the giving of time as an end in itself and as a means to an end – the development of the child's potential (Hallden, 1988). Despite these mothers' full-time employment which heavily constrained the time they could be available to their children, and despite their considerable reservations about being at home (even during maternity leave), their accounts of motherhood constructed mothers as the principal figures in bringing about 'normal' developmental progress principally by giving as much time as possible to the child. In order that this task should be fulfilled they also stressed how important it was that they should enjoy the mothering work.

In contrast to these general, open-ended questions designed to get women to talk openly about motherhood, some of the direct, focused questions produced the admission of strong negative and positive feelings in connection with their employment status. These were noticeably absent from their general accounts of motherhood. In particular, when asked if they ever felt guilty many owned up to this feeling, describing in detail the particular conditions which provoked it.

When asked directly whether there were any benefits to combining full-time employment with motherhood, and the relative balance of costs and benefits, the great majority were more positive than negative (80 per cent). In particular, many testified to a heightened quality in their relationships with their children because they were not with them all the time, thereby suggesting yet another meaning to giving children time. In addition, many asserted that they were better mothers and better people as a result of their paid employment. Some were at pains to demonstrate that they had not 'missed out' on their children through their employment, mentioning that they had in fact witnessed their children's first words and first steps. But by implying that they were exceptional in this respect, working mothers constructed their experiences according to the dominant paradigm.

> I've been very lucky. I've seen firsts with both of them. And I gather that's quite unique not being there all day. The chances of them doing something.... I sometimes wonder if [nanny] isn't telling a fib so I'll get the pleasure.

It was also notable that, among those who felt that motherhood had changed them, more returners than non-returners felt that the change had been a positive one. The emphasis upon motherhood as an enjoyable activity, both for the child's well being as well as the mother's, is a possible beginning to a countervailing ideology with respect to maternal employment – namely that if a woman is unhappy as a full-time mother then it may be better to go out to work, both for herself and her child. However, it was one which largely remained under-played and under-developed, overshadowed by the dominant paradigm.

Women's accounts of their experiences of combining employment with motherhood are therefore somewhat piecemeal and contain contradictory elements. They reflect both the substantive and ideological divisions in women's lives between the public and private spheres and the divisions within the interviews themselves – the separation of questions concerning motherhood and employment. Through the process of compartmentalisation women achieved a degree of integration between the ways in which they reproduced the dominant ideologies of motherhood and the specific practices which contravened these ideologies, namely returning to full-time employment in the child's first year of life.

CONCLUSION

The process of making sense of these data concerning households in which both parents are employed full-time with a young child has uncovered a number of discrepancies between the ways in which the mothers reproduced dominant ideologies with respect to family life – breadwinning, marriage and motherhood – and their practices in the labour market. In addition the chapter has highlighted the interview process and the mechanisms whereby the discrepant elements in women's accounts are welded together into some kind of whole without respondents necessarily confronting the inherent contradictions. The failure on the part of human beings to connect the fragments of the reality they construct – what they believe, what they do and what they report – is both a human frailty and a human strength. It is therefore not so surprising that a change in women's behavioural attachment to the labour market should generate, not a domestic revolution, but a process of accommodation to existing inequalities in domestic roles.

5 Employment and Domestic Work: A Comparison of Samples of British and French Women[1]

Ian Procter and Peter Ratcliffe

Increasing attention has recently been paid to the comparative analysis of women's labour force participation (Jenson, 1988; Mincer, 1985; Paukert, 1984; Rubery, 1988). Whilst labour economists have highlighted a converging trend, linked with hypotheses on the role of human capital (Mincer, 1985), sociologists have focussed upon significant differences associated with variation in the social institutional context in which the labour market operates.[2] Here the comparison of Britain and France becomes clearly relevant (Beechey, 1989; Benoit Guilbot, 1987; Dex and Walters, 1989; Walters and Dex in this volume). Both are developed industrialised societies with roughly similar rates of overall female labour force participation.[3] Yet two differences stand out, the propensity to continuity of women's employment over their working lives and the proportion of women who work part-time.

Figure 5.1 illustrates these differences. In Britain 60 per cent of women in the 20–24 age range are in employment. This drops to just over 50 per cent between the ages of 25 and 34 before moving towards 70 per cent of women in their forties. But for full-time women workers the initial high point of the early twenties is never recovered – women's participation in full-time employment varies between a quarter and a third of all women until the early fifties age group. In France, the situation differs on both points. The employment rate of women in their early twenties is rather lower than in Britain (55 per cent) but continues to rise in the later twenties and remains steady at over 60 per cent until after the late forties age group. Looking at women in full-time employment the same pattern is evident – a rising rate of full-time employment in the twenties which holds up at around 50 per cent

Figure 5.1   Employment participation rates, women aged 20–64, by five-year age groups, Britain and France

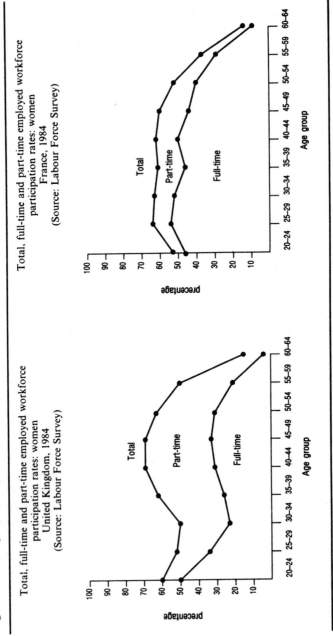

Total, full-time and part-time employed workforce
participation rates: women
United Kingdom, 1984
(Source: Labour Force Survey)

Total, full-time and part-time employed workforce
participation rates: women
France, 1984
(Source: Labour Force Survey)

Source: A. Dale and J. Glover, 'An Analysis of Women's Employment Patterns in the UK, France and the USA: the Value of Survey Based Comparisons', Research Paper No. 75 (London: Department of Employment, 1990), Figure 18, pp. 53.

until the late forties. In sum, British women still show a much higher rate of labour market withdrawal in the peak child-rearing phase of life and tend to return to part-time employment after this; French women show a much lower rate of withdrawal when children are young and remain in full-time employment to a far greater degree.

Turning to explanation of these differences, a number of avenues have been explored. In terms of the demand for labour, Jenson (1988) and Dex and Walters (1989) have indicated how state regulation of 'non-standard job forms' (particularly part-time employment) differs markedly in the two countries, with the British state adopting a permissive stance and the French attempting to regulate employers' use of such practices.

State policy has also been invoked on the supply-side of the labour market in its differential support for working mothers in the two countries (Walters and Dex in this volume). In an exploratory paper, Beechey (1989) pursues the supply side argument by highlighting child care provision and the cultural definition of women as mothers and workers. Her case is that women's continuous, full-time employment is facilitated in France by an extensive system of child care provision and cultural support for working mothers. By contrast, women's continuous, full-time employment is inhibited in Britain by the lack of child care provision and a cultural context in which the working mother has been defined as the source of social problems.

Historically, these two factors are probably linked. In their classic comparison of employment and family in the process of British and French industrialisation, Tilly and Scott (1987) show how the British demand and supply of young, single women workers differed from the demand and supply of married women workers in France. The social policy implications of this are described by Jenson (1986) in her discussion of the French state's preoccupation with the low fertility of French women in an economy of *de facto* working mothers in peasant and workshop enterprises which contrasts with the British state's preoccupation with the pathologies associated with working mothers. The differing pattern of employment, family formation, and state policy in the process of industrialisation thus come together to encourage the state, employers and women workers to adopt contrasting attitudes to working mothers and different practices for the care of young children.

The question remains how far these historical differences remain and are efficacious in shaping the supply of women workers. A further question is their interrelationship, especially whether child care provision and its use by mothers is dependent upon a culture supportive of working mothers.

In this chapter data relevant to these questions is presented, drawn from a comparative survey which included items on British and French attitudes to women's family and employment roles and actual use of child care facilities. The following sections describe the two samples used, the pattern of economic activity during the time respondents had young children, and the value of child care and culture as explanatory factors.

THE TWO SAMPLES

The chapter draws upon work history and attitudinal data from two samples of women interviewed during 1987–8 in Coventry, England, and Rouen, France. The Coventry sample included 183 women, the Rouen group 181. In constructing the samples the research team was clear that the intention was not to claim that the data would be representative of the national or urban populations as a whole but of specified groups within the population. It was intended to match the British and French samples as closely as possible to facilitate cross-cultural comparison for a specified group within the two societies.

Those included in the samples were all married, or living as married with a partner, and all had at least one dependent child. The samples were drawn from a district of each city selected on the grounds of high proportions of male manual workers, unemployment rates at about the average for the urban area and relatively low proportions of ethnic minority residents. In constructing samples in such terms the intention was to focus on specific groups within the population and this clearly has implications for the generality of the results. To repeat, the sampling strategy excluded single people, favoured people in the twenties to forties age range and people with 'working-class' occupations, and was unlikely to include large numbers from ethnic minorities.

To attain the various purposes of the research project,[4] it was also our intention to obtain samples equally matched in terms of numbers of employed, unemployed and non-active.[5] To achieve the samples, interviewers were allocated target numbers for these three economic statuses in geographically delimited areas of the districts. A 'random walk' technique was employed to move through the area until the quota was filled. This worked up to a point, being successful in achieving the desired sample in terms of sex, marital status and family composition but rather less so in terms of economic status.

Here two problems were met. In France the random walk technique was difficult to operate and it was decided to shift to a sample frame of the unemployed supplied by Agence Nationale pour l'Emploi. In other words, all but two of the French unemployed are registered as unemployed. The second problem concerned the British sample. Initially, this was split equally three ways but on closer inspection of information provided, it was decided to reclassify some respondents from 'unemployed' to 'non-active'. This means that the British sample under-represents unemployed women and over-represents non-active women. To compensate for this imbalance in sample composition, the British unemployed have been weighted at 1.3 and non-active women at 0.7 in the tables presented in this chapter.

Some key features of the samples can be examined in Table 5.1 to check the degree to which they are matched. The two samples are well matched in terms of the average age of the respondent (33 in Coventry, 35 in Rouen) and number of children (2.1 and 2.2). The children of British repondents are rather younger: 31 per cent were all under five years as against 20 per cent of the French. Eleven per cent of the French children were all over 16 years as against only 4 per cent of the British. Although the difference in the ages of children is statistically significant at the 0.05 level it will be seen that these hardly seem material differences as compared to the patterns of labour market activity considered in the next section.

The figures for occupation and industry refer to the woman's current job if she was employed or to her last job.[6] Occupationally and industrially, the two samples are remarkably similar. In both, women's occupations bunch in lower non-manual and partly skilled manual work, their industries in manufacturing, distribution and other services, especially public services. The main difference lies within industrial concentration: in Britain 45 per cent are found in other services and 24 per cent in distribution, in France 30 per cent in other services, 35 per cent in distribution. This difference does not appear to be a material one in the present context.

With the caveat regarding statistical weighting and within the limits specified above, two comparable samples can thus be deployed to investigate women's labour force participation.

Table 5.1   Demographic and economic characteristics of the Coventry
and Rouen female samples

	Coventry	Rouen
Average age	33 years	35 years
N = *	(170)	(181)
Average no. of children	2.1	2.2
N =	(172)	(179)
Ages of children	% of respondents	
All under 5 years	30	20
At least one < 5	24	26
All 5 to 16 years	28	30
At least one 5 to 16	13	13
All over 16 years	4	11
Total	100	100
N =	(172)	(179)
Current economic status	% of respondents	
Employed	36	34
Unemployed	32	33
Non-active	32	33
Total	100	100
N =	(171)	(181)
Occupation	% of respondents	
Not determinable	9	8
Small self-employed	1	1
Manager/professional	4	2
Supervisory and technical	14	10
Lower non-manual	45	49
Skilled manual	6	6
Partly and unskilled	22	24
Total	100	100
N =	(172)	(176)
Industry	% of respondents	
Agriculture	1	1
Energy	1	1
Manufacturing	21	24
Construction	1	3
Distribution	24	35
Transport and communication	3	3
Financial services	4	4
Other services	45	30
Total	101	101
N =	(152)	(155)

* Weighted *N* is used in all tables, see text.

ECONOMIC ACTIVITY IN THE 'PEAK CHILD-REARING PERIOD'

The 'peak child-rearing period' is defined as the time in a woman's life between the birth of her first child and when her last child reaches five years of age, or the time of interview if her youngest child was not yet five.[7] This is a crucial period from the point of view of women's employment, as it marks the time when combining domestic and employment responsibilities is most difficult. However, there are significant differences between the two samples in the extent and kind of labour market activity in this period. On average, the Coventry women had spent 45 per cent of the period economically active, the Rouen women, 57 per cent. Whether a woman had spent all, some, or none of the peak period economically active is shown in Table 5.2.

Table 5.2 Percentage of 'peak child-rearing period' spent economically active by country

	Coventry	Rouen
None	25	23
Some	54	35
All	21	41
Total	100%	100%
N =	(172)	(181)

A far higher proportion of the French women (41 per cent) had spent all the peak child-rearing period in the labour market than the British (21 per cent). There was no difference in the proportions who had spent none of the period economically active, but a difference is apparent amongst those who spent some time in the labour market. In Britain this applied to 54 per cent of the sample, in France 35 per cent. Thus our data are consistent with the lifetime participation patterns noted earlier: in France a higher proportion is active continuously, in Britain a large proportion become non-active for a period around the time of child bearing and the most demanding child care.

The data are also consistent in terms of part-time and full-time employment. Looking first at the employed respondents in the samples, amongst the British only 27 per cent were employed full-time, 73 per cent part-time. Amongst the French, almost the opposite is the case, 65 per cent were employed full-time, 35 per cent part-time. This is also apparent in the amount of time spent in full- or part-time employment in the peak child-rearing period. The mean proportion of the period spent in full-time employment in Britain was only 9 per cent, in part-time employment 19 per cent. In France women had spent an average of 35 per cent of the period in full-time employment, only 6 per cent of the period in part-time employment.

SOME EXPLANATORY FACTORS

Turning to consideration of possible explanatory factors on the labour supply side of the market, to which we are confined by the data, Beechey's suggestions can act as the point of reference. These are that child care facilities in France enable women to continue in the labour market in the child bearing and rearing phase of life and that French culture gives greater support to maternal employment than British (1989, pp. 371–2). She argues that the supply of labour is socially constructed and not simply the natural product of immutable demographic trends. Two facets of state policy are highlighted in support of this position. First, the degree to which the state makes provision for young children whilst their parents are at their workplace. In France, 95 per cent of 3 to 5-year-old children enter 'pre-primary schooling' and there is an array of nursery facilities for children under 3 years of age (Moss, 1988, p. 93, see later for further discussion). Furthermore, the fiscal attitude of the state has supported the working mother by granting the cost of child care as an allowance against tax (Moss, 1988, p. 72). By contrast, in Britain, only a minority of under fives attend school and then on a part-time basis. Provision for very young children is minimal (Moss, 1988, p. 96). In addition, until the 1990 Budget, the use of employer provided nursery facilities by a working parent was regarded by the Inland Revenue as taxable income. The concession in that Budget affects only a tiny number of people and does not begin to move to the French position of allowing the expenses of child care to be offset against tax.

   But state policy and provision do not emerge in a vacuum. Beechey's second claim is that labour supply is shaped by 'cultural constructions' (1989, p. 372) arising from ideological struggles. Here she draws upon Jenson's (1986) analysis of the origins of state family policy in Britain and France. Jenson identifies the thirty year period before the First

World War as crucial. This was a context in which otherwise opposed social forces came to agreement on some social problems and state responses. On the one hand, imperialists and militarists were preoccupied with the size of the population and the health of the potential soldier. On the other hand, feminists and organised labour agitated for the rights of women and workers. Both sides agreed that the high rates of infant mortality were a serious social issue and that the state should intervene. But the consensus around the nature of that intervention differed in Britain and France. In Britain, the diagnosis of the infant mortality problem focused on its link with maternal employment, and the solution was to discourage the working mother. In France, 'state policy-makers. . . indicated their acceptance of women's employment as a fact of life' (Jenson, 1986, p. 19) and the solution focused upon demands for paid maternity leave, introduced in 1913.

Culture as an Explanatory Factor

Data from a sample survey cannot test such interpretations of the past but, insofar as historical struggles have shaped cultural assumptions, these should be manifest in people's expressions of their attitudes. The Coventry–Rouen study was based on a common questionnaire which included a range of questions on employment and domestic responsibilities. Material on the domestic division of labour, attitudes to working mothers, and early socialisation into attitudes to work and motherhood is presented next to consider cultural definitions as represented in attitudinal data.

To the extent that French culture is more conducive to maternal employment, a more equitable division of domestic labour might be expected as compared to Britain, in that a woman's role is not associated wholly with homemaking and child care. The data shows this *not* to be the case, indeed there was a remarkable similarity between the two samples. Thus, in Coventry, 69 per cent of women told us that they did almost all or most of the routine domestic work, and in Rouen the figure was 74 per cent. Furthermore, French women seemed more inclined to accept this imbalance, 66 per cent saying that the division of labour was as it should be as against 51 per cent of the British women. Similar proportions of both samples agreed with the statement 'I am not against women working but men should be the breadwinners in the family', 51 per cent of the Coventry women, 46 per cent of the Rouen women. Whilst the pattern of domestic labour seemed quite traditional in both samples and seemed to be accepted as such by around half of each, there was a common recognition that combining such a division of responsibilities with employment caused problems for women: 83 per cent of both samples agreed with the statement 'For most working women it causes a lot of strain trying to combine work and family life'. So from the point of view of coping with the tasks of domestic life, French culture clearly gives no more support to the woman waged worker than the British.

A range of questions about working mothers was included. The picture which emerges is not unequivocal but there is some indication here of more positive support for maternal employment in France. Sixty per cent of British women and 62 per cent of the French perceived a general social disapproval of working mothers insofar as they agreed with the statement 'Most people disapprove of women who go out to work when their children are young'. However, when asked their own view, 26 per cent of the Rouen sample thought that 'A woman should keep her job even when she has young children' as against 19 per cent of the Coventry women. Again, 35 per cent of the Rouen women thought that a woman with young children should leave her job, rather lower than the 44 per cent of Coventry women who thought this was what women should do.[8] When asked what their husbands thought about this, 26 per cent of the French said their husbands would say that a working mother should keep her job, rather higher than the 19 per cent of Coventry women who took this view. Conversely, the proportion of French women who said their husbands would approve of women leaving their job was rather lower (49 per cent) than the British (60 per cent). So in both samples only a minority of women felt that women with young children should continue in employment and only a minority felt their husbands would agree with them, but the minority is rather larger in France than in Britain. On the other hand, only a minority felt that a mother should leave her job, but that was rather smaller in France than in Britain, and fewer French women thought that husbands would expect women with children to leave jobs.

On a number of other questions, the French respondents displayed a more positive attitude to maternal employment than the British. Far fewer of them agreed with the statement 'Being at home with the family is more enjoyable than going out to work', 43 per cent as compared to 65 per cent of the British women. Fifty-three per cent of the Rouen sample agreed that 'A woman who goes out to work is more respected within her own family' as against only 37 per cent of the Coventry women. On the other hand, rather more of the Coventry sample thought that 'A mother who goes out to work is likely to be a better mother because she will be more stimulating for her children', 32 per cent as compared to 25 per cent of the French, but this difference was not statistically significant. Finally, when asked whether women should withdraw from employment in times of high male unemployment, only 25 per cent of British women agreed, much lower than the 41 per cent of the French. However, the significance of this is ambiguous. It is arguable that the higher French figure reflects French women's perception of their role as full-time workers and to that extent, replaceable by male workers, a scenario much more unrealistic for Britain's large proportion of female part-time workers.

Questions were asked of unemployed women which are relevant as indicators of the significance of employment to them. In both samples about half agreed that they felt 'rather useless', and said that they got depressed. Rather larger proportions missed the routine of a paid job and agreed that unemployment inhibited sociability with friends. However, there were also some differences here. Interviewees were asked what they thought of the statement 'Other people sometimes look down on me because I haven't got a paid job'. Only 20 per cent of the Coventry women agreed that this was the case, 80 per cent clearly rejecting it. In Rouen, however, 56 per cent agreed and only 37 per cent disagreed. Again, whilst 57 per cent of the Coventry women agreed that unemployment 'makes me feel too dependent on the income of other people in the family' the figure in Rouen was 70 per cent. When asked whether they needed the money from a paid job, 67 per cent of the Coventry women said that they did, while in Rouen the proportion was as high as 86 per cent. So, whilst there was agreement among both British and French unemployed women that the consequences of unemployment were wholly negative, some of these are much more strongly pronounced amongst the Rouen respondents, possibly indicating a more employment oriented culture for married women.

To begin to explore early socialisation into work and family roles, respondents were asked to recall what, in their last year at school, they expected to do in the future, choosing from the following options:

To stop work on marriage and not to work again.
To stop work at the birth of a first child and not to work again.
To stop work at the birth of a first child but to go back to work after several years.
To continue work throughout life except for short breaks at the birth of children.

Table 5.3 displays the responses to this question amongst the French and British respondents, amalgamating the first two possibilities as both indicated an expectation of a temporary sojourn in the labour market followed by permanent withdrawal.

Table 5.3   Recollections of labour market participation intentions in last year of school (column percentages)

	Coventry	Rouen
To work until marriage/first child only	16	19
To return to work after a break for children	46	28
To work continuously except for short breaks	37	53
Totals	99	100
$N =$	(154)	(152)

What is suggested here is that early socialisation reflects national patterns. A much larger proportion of the British women anticipated breaking their employment for children and then returning. Conversely, more of the French had anticipated working continuously throughout life. This suggests a cultural influence but unfortunately the nature of that influence is difficult to pin down. Two possibilities were envisaged, mothers as role models and expectations deriving from education.

With regard to mothers, the hypothesis was that French mothers would have been more likely to have been employed, even if in the 'traditional' sector as indicated by Tilly and Scott (1987) and Berger (1980). However, the data do not support this: 52 per cent of Rouen respondents said that their mothers had never been employed when they were children, much higher than the 27 per cent of Coventry mothers.

Turning to education, human capital theory is frequently invoked to explain cross-cultural variations in women's economic activity (see, for example, Mincer, 1985; Hage, Garnier and Fuller, 1988; Brinton, 1988). A key idea here is that increased educational provision leads to higher participation rates. Within the samples, the average age at which women left school was almost identical, 16.2 years in Britain, 16.4 in France. However, there was some variation in the highest educational qualification women had obtained.

The comparison of qualifications must not be regarded as exact as this involves the complicated task not only of matching qualifications cross-culturally but different qualifications over time.[9] However, rather more of the Coventry sample had no qualifications at all, 41 per cent, as compared to 30 per cent of the Rouen sample, whereas more of the Rouen sample had 'lower secondary' qualifications than the Coventry women. Whilst more of the British had secondary qualifications, rather more of the French had non-professional vocational credentials. Finally, of the more qualified, the British tended to have higher secondary qualifications, the French higher education and professional. The human capital expectation that higher qualifications explain greater labour market participation is now examined (Table 5.4).

Table 5.4   Percentage of 'peak child-rearing period' spent economically active by level of qualification and country

Highest qualification	Coventry		Rouen	
	%	N	%	N
None	37	(70)	41	(54)
Lower secondary	39	(18)	54	(39)
Secondary	58	(35)	55	(16)
Non-professional vocational	44	(24)	62	(45)
Higher secondary	53	(7)	62	(7)
Higher education/professional	55	(18)	93	(20)
All mothers	45	(172)	57	(181)

For the French respondents, there appears to be a relationship between qualification level and degree of participation. But in Britain the pattern is not evident. Furthermore, at *each* qualification level (excepting the secondary), the French participation rate is higher than the British equivalent. These findings go against human capital theory, since it is not that the French respondents were more highly qualified that matters, as at any level they were more economically active than the British.

This concludes the discussion of national cultural influences on women's labour market participation. The broad expectation was that if French culture is more supportive of women's employment than British, then this would manifest itself in the domestic division of labour, attitudes to working mothers, the significance of employment to unemployed women and pre-adult expectations. Some support for this hypothesis comes from the apparent differences between British and French data on girls' expectations of their working lives and the significance of employment for unemployed women. But against this there is no difference between the French and the British on the domestic division of labour. On working mothers the data is equivocal, some questions reveal a more employment centred culture, but others do not. The conclusion must be that differences in women's labour market participation cannot be accounted for in terms of the two national cultures, the variation in cultural attitudes revealed here is unlikely to be sufficiently strong to have such an effect.

Child Care as an Explanatory Factor

Beechey's second claim is that labour supply is shaped by the availability of child care and that there is a substantial difference here between Britain and France. Moss's (1988) report to the European Commission brings out the extent of the difference both in provision and the state's fiscal attitude to child care. In the UK he estimates that only 2 per cent of children under three years of age are in publicly funded nurseries, rising to 44 per cent of three to four-year-olds in pre- and early primary schooling. The latter figure has to be severely qualified as in pre-primary schooling the child attends for only a few hours each day, whilst early primary schooling is essentially a brief period of introduction to school for four year olds who are 'rising 5'. In addition there is an unknown proportion of children looked after by nannies and childminders for whom no public support is given either through the tax or social security system.

In France the most significant fact is that almost all children start pre-primary education at 3 years of age for 5–6 hours per day with care extended outside school hours in a 'substantial proportion of schools' (Moss, 1988, p. 93). For younger children, there is provision for 20–25 per cent of children in publicly funded nurseries. In addition there is an array of non-publicly funded but supervised facilities – *multi-accueil, jardins d'enfants, haltes gardineries and crèches familiales* (M.S.S.P.S., 1989).[10] However, both in hours of care and the number of places it is doubtful whether these provide much of an extension to the nurseries. Rather a key role is played by *assistantes maternelles* or childminders and, less significantly, women who come to the child's home to care for her/him (see later).

French state financial support for child care is extensive (Moss, 1988, pp. 72–3). For families where both parents are employed and children are looked after outside the family home, the mother can claim a tax allowance, of 10 000 FF per year in 1989, to cover the cost of care for each child. With regard to social security, two systems operate depending on whether the caregiver works in the child's home or the caregiver's. In the former, a state grant of 2000 FF per month is available, in the latter a grant of 300 FF per month for each child. These are dependent upon registration of the caregiver, which involves payment of social security contributions. The grants to parents are in fact explicitly intended to cover these contributions and incorporate such caregivers into the employment system.

The French and British systems thus offer significantly different levels of provision. The question remaining is the level of actual usage of child care by women workers. Here the evidence of the Coventry and Rouen samples can be deployed. Respondents were asked if they had ever had to leave a job because of pregnancy or the need to look after children: 69 per cent of the Coventry women said that they had left a job in such circumstances, whereas only 29 per cent of the Rouen women said they had been in the same position. They were further asked whether anyone else but themselves had looked after their children during their pre-school years. Amongst the Coventry women, 44 per cent replied yes; in Rouen 64 per cent of respondents had had assistance with child care. There was a further difference in the kind of assistance received (this was a multiple response question). Of the British responses, fully 75 per cent included assistance from family and friends and only 25 per cent childminders, playgroups and nurseries. In France, only 44 per cent of assistance came from family and friends, with 56 per cent from more formal providers. Finally, respondents were asked whether difficulty in finding adequate child care facilities had ever prevented them taking a job. Twenty-two per cent of the British said that this had been the case, significantly higher than the 13 per cent of French women who had been deterred from taking employment for this reason. Thus, amongst the French respondents, many fewer had had to leave jobs because of children, far more had used child care assistance, which tended to be from more formal rather than informal sources, and fewer said they had been prevented from taking employment by lack of child care.

However, some points of qualification should be added with regard to French provision for the care of children under three years of age, particularly in the case of child care outside nurseries. As already noted, Moss estimates that publicly funded nurseries are provided for 20–25 per cent of young children.[11] In France a key role is played by *assistantes maternelles* and women employed in the child's home. The bulk of formal support for mothers in the Rouen sample came in fact from childminders (53 per cent as against only 3 per cent from other formal sources).

The French system allows a parent paying a childminder to claim costs against tax up to 10 000 FF per year and to claim a grant to cover the childminder's social security contributions. But as Moss points out 'the actual subsidy to parents from tax relief comes to well under half parents' total child care costs where they are a service which is not publicly funded' (1988, pp. 72–3). Furthermore, whilst the inclusion of caregivers in the social security system should be noted, there remains the possibility that the French child care system encourages the use of cheap female labour outside nursery provision for many young children. The Ministry estimated the number of *assistantes maternelles* to be 133 300 in January 1989 (M.S.S.P.S., 1989).

Nevertheless, with this caution against complacency, it is clear that there is a significant difference between the extent of formal provision for the care of children of working mothers in Britain and France and in the fiscal arrangements in the two countries which deter or encourage such provision. This is reflected in the evidence from the two samples of mothers where the 'problem' of child care is much less significant within the Rouen group as compared to the women in Coventry. The data is consistent with Beechey's hypothesis that there is a social institutional difference which shapes the supply of labour and plays its part in the different pattern of women's employment in the two countries.

CONCLUSION

This chapter has used work history and survey data drawn from matched samples of women living in Coventry and Rouen. The work history data is consistent with national aggregate labour market participation patterns. French mothers have a greater propensity to work continuously and to work full-time through the main child bearing and rearing period. British mothers tend to withdraw temporarily from the labour market at this period and have a higher propensity to part-time employment.

In seeking to throw light on these differences, Beechey's suggestions about the shaping of labour supply by social factors have been developed. These are that the cultural construction of motherhood in

Britain and France and the extent of child care provision in the two societies may account for the different patterns of economic activity. The evidence with regard to manifestations of culture in a range of attitudinal data is ambiguous. There are certain indications that French culture is more supportive of maternal employment than British, but this is equivocal and the conclusion must be that this argument is not a strong one. Certainly there appears to be a greater use of formal child care provision by the French respondents. Here the sample data showed clear differences in the extent and type of child care usage by working mothers. Labour force participation had been far less inhibited in the case of French respondents. This is consistent with the far more elaborate range of provision in France and the financial support given by the French state to working mothers who employ others to help look after their children.

Perhaps the most interesting policy implication of these findings is the lack of interconnection of the cultural and child care factors. It might be argued that a supportive system of care for young children is dependent upon a more diffuse cultural context in which child care by caregivers other than the mother is normatively acceptable. The data deployed here do not tally with this, indeed, just about the same proportion of Rouen (62 per cent) and Coventry (60 per cent) respondents felt that there was a general social disapproval of working mothers with young children. Yet the French system of child care works by facilitating continuous, full-time labour market participation despite the absence of a broader culture which legitimates it. This has implications for the 'transferability' of French child care policies to a society such as Britain. An argument that such policies would not be successful within Britain because of British cultural attitudes to working mothers is not consistent with the evidence arising from the Coventry–Rouen study. Greater equality in the labour market participation of men and women is not dependent upon a culture of maternal employment but is encouraged by child care provision.

Con c.

Notes

1. This chapter draws on material from the ESRC/CNRS supported research project 'Unemployment and Attitudes to Work in Britain and France' (Franco-British Programme Grant No. RI01230008). The authors gratefully acknowledge the assistance of the two funding bodies in facilitating the research. In addition to the two authors named here the research team included Duncan Gallie and Odile Benoit Guilbot. Whilst

responsibility for the present chapter lies entirely with the authors we acknowledge the part played by fellow team members in conducting the research.

2. See the discussion of comparative analysis by Lane (1989) in which she advocates the 'institutional' approach. The present chapter continues to extend this to women's work and employment (Benoit Guilbot, 1987).

3. The female civilian labour force participation rate for 1985 was 60 per cent in the UK and 55 per cent in France (Dale and Glover, 1990, p. 3).

4. These were wider than a concern with women's employment and covered a range of issues around the impact of rising unemployment on attitudes to work in Britain and France.

5. A non-active person is neither available for nor has been seeking employment within the previous four weeks.

6. Except in a few cases where the woman's last job was many years earlier and it would have been misleading to use this information for current purposes.

7. Bearing in mind that French children can start school earlier than British, at three years old, we used two definitions of the peak period, one up to five, the other up to three. There was no significant difference between the two.

8. As these figures imply, large proportions of women either expressed no strong feelings or provided another answer (36 per cent in Britain, 39 per cent in France).

9. To exemplify our categories: in Britain 'lower secondary' is typically CSE (other than grade 1) and lower grades of GCE O level, in France the Diplôme de Fin d'Etudes Obligatoire: 'secondary' includes higher grades of GCE O level in Britain and the Brevet d'Etudes du 1er Cycle in France; 'non-professional vocational' in Britain include City & Guilds and RSA, in France the Certificat d'Aptitude Professionnelle and the Brevet Professionnelle; 'higher secondary' is GCE A level in Britain, the baccalauréat in France.

10. Ministère de la Solidarité, de la Sanie et de la Protection Sociale.

11. This is consistent with figures which can be calculated from French official sources (M.S.S.P.S., 1989). Each year in France approximately three-quarters of a million children are born alive. The rate of economic activity of women in the 25–44 years old age range is 74 per cent meaning that around 555 000 children of economically active mothers need care. Nursery provision covering the working day amounts to 158 000 places leaving nearly 400 000 children without nursery places. We are indebted to Odile Benoit Guilbot for this information and for drawing the point to our attention.

6 Feminisation of the Labour Force in Britain and France

Patricia Walters and Shirley Dex

Similar trends in women's employment have been visible in Britain and France over the period since the Second World War. In both countries women's participation rates have increased, so that by 1987, 62.6 per cent of women of working age in Britain and 55.7 per cent in France were in the labour force (Eurostat, 1989). The percentage of women in the labour force was similar in the two countries: 43.1 per cent in Britain and 42 per cent in France. In the post-Second World War period both societies have experienced change in the pattern of female labour force participation over the life-cycle: in France the M-shape of the participation rates by age has now virtually disappeared giving a relatively smooth pattern of participation over prime age ranges. In the UK an M-shape pattern still prevails, although the dip in the twenties and thirties age brackets have been moderated.

The prevalent view underlines the similarity of women's increasing employment in industrialised countries. Albeit various theories – Marxist theory, segmented labour theory, patriarchal theory – differ as explanations of feminisation, they agree on the uniformities of women's increasing labour force participation in low-skilled, low-paid, alienating jobs with occupational segregation between men and women becoming reinforced by the rise of part-time work as a feminised sector. However, when comparisons become more detailed, an emphasis on differences and diversity between industrialised societies emerges. This is the case, for instance, in Jenson's recent collection on the *Feminisation of the Labour Force* (1988) and Rubery's recent comparative collection on *Women and Recession* (1988) where both authors argue that diversity of experience is evident through a range of national comparisons.[1]

In this chapter we address the question of the similarity and diversity of women's experience between countries by considering the employment histories of French and British women, focusing on the amount of continuous employment. Procter and Ratcliffe (this volume) deal

89

with the same phenomenon in the two societies exploring the role of cultural differences. We, however, explore how social and employment policies influence women's work histories in the two countries. Our focus is not equal opportunities policies but other social policies which we argue affect women's employment continuity. We suggest that our analysis can usefully contribute to the critical development of general theories of women's employment, in particular the debates over the existence and nature of patriarchy.

Comparative work between Britain and France on women's employment and the role of social or state policies offers one strategic testing ground for the debates over the existence and nature of patriarchy. The patriarchy debate is about whether a separate and independent system of patriarchy exists, such that men oppress women and can be seen to have done so across time and cultures.[2] It is proposed that patriarchy and capitalism together constitute a 'dual system'. In opposition, some Marxists question the need for any concept other than that of capitalism for understanding the material and social relations of production. An alternative Marxist-feminist view has been proposed by Acker (1989), that gender relations are woven into all other relationships although not as a separate system; rather, there is just one system of relationships. Those who accept a dual systems approach elaborate how it operates, and how it has changed its form over time. Hartmann (1979) was one of those initially arguing for a material and independent system of patriarchy. More recently, on the basis of British material Sylvia Walby (1986, 1990) has developed an argument documenting women's systematic exclusion by men in Britain from access to better jobs and from full participation in the labour market. She argues that the exclusion and marginalisation of women in the labour force relates with, but is not reducible to, their subordination in other spheres and that gender inequality cannot be understood without the concept of patriarchy.

What is the role of the state and its policies in this issue about the existence and nature of patriarchy? All parties see the state as having a role to play. In the case of Walby's dual systems theory the state is one of the structures of patriarchy, and men are seen as oppressing women through the vehicle of the state and its policies. Waters (1989) points out that contemporary viriarchy is likely to operate through the state but it can have either direct or indirect effects. Acker's suggestion that we focus on gender expects that state policies will always have gendered implications, and that if policies appear to be gender-neutral, for example in their description or motivation, they will not be neutral in their effects or implications. Acker's position does not specify that the gendered effects must be necessarily oppressive to women, although that is probably implied. That the state has a role is therefore not at issue. Dual systems theory leads us to expect, however, that state policies will act to oppress women systematically across countries.

Our analysis of the way in which women's employment is influenced by social policies in two countries is clearly of relevance to these issues. Do we find evidence in the employment patterns of women of systematic oppression across countries, and of systematic oppressive effects on women's employment patterns from state policies across countries?

DATA AND METHOD

The research project that we are drawing upon (Dex, Walters and Alden, 1988) gives a picture of the early 1980s and is based on comparisons between the Women and Employment Survey (WES) in Britain (1980) and a survey of French women, *Vie Familiale et Vie Professionelle* (1981) undertaken by the Centre d'Etudes des Revenus et des Couts, Paris (1985). Whilst there were differences between the two survey populations they had sufficient overlap to yield two similar samples of mothers. Our analysis was based on a comparison of British and French mothers aged between 18 and 54 with at least one child under 16 at the time of interview.[3]

The work histories of mothers are particularly interesting to compare since motherhood can be a cause for systematic interruptions to employment for women. We are particularly interested in the way social policies operating in different countries can influence women's decision making and hence their employment histories in and around the family formation period of their lives. We explore the way social policies influence and help to construct gendered experiences in labour markets.

In comparing the two samples of mothers, we excluded most of the group of farm and family workers and the self-employed from the French sample. A comparison by Dale and Glover (1990) of the French and British Labour Force Surveys revealed that since these groups are far more predominant in France than in Britain, for historical and cultural reasons, they tend to account for much of the differences visible in national comparisons. By excluding these groups from the

French sample, we restricted our comparisons to a group of women who are more directly comparable; one could call them, the women of the modern industrial sector of each economy.

By this truncation, we also restricted our comparisons to those mothers who come within the sphere of the state's social policies for employees. The group of French women we have excluded (family workers and the self-employed) are those who largely fall outside the scope of such state social security benefits and contributions. The same is true of these groups in Britain, but in Britain they are a far smaller group of women. Since our main aim is to compare the effects of social policies it makes sense to compare those who are subject to these effects, with certain qualifications.

This restriction of the sample has implications for our aims of testing out theories of patriarchy. We are excluding from the French sample a group who are likely to be at the bottom of the status and rewards hierarchy, and who because they often work for fathers, husbands and brothers are likely to be more subject to patriarchal oppression than are women in general. We need to remember this fact in drawing conclusions.

DIFFERENCES IN FRENCH AND BRITISH WOMEN'S EMPLOYMENT CONTINUITY

Our analysis makes clear that similar overall participation rates between French and British mothers are allied with very different patterns of mothers' lifetime working in the two countries. Compared with British mothers, more French mothers work continuously, taking only short breaks for maternity leave over their child-bearing and child-rearing years (Table 6.1). We defined continuous employment as occurring when a woman does not have any breaks in employment lasting longer than six months. French mothers also tend to maintain full-time employment throughout.

Working continuously through child-birth and through child rearing is spread through French society. For instance, there is a substantial amount of continuous working amongst mothers of all ages: over a third of mothers in their twenties and, notably, over a quarter of mothers in their forties have always worked (Table 6.2).

Almost half of all French mothers with one child have always worked, but so too have a third of mothers with two children, and one in eight of all French mothers with three children (Table 6.3).

Table 6.1   Employment indicators of British and French mothers*

	British 1980	French 1981
Percentage employed on total sample of mothers	51.4	51.2
Percentage employed part-time of total sample of mothers	34.6	8.8
Percentage continuously employed of total sample of mothers†	3.4	31.6
N =	(2631)	(3977)

* Mothers are aged 18–54 with at least one child under 16 in this and subsequent tables.
† Continuously employed means that a woman has not had any breaks from employment lasting more than six months.

Table 6.2   Percentage of mothers continuously employed by (a) age, and (b) number of children

Percentage continuously employed	*British*	*French*
(a) Age		
20–29	4.6	36.2
30–39	3.4	33.8
40–49	2.2	25.1
(b) Number of chilren under 16		
1 child	8.0	47.9
2 children	2.3	33.7
3 or more children	1.1	15.5

There is a substantial amount of continuous working by French mothers at all socio-economic levels (Table 6.3). In our analysis we re-classified the occupational categories of the French data into those of the Women and Employment Survey, collapsing the original twelve WES categories to ten. Even in those occupations with terms of employment most likely to generate intermittent employment, e.g. sales, semi-skilled and unskilled work, a fifth of all French mothers have maintained continuous employment.

It is not the case that one can explain variations in French and British mothers' employment continuity in terms of the French having

Table 6.3   Percentage of mothers continuously employed in each
occupational group*

Occupational category	British	French
Professional	6.7	66.3
Teacher	9.0	60.4
Nursing	1.8	52.9
Intermediate non-manual	8.9	45.9
Clerical	4.0	42.3
Sales	1.4	24.4
Skilled manual	3.6	34.3
Child care	0.0	37.1
Semi-skilled factory	2.5	21.8
Other semi-skilled, unskilled	2.6	22.1
N =	(2631)	(3977)

* All mothers' current or most recent occupation.

smaller families, or experiencing a different occupational structure, or
being younger than British women, nor indeed of French women being
more educated. The difference in the amount of work continuity
between French and British women is something that exists as a
national pattern irrespective of any socio-demographic differences.

Table 6.4   Summary of women's employment patterns

Lifetime working pattern	British (%)	French (%)
Continuously employed	3.4	31.6
Never worked*	1.2	1.8
Not worked in last 10 years*	11.0	22.5
Intermittent working: Less than or equal to 50 per cent of time spent working	27.1	18.3
Intermittent working: More than 50 per cent of time spent working	57.3	25.8
N =	(2361)	(3977)

* Mutually exclusive categories. Included in never worked first and 'not worked in
last ten years' second.

French and British mothers have different overall patterns of life-time working experience. French womens' life-time working experience is more polarised than that of British women. French mothers either work fairly continuously, often for the same employer, or leave the labour force and do not work at all (Table 6.4). In Britain intermediate points on the spectrum appear to be more common: most mothers intermittently combine not working and paid work, often with a range of employers.

THE EFFECTS OF CONTINUITY OF EMPLOYMENT

Do French women appear to benefit from their continuity of labour force participation? From our analysis there is evidence which we think points to continuity of employment leading to some improvement in French women's position in the occupational hierarchy and hence in status and earnings. Occupational downward mobility resulting from their breaks from work for family formation has been recognised as a problem for British women. Our data permit a limited examination of this topic.

Looking at the occupational status of women working at the time of the interview in France and Britain, our data showed that, taking the top four occupations to represent the higher grade occupations, 18 per cent of British working mothers were in these higher grade occupations in 1980 compared to 29 per cent of French mothers (Table 6.5). At the bottom end of the hierarchy, 39 per cent of the British women were in the semi- and unskilled categories compared with 21 per cent of the French women. We have recently argued (Dex and Walters, 1989) that it is the proliferation of part-time employment in low-status jobs in Britain which is partly responsible for the lower proportion of higher grade jobs overall for British women; 29 per cent of British full-time workers were in the top four occupations, the same percentage as both the French full-timers and part-timers. Only 12 percent of British women working part-time were in higher grade jobs.

These figures tend to suggest that there are better opportunities for women overall in France than in Britain, but that the difference is largely due to the amount of low status part-time jobs done by women in Britain. However, since our data are restricted to a sample of mothers only we cannot be more definite about this inference. Also, we need to remember that the agricultural family workers and self-employed have been excluded from the French sample. We can obtain

Table 6.5 The occupational status of British and French mothers working at the date of survey

Occupation	All	% British Full-time	Part-time	All	% French Full-time	Part-time
Professional	0.5	0.5	0.3	4.8	3.0	13.7
Teacher	5.2	10.4	2.6	8.0	8.7	4.1
Nursing	7.3	9.1	6.4	6.7	7.1	4.7
Intermediate non-manual	5.0	9.1	3.0	9.9	10.7	5.8
Clerical	23.7	30.6	20.3	28.2	30.0	19.5
Sales	10.1	6.8	11.6	7.3	6.7	9.9
Skilled manual	5.9	6.6	5.6	14.4	14.8	12.5
Child care	3.6	1.6	4.5	2.5	2.7	1.7
Semi-skilled factory	10.4	16.3	7.5	10.2	11.4	4.4
Other semi-skilled	28.6	9.1	38.2	11.1	4.8	23.8
Total	100.3	100.1	100.0	100.3	99.9	100.1
N =	(1351)	(441)	(910)	(2036)	(1692)	(344)

a better picture of women's occupations as a whole from Dale and Glover's (1990) analysis of the Labour Force Survey data.

Dale and Glover's occupational distributions show all British women as having a slightly higher proportion than all French women in the top two occupation groups: 'Professional and Technical' plus 'Administration and managerial'. British women have 19.4 per cent in these two categories compared with 16.9 per cent of French women. It is obvious from the figures that the inclusion of agriculture is what makes the difference to the proportions. Our conclusion still holds, therefore, that French women in the modern industrial sector probably have slightly better opportunities than British women.

The negative effect of low status part-time work on British women's occupations can be seen when employment continuity is controlled. Continuous workers always have larger proportions in the higher grade non-manual occupations than the sample as a whole. In France, continuous workers who are working part time at the interview have 36 per cent in higher grade non-manual occupations compared with 33 per cent for full-time French workers. In Britain, only 15 per cent of the part-time continuous workers are in the top occupations, whereas 44 per cent of continuous full-timers are in these better occupations.

French mothers were asked about their occupations and their employers, either side of breaks from employment of more than six months. Those who said that they had not had any such breaks were not asked about these details: it is reasonable to assume mothers who did not have a break of six months or more took maternity leave and returned to the same occupation and same employer. The latter group is substantial and they are likely to weight the French results heavily towards those who did not have occupational mobility over family formation. Rather than being a biased picture, however, we think this is an approximately accurate reflection of French in comparison to British mothers' experiences. We are restricted to examining some summary measures of occupational mobility since French mothers were not asked for the precise occupation either side of a break, but only if it had changed. These figures allow us to see the limits of the range of experiences but not to quantify them precisely.

The distributions of the various experiences for all mothers are set out in the first two columns of Table 6.6. If we assume that getting the same job, but with another firm, does not involve occupational mobility, but that getting another job either with the same or another employer does involve occupational mobility, certain conclusions

Table 6.6   Job and employer history from last job before first break
from employment to first job after

History	All women French	British	All women with at least one employment break* French	British
Same job/same firm	67.4	8.7	26.7	3.3
Another job/same firm	1.3	0.1	2.9	0.1
Same job/another firm	8.9	42.6	20.1	45.2
Another job/another firm	22.4	48.6	50.3	51.4
	100	100	100	100
N =	(2354)	(1618)	(1047)	(1528)

* Only breaks in employment of six months or more were recorded.

follow. French women clearly experience a lot less occupational
mobility than British women under these assumptions; 76 per cent of
French women were in the same job either side of their first childbirth
in comparison with 51 per cent of British women. Although we cannot
be sure how many of the dissimilar jobs are downwardly mobile, the
scope for downward mobility is clearly much greater for British than
for French women. Other studies of the WES data confirm that
occupational downward mobility is common at this time for the
British mothers (Dex, 1987). Also, British women are much more
likely to change their employer at this time (over 90 per cent), even
when they get the same job on their return to work. It is uncommon in
either country for women to get a different job with the same employer
after childbirth.

We can see the extent to which the lower amounts of French
women's occupational mobility are due to their continuity of employment by subtracting the continuous workers from each sample. The
resulting samples, of women who have had at least one break for six
months or more, are displayed in the last two columns of Table 6.6. In
this case the French and British samples have almost identical amounts
of job mobility although British women have considerably more
employer mobility than French women. These results suggest that
British women's larger amount of occupational or job mobility over
childbirth is mainly attributable to their more intermittent and
discontinuous working patterns; in practice for British women this
means not taking maternity leave, staying out of employment longer

and returning to a part-time job with a different employer. The figures also suggest, although we are unable to confirm this, that French women use the maternity absence provisions and hence stay with the same employer, or retain links with the same employer, much more than British women in similar circumstances.

So far we have highlighted the phenomenon of French mothers' greater career continuity compared with British mothers and have discussed some possible consequences of this. Our evidence dates from 1980/81 and reflects the experiences in the years preceding that. In the 1980s British mothers may have moved in the direction of greater amounts of continuity, but we would doubt that overall differences between the two countries have changed much. Compared with British mothers, French mothers who work have a form of labour force participation which incorporates them more permanently into the labour force and this has had some positive consequences for French mothers' occupational status. French mothers lifetime employment experience is more polarised than that of British mothers. There appear to be stronger forces operating on French mothers in two contrary directions – continuity of work and continuity of *not* working. British women's more intermittent pattern of working (resulting in lifetime working of 50 per cent of time or more, but rarely 90 per cent or more) can be attributed to the lack of strong incentives, in comparison with France, either to work continuously or to give up work altogether. An analysis of the contribution of social policies to the greater employment continuity of French mothers has also to consider the polarity of their experience.

THE IMPACT OF FRENCH POLICIES

Different outcomes for French and British women's employment through their lifetime are influenced by a number of policies interacting. What follows is a brief indication of the main policies contributing to greater employment continuity among French women.

It is possible to distinguish policies according to their specified intentions and target groups. Thus there are general policies, e.g. provision of nursery education, structure of taxation rates, and redundancy policies, which have an effect on mothers' employment continuity in the two countries. There are also specifically gendered policies which intentionally address mothers' labour force participation, e.g. maternity leave policies, and policies of child care provision for working mothers.

French maternity leave and pay provisions at the time of survey were more generous with less restrictive eligibility conditions than in Britain. The nationally standard period of paid maternity leave in France was then sixteen weeks, paid at a rate of 90 per cent of salary. The period of paid leave increased for a third child, for multiple births and for reasons of ill-health in pregnancy up to a possible maximum of 34 weeks. To be eligible for the statutory provisions women had to have paid social security contributions for ten months before the birth. Employment protection for pregnant women and women on maternity leave was established in France at about the same time as it was in Britain. The fact that a high proportion of currently employed French women with dependent children have no recorded break greater than six months suggests that the use of paid maternity leave was widespread. Up until 1980 it was clear that maternity absence had not had a major impact on British women, possibly because some were ineligible but also because some British women clearly wanted to take more time out of employment for childbirth than maternity absence provisions permitted. The limited nature of British maternity rights legislation is discussed by Brannen in Chapter 4.

Our analysis indicated that age of youngest child had very little influence on French mothers' employment participation compared with that of British mothers. When we looked at factors affecting employment continuity in a regression analysis British mothers were twice as likely as French mothers to have breaks in their continuity of employment because of having a child under three (Dex, Walters and Alden, 1988).

French child care provisions and nursery school provisions seem to have an effect in promoting employment continuity (Procter and Ratcliffe, this volume). The two kinds of facilities, nursery schools and day nurseries, are distinct in France as in Britain. Full-time free nursery schooling is almost universally available for children aged three upwards in France. For children under three, Moss (1988) calculated in 1986 that in France 23 per cent were in publicly-funded places in day nurseries and nursery schools. In Britain, the corresponding percentage was 2 per cent; this included two to three year old children in pre-primary public schooling but excluded children in play groups. In our survey 44 per cent of French working mothers with children under three used paid childminders to provide care; family care was the next most frequent kind. In Britain, for children of the same age group, partners were the most frequent carers.

In other work we have done we identified a strong pull from French women's earnings encouraging their employment continuity (Dex and Walters, 1990). There is relatively greater financial profitability in continuing employment for French women. This derives from a number of aspects. First, the work is full-time and the contrast financially between working and not working is very marked indeed: second, compared with Britain more of the jobs are amongst the higher occupational categories, and, finally, there is the marked effect of the French income tax system on women's earnings. Full-time working women in France retain much more of their earnings after tax than do British women.

Differences of labour market organisation are likely to contribute to higher levels of employment continuity amongst French mothers and to their enhanced occupational status. Marsden (1989) has argued that an external/occupational labour market model is more highly developed in Britain whereas in France internal labour markets are more developed. From our analysis there was evidence that mothers' continuous employment in France was frequently for the same employer and that mothers' discontinuous employment in Britain was with different employers. It is likely that French mothers' employment continuity is structured by nationally specific labour market policies: for instance, French unions have pressed for greater protection from redundancy than their British counterparts (Marsden, 1987). It is also the case that internal upgrading from semi- and unskilled jobs to skilled jobs is considerably more developed in France than in Britain (Marsden, 1989).

It would seem that different structures of labour markets in the two countries, different national policies and different employer-level policies help to create differences in women's employment histories between France and Britain. Whilst we have argued that in France a range of policies help to promote women's employment continuity, French child-benefit payments have an opposing, disincentive effect. For larger family sizes, especially where children are older, benefits are considerably higher in France than in Britain, and are likely, all other things being equal, to constitute a greater disincentive to mothers' employment. The really strong contrast between the two countries occurs in families with more than two children. Levels of benefit in France increase with three or more children unlike in Britain: age premiums for children in France, first for children over ten years of age and further for children over fifteen years of age, enlarge the difference between the countries even more. These disincentives are visible in an econometric analysis of earnings undertaken by the authors (Dex and Walters, 1990).

CONCLUSIONS

To return to the questions that we raised from our discussion of patriarchy: comparing the two countries, do we find evidence in women's employment patterns of systematic oppression and of systematic oppressive effects from state policies?

Our comparison of the employment patterns of French and British mothers has shown that as well as differences there are some similarities in the position of mothers in the occupational, and therefore in the status and rewards, hierarchies in the two countries. The similarities would probably be more striking if the excluded sample of French agricultural women were added back into our comparisons. These similarities are in line with the possibility of a systematic and across-cultures operation of patriarchy.

Our examination of social policies suggests that a somewhat more complex picture emerges with respect to the role of the state. Whilst distinguishing between general and gendered policies according to their specific intentions, we agree with Acker that there do not appear to be general policies which are gender-neutral in their effects, and our analysis has shown this quite clearly. Other recent analyses of women's employment, for example Ruggie (1988) and del Boca (1988), have emphasised the importance and contribution of general as well as gendered policies to gender inequalities in employment. We have found a mixture of advantageous and disadvantageous effects on women's position in the labour market from the operation of both general and gendered state policies in our two countries.

We conclude therefore that state policies, both gendered and general ones, have effects on women's and mothers' employment in these two countries; that some general and some gendered policies have worked to improve the position of women, whilst others have either left their situation unchanged or possibly worsened it. Policies have worked in different ways in the two countries. Whilst the improvements to women from the state policies are by no means a panacea, we think that they are sufficient to question the claim that there is a systematic operation of patriarchy working through the state, and across states in different industrial economies. Thus we are suggesting that the state is not clearly a simple patriarchal force, that the state does not work systematically in all countries, and that this casts doubt on the accuracy of current versions of the dual systems theories of patriarchy and its operation.

Notes

The analysis reported in this chapter was funded by the UK Department of Employment. The views expressed are those of the authors and do not necessarily represent those of the Department.

1. Jenson, introducing essays on women's economic role in seven OECD countries writes that 'there is a great deal of diversity in women's actual work experience. No clear trend has emerged that could adequately characterise the present status or future of the female labour force' (1988, p. 4). Rubery, concluding a study of women's employment in Great Britain, France, Italy and the USA argues 'there is a need to redress the balance of the debate in comparative analysis which has so far tended towards the universalist type, stressing the similarities in women's role' (1988, p. 254).

2. There is a recent argument by Waters (1989) that what is being discussed here is the existence of what he calls viriarchy (rule by adult males), rather than patriarchy which should be reserved for the fathers' oppression of other household members. We tend to agree that this refinement in the terminology would benefit the discussion.

3. The sample sizes for our comparison of mothers were as follows: 2631 British women and 3574 French women. The French sample had to be weighted to maintain its nationally representative character and a weighted sample of 3977 women was therefore used. The samples of mothers in both French and British data were collected from nationally representative samples of households. More details of the two surveys are available from Martin and Roberts (1984) and CERC (1985).

7 Demographic Change and 'New Opportunities' for Woman: The Case of Employers' Career Break Schemes

Carole Truman

It is predicted that as a consequence of a shortfall in the number of school leavers there will be severe skill shortages in the United Kingdom in the 1990s. However, an estimated 900 000 jobs could be filled by women's increased participation in paid employment. The majority of these women will be mothers. In a political and economic climate where market forces prevail, the onus has been placed upon individual employers to make provisions which will help women to combine a career with a family. This has been seen by some as a period of new opportunity for women.

This chapter examines the initiatives that employers are using to encourage women with children to remain in or return to paid employment. Breaks in full-time paid employment during family formation are a significant factor in women's disadvantaged position in the labour market. The chapter considers whether the career break initiatives devised by employers will actually provide a solution to predicted skill shortages. The question will be addressed, do career break schemes provide an effective means to help women to continue a career. It is suggested that inconsistencies between policies and practice are such that career break schemes actually reinforce gender inequality through the existing sexual division of labour. As such, they do comparatively little to enhance women's position in the labour market.

DEMOGRAPHIC CHANGE AND THE DIVISION OF LABOUR

The problem of skill shortages is one which has received considerable attention by the press, radio and television. Reports and features suggest a need for women in the UK to return to work to meet the skill shortages of the 1990s. By the end of the decade, it is predicted that women will comprise more than half of those in paid employment. Lady Howe, non-executive director of a large retail company, is typical of those raising these concerns:

> We need to find out what more has to be done to help women realise their full potential as contributors to our economic life. We need to do this because not to do so is to waste an enormous asset which can enrich and stimulate our business by tapping new talent. We need to do it now more than ever because future population trends show that business success and industry is going to have to rely increasingly on women in the 1990s and beyond. (Lady Howe, 1988, p. 3)

Predictions about skill shortages have stemmed from official government statistics (*Employment Gazette*, 1989) which report that manufacturing firms have faced recruitment difficulties since 1987 and that the service sector is experiencing shortages of professional and managerial staff. A shortage of school leavers will lead to a reduced pool of labour that can be trained to meet the skill requirements of the future. Employers are being encouraged to look for alternative sources of labour such as the unemployed, women, older people, people from ethnic minorities and people with disabilities. Employers may also introduce policies to make better use of existing workers by improving recruitment practices, career structures, working conditions and so on (Training Agency, 1989).

Official statistics have rightly been criticised for inadequately representing women's participation in paid employment and there may be good cause to question them (Allen and Wolkowitz, 1987a; Allen and Truman, 1989). It is beyond the scope of this chapter to consider details of the origins and accuracy of such statistics. Instead, the focus rests upon the assumptions behind what, in the words of Lady Howe, 'is being done to help women realise their full potential as contributors to our economic life'.

The discussion of demographic change must be analysed within the framework of the sexual division of labour. Two major assumptions may be challenged. The first is that both historically and at present, women are a wasted resource and as a society we are failing to realise their full potential in economic life. In other words, women's unpaid work in the home fails to maximise their economic potential.

Yet, the assumption that women's potential is at present being under-utilised is open to question. It has been argued that capital requires women to reproduce children and male labour power whilst remaining available as low paid casual workers in the labour market (see, for example, Coulson *et al.*, 1975; Secombe, 1974; Smith, 1978). Analyses of patriarchy claim that women's work in the family is primarily for men rather than for capital (Delphy, 1977). We might also question the extent to which women's labour represents a 'new talent' for business to tap when skill shortages occur.

The second assumption relates to the extent to which employers are able to provide working practices which enable women to improve their contribution to our economic life. If women's unpaid domestic commitments are the main reason why their economic contribution has so far been stifled, then employers need to find ways to allow women to combine paid work with domestic commitments. But the sexual division of work and women's unpaid labour are constructed within both patriarchy and capital: if demographic change is to bring about significant changes in women's position in the labour market, the construction of paid and unpaid work must also be altered.

The debate about skill shortages and women's work thus raises important practical and theoretical questions about the intersection of paid and unpaid work. Women care not only for children, but also for the elderly and the infirm. Whilst demographic change will lead to fewer school leavers, it also means that there will be a greater percentage of the population who are past retirement age and that women will be increasingly called upon to care for the elderly. The discussion and analysis which follows suggests that women will derive no long-term benefit from what have been termed 'new opportunities' stemming from demographic change. Indeed, it will be argued that as long as discussion is restricted to reactions by women to the policies of individual employers, the sexual division of labour and inequalities between men and women will only be reinforced.

WOMEN'S WORKING PATTERNS

In discussions of women as a wasted resource it would appear that some believe that many women in Britain do not work at all. Yet women already make up 42 per cent of the workforce, and up to 50 per cent in certain regions (EOC, 1989). Despite the extent of women's participation in paid employment, they are clearly still considered by some to be a marginal component of the labour market.

Part of the problem in 'making better use' of women may rest in the type of paid work that women perform. Official statistics report that 44 per cent of British women who are employees work part-time (Eurostat, 1987 and see Chapter 1). Part-time jobs may involve a variety of working schedules: some may require a person to work a few hours each day whereas others require someone to work a number of full days each week. As Hurstfield (1987) points out, official figures on part-time workers refer to jobs rather than people. From official statistics, it is unclear how many workers perform more than one paid part-time job. In Britain, there is no single consistent definition of part-time work. Indeed, it has been proposed that measuring female activity rates is comparable to measuring a length of elastic (Joshi and Owen, 1987). It thus remains unclear exactly how better use can be made of female labour, since much of women's paid employment is unrecorded in official statistics.

One strategy employers might adopt to improve women's economic contribution would be to encourage them to work full-time rather than part-time. However, this proposal implies that the time that women devote to household organisation and caring for dependents is wasted. But women's unpaid domestic labour is a fundamental feature of both patriarchal and capitalist structures. Women's participation in part-time paid work allows them to serve the requirements of capital and of men. One would expect there to be considerable vested interest from patriarchy and capital to maintain working structures which allow women to perform both paid and unpaid labour. The extent to which the actions of individual employers can fundamentally alter women's labour market position is likely to be limited.

Another feature of women's paid employment is that they perform different jobs to men and receive lower rates of remuneration for the work that they do. Cockburn (1988) describes how part-time work reinforces gender segregation in paid employment: 92 per cent of part-time workers are found in selling, clerical, education, health and welfare, cleaning, catering, and hairdressing. Most of these jobs are characterised by low pay and low skill. It might seem to be in employers' interests to encourage women doing these jobs to move into more skilled work. But the reasons why women are found in jobs with low pay and low skill cannot be ignored. Women do not actively choose to supply low paid, low skilled labour. It is more the case that a large section of industry demands and depends on the cheapness and 'flexibility' of women's labour to stay profitable. Beechey and Perkins (1987) clearly demonstrate that the introduction of part-time working or the re-organisation of part-time workers' hours is a strategy carried out by employers with little or no consideration of women's needs. Evidence suggests that employers' requirements for flexibility will lead to an increased casualisation of women's work in Europe (Huws, Hurstfield and Holtmaat, 1990). It is therefore too simple to suggest that industry and commerce are wasting women's potential talents and abilities by confining them to part-time, low paid, low skilled work. On the contrary, it would seem that large sections of the economy are dependent upon sustaining the existing situation. As Dale (1987) has argued, demand factors interact with supply conditions to segment the labour market to the disadvantage of women.

The number of hours worked for an employer is not the only feature which differentiates women's paid employment from that of men's. As Hakim (1979) has pointed out, the labour market features occupational segregation with both horizontal and vertical dimensions. Her study of vertical segregation shows that women are found at lower levels of the occupational hierarchy.

The work histories of British women also differ from those of men and it is suggested that women experience distinctive labour market barriers (Dex, 1987). The nature of the differences between men's and women's work histories has particular implications for their relative positions in occupational hierarchies and their opportunities to follow conventional career structures. The concepts of a career and career progression have been developed in terms of the working patterns of men. They imply full-time work, continuity of employment and progression through increasing levels of job responsibility. When women embark upon career paths, they frequently experience interruptions which affect their prospects and positions in paid employment. In her analysis of the Women and Employment Survey (Martin and Roberts, 1984), Joshi showed that:

> Interruptions to women's work histories are predominantly associated with children, but these interruptions are not the only consequences of child bearing on women's working lives, for the nature of the employment to which many mothers return is different to what it would have been had they had uninterrupted careers. (Joshi, 1984, p. 1)

Dex (1984) describes how the most common pattern of women's working changes from being full-time before childbirth to a mixture of part-time and full-time after the birth of the first child. She describes how the transition from full-time to part-time work is marked by downward occupational mobility. This, together with the period of 'non-employment' when women are absent from the labour market after the birth of a child, is perhaps the lost economic contribution at the centre of the discussion on demographic changes. British women are far more likely to experience breaks in employment than other European women. Walters and Dex (this volume) describe how French women accrue benefits relative to British women through higher levels of employment continuity. Procter and Ratcliffe (this volume) assert that the provision of extensive child care supports French women's more continuous and full-time role in the labour market.

The consequences for women of gaps in paid employment are various. Interruptions in employment may be unpaid since many women fail to qualify for statutory maternity benefits (Trades Union Congress, 1985). Gaps in paid employment will lead to women missing increments on salary scales. There is no doubt that women also suffer financially as a result of the downward occupational mobility which may follow a career break. Part-time work in itself provides lower levels of remuneration and skills may be temporarily or permanently downgraded with a consequent loss in earnings. Joshi concluded, from analyses of the Women and Employment Survey, that 'the gross cash earnings forgone by women as a result of family formation could be about double the loss of woman-years to the labour force' (Joshi, 1984, p. 1).

Individual women carry most of the burden of breaks in employment. However, employment structures and policies relating to child care are such that there is little that individual women in Britain can do to lessen the burden. But, when employers recognise that they too experience losses if they are unable to retain trained and experienced staff, there is the potential for change to occur.

Initiatives which facilitate women combining paid and unpaid work are neither new nor innovatory. There was a need for women's labour in the Second World War, but change was short-lived since in both the USA and the UK, post-war propaganda forced women back to domesticity and secondary forms of paid employment, as shown in Brown's analysis (this volume). Summerfield argues that:

> in spite of [the] challenge of expectation and change during the war, continuity with pre-war attitudes and practices towards women was considerable in the areas of domestic work and paid employment. (Summerfield, 1984, p. 1)

Although the data for this chapter were collected in the context of the British labour market in the 1980s and 1990, some of the organisations that were interviewed have experienced local skill shortages since the 1960s. Steps have been taken to offset skill shortages since that time, long before those precipitated by current demographic trends.

The next part of this chapter examines whether the problems of absence from paid employment and downward occupational mobility which are experienced by women can be eliminated or reduced by the actions of employers. A research study has been carried out which explored the types of initiatives introduced by employers to address the problems of discontinuous working patterns. In-depth interviews were conducted with senior personnel of twenty organisations in the public and private sectors known to be actively developing equal opportunities policies. They were asked to describe the characteristics of their organisation's initiatives. Details were requested of the actual and perceived benefits to the organisation of introducing such initiatives. Interviewees were asked to quantify the costs and benefits where this was possible and appropriate. The data from this study are contained in a report to the Manpower Services Commission (Truman, 1986).

EMPLOYER RESPONSES

From the point of view of employers, it is women with career paths, rather than women in general, who experience downward occupational mobility on returning to work after taking a break in paid employment to have children. The sexual division of labour whereby women are assumed to take the major responsibility for the care of children means that it is women's careers that are disrupted by family formation rather than men's. Therefore career break initiatives are aimed at women in the labour market rather than parents of either sex. This is an important factor since all career break initiatives are based on assumptions relating to motherhood rather than promoting a more egalitarian division of domestic labour.

There are various reasons why employers might want to introduce initiatives of this nature. Whatever the primary purpose of the initiative, it is likely that from the employer's point of view, the benefits to the organisation of career break initiatives will be greater than the costs.

On the other hand, the extent to which career break initiatives are in the interests of women needs to be examined. For example, do career break schemes provide women with new opportunities or greater equality in the labour market? The absence of coherent trade union or government policies on rights for working parents means that in all cases, the impetus to introduce career break schemes has to come from individual employers.

The over-riding aim of all career break policies examined in the study was to devise employment practices which either eliminated or reduced the need for women to take a break in paid employment during the years of family formation. The policies deployed by employers can be divided into four main types:

1. Workplace nurseries.
2. Part-time, 'flexible' working and job sharing.
3. Working from home.
4. Re-entry and retainer schemes.

The remainder of the chapter describes the characteristics and assumptions behind these four types of career break initiatives which employers have introduced. The range of benefits to employers are discussed as is the extent to which women obtain improved opportunities in the labour market.

Workplace Nurseries

The care of young children has been seen to be one of the major constraints on women's participation in paid employment. Pre- school child care provision in Britain is amongst the lowest of any EEC nation (EOC, 1989). There has been a vigorous campaign to encourage employers to offer the child care which in other countries might be provided by the state. In 1990, the British Government removed the tax on workplace nurseries as a benefit in kind. Whilst in force, the tax meant that many parents whose children were in a nursery provided by their employer faced paying tax on the value of employer subsidies to workplace nurseries. This could mean that the stage is set for work-place nurseries to provide parents with the opportunity to continue to work whilst their children are young.

Employers undoubtedly face substantial costs when they invest in and maintain workplace nurseries. There is evidence, however, that at least some of those costs can easily be offset. One employer, the Greater London Council, found that as a result of providing two fifty-place nurseries, it made savings of more than £200 000 through reducing the hidden costs that resulted from the impact of child care responsibilities upon labour turnover and work efficiency. These savings came from the costs of advertising posts, costs associated with recruitment, the value of the work lost whilst a post is vacant, and the value of the work lost whilst a new recruit is learning the job (Greater London Council, 1986). From this evidence alone it would seem that workplace nursery provision can be justified on strict financial criteria. If skill shortages materialise, the value of lost personnel may exceed the current costs of that labour and workplace nurseries would be of even greater benefit to employers. But what of the advantages to women?

It is probably true that workplace nurseries are better than no provision at all. But as one campaigner pointed out, 'a policy which ties nursery provision to the marketplace could prove to be a curse' (*Guardian*, 20 March 1990). The practicalities of commuting with a child to a nursery based at work rather than near its home are just one part of the problem. The nature of workplace nurseries mean that unless the business is a large local employer in a relatively small area, the children who use it will not necessarily live in the same community. They would therefore come together in an artificial environment far away from the neighbouring children where they live.

A further consideration is that emphasis on workplace nurseries focuses attention on care for the under-fives who are in good health. Children also require care when they are sick, and older children require care during school holidays and after school. For the parents of these children, workplace nurseries provide no help whatsoever.

Part-time, Flexible Work and Job Sharing

Another way that employers have sought to enable working parents to continue with their careers is to offer alternatives to the narrowly defined concept of what constitutes 'normal' working patterns. For example, a major retail chainstore had always maintained a policy of re-employing staff who had left, as and when vacancies arose. However, if someone wanted to return to work on a part-time basis, they could not be employed at a level higher than shopfloor supervisor. This meant that women who had previously been in management positions experienced downward occupational mobility. From the company's point of view this represented an under-utilisation of resources. On average, it took a recruit nine years to progress to a managerial position, and the company recognised the need to put their training and experience to good use. It therefore introduced part-time working for managers on a trial basis. It soon became evident that the part-time managers provided the company with a new 'flexible' labour force. Extended shop opening hours meant that full-time managers were being put under increasing pressure and the part-timers were able to fill the gaps. The firm thus gained considerable benefits from employing women as part-time managers.

The unsociable hours that the part-timers were asked to work meant that the benefits they gained were reduced, but the fact that part-time work was seen as a concession rather than a right implied that the women should be grateful for being offered some work rather than no work.

Job-sharing is another strategy that has been used to help women gain access to better jobs on less than a full-time basis. During interviews, many employers reported how employing job sharers is a practical demonstration of two heads being better than one. However, implicit within job sharing and other strategies which offer less than full-time hours of work, is that two employees can survive by sharing one full-time wage. There are also many other examples of employers offering women temporary or flexible work to accommodate their other commitments. In the context of increasingly casualised working arrangements, the benefits of a flexible contract are at best limited, and at worst potentially dangerous in terms of the deregulation of working conditions.

Working from Home

Another type of career break initiative aimed at minimising the conflicts between home and work is to provide women with the option to work from home. One of the earliest schemes for off- site working was introduced by a computer company who faced skill shortages as early as the late 1960s. The scheme was introduced as an experiment and a small group who were termed 'pregnant pro-grammers' were employed to work part-time from offices in their own homes. The company's objectives were to retain the skills and expertise of staff whilst enabling them to combine career and family commitments. The selection of staff was seen to be crucial to the scheme, and employees were not offered off-site employment as a matter of right. They first had to prove their technical capability and personal suitability through a rigorous selection procedure.

Those staff who qualified were provided with computers and a telephone link to the main offices and were contracted to undertake a maximum number of hours work each week. The company would not expect employees to work more than the hours they were contracted to work. However, if insufficient work was available, the company agreed to pay a retainer. In practice, it was rare that off-site workers had insufficient work. The minimum number of hours an employee could contract to work was 25. The costs of the computer and telephone link were borne by the company while employees paid for their other overheads. Since the 1980s, employees have received exactly the same fringe benefits as on-site staff, although these have only been offered as a result of collective bargaining over the years.

Whereas child care commitments were the main reason that women moved into off-site employment, it was recognised that employees could not combine paid work and child care at the same time. Therefore most had to employ childminders or use nurseries during the hours they were working.

Since the scheme was first introduced, employees have been paid at the same hourly rate as on-site staff for the number of hours that they work. This might suggest that they had equal treatment. However, when child care, heating and lighting costs are taken into consideration, it is clear that women bore many of the costs of the initiative. In practice, it soon became clear that off-site working was more efficient than office based work from the employer's perspective. The nature of office work, with rest breaks, interruptions and interaction with colleagues, means that the productivity of the working day is lower than when working in isolation. Lack of interruptions mean that off-site workers carry out the same amount of work in 25 hours as an on-site worker would do in 40.

The social problems associated with off-site employment with new technology have been well documented by Huws (1984). It would seem that off-site working is another scheme aimed at using the otherwise wasted resources of women's labour which has more benefits for the employer than the employee.

Re-entry and Retainer Schemes

Martin and Roberts (1984) showed that 90 per cent of women who leave paid work for 'domestic' reasons eventually return and that since the 1950s, the average total length of breaks has reduced from fourteen years to only five. There is evidence that the average period women spend away from paid employment has decreased further since the

Women and Employment Survey (EOC, 1989). However, the average length of break in paid employment is considerably longer than that permitted by statutory maternity leave.

Statutory maternity leave allows women the right to stop work eleven weeks before the birth of a baby and to return to existing employment up to 29 weeks following confinement. Unless women resume paid employment immediately after maternity leave, they have no statutory right to return to their previous employer. There are a number of criteria which have to be met before a woman qualifies for statutory maternity leave and only one in six women having babies qualify for maternity pay (Land, 1986).

A number of employers have recognised that the inadequacies of statutory maternity leave and lack of alternative support for women with children influence their ability to return to work. In response, re-entry and retainer schemes have been introduced to give selected employees rights to return to their previous jobs after taking extended unpaid leave.

The nature of these schemes varies from company to company. Some allow employees to take one break of up to five years whilst others permit two extended breaks of two years. Most schemes require that employees work for at least two weeks in each year they are on leave so that they keep in touch with the employer. In practice, those who work in retailing or retail banking often work on Saturdays throughout the year. The employer thus not only retains a worker that might otherwise have been lost, but also obtains additional flexibility to cover extended opening hours. Re-entry and retainer schemes are often part of employer's equal opportunities policies and are thus open to both men and women. In reality, they are much more likely to be a feature of women's careers than men's: until 1989, only one man had taken a career break in the ten years that a major high street bank had operated a scheme.

The right to return to work at the same level as before after a period of extended unpaid leave may be seen as a bonus. But the staff who qualify have to be seen to be of intrinsic value to the organisation. They also need to be in a position where they can afford not to work for up to five years. Since it is almost exclusively women who take career breaks, such schemes assume women's dependency upon men. Such schemes also tie women to the same employer at a period in their careers when their male counterparts are free to take advantage of career moves to new employers.

CONCLUSION – WILL CAREER BREAKS HELP WOMEN?

An over-riding consideration of all of these initiatives is that they are primarily aimed at women because it is women who bear the burden of organising children and the home. Additionally, career break initiatives will only be offered to a comparatively small group of women who are deemed by their employers to have intrinsic value. One longer-term effect may be to bond such women to their employers. Consequently, there is cause for concern if employers use the basis of this dependency to depress women's wages and dilute their union activity.

The other side of the demographic change equation is that Britain will have an increasingly ageing population. As mentioned previously, women also care for the elderly and the infirm, but none of the initiatives which have been mentioned encompass that possibility. Government policy which advocates care in the community shifts an increasing burden onto women as the unpaid carers of the sick and elderly, taking them out of the pool of labour that can be called upon to fill skill shortages.

This chapter has demonstrated that the current debate about women's paid employment appears to be misdirected. In practical terms, career break policies represent little more than opportunities for a small group of women to derive short-term benefit from variations in employer's career structures. Even where this is the case, it is possible that women will follow the new career paths, whilst those of men remain as they have always been. If this is the case, the dominant concept of a career may remain largely unchallenged.

The chapter has exposed inconsistencies in the argument that the economy will become more dependent upon women's paid employment over the next decade. From existing data, it would appear that large parts of industry are already dependent upon women's economic contribution through their participation in part-time work. Moreover, it is apparent that society is dependent upon women's unpaid labour in the home and the community. The flaw in the argument about women filling the gaps created by demographic change rests on two contradictory assumptions: firstly, that the downward occupational mobility which women experience when they move from full-time to part-time work implies that employers are failing to make optimum use of women's labour in paid employment; and secondly, that industry remains dependent upon the supply of women's labour into low paid, low skilled jobs in the casualised labour market. There appears to be an inherent conflict over how women's labour might best be deployed.

Moreover, the relative costs and benefits of career break initiatives suggests that even without skill shortages, employers will find these initiatives a cost effective component of their employment policies. As long as the design of career break initiatives rest in the hands of individual employers, women will have fewer choices in the labour market. This is because they will be bound not only to their domestic commitments in the home, but also to the specificities of whatever type of career break initiative their employer chooses to make available.

The debate about demographic changes need not be dismissed, however. It is important that feminists enter the discussion because its very nature places women's participation in paid and unpaid employment at the forefront of public concern. For the debate to be of ultimate benefit to women, it is essential that women, not employers, politicians or newspaper editors, define the parameters of the discussion. The consequences of demographic change should not be limited to how employers or individual women might respond, but how the ideological, economic and social relations between men and women might change to give women real choice.

8 Women under *Glasnost*: An Analysis of 'Women's Place' in Contemporary Soviet Society

Kay Richards Broschart

In the last decade of the twentieth century, women in many industrial nations still lack constitutional guarantees of equality and equal access to employment opportunities. Over the past seventy years, however, women in the Soviet Union have acquired the same legal rights as men and have established an unprecedented pattern of full employment. In addition, Soviet women are protected by an extensive programme of labour legislation which recognises their unique reproductive capacities as well as their rights as workers.

The Soviet Union provides a strategic research setting for examining several critical questions about the working lives and status of women. For example, to what extent is the social and economic position of women in a society a reflection of the level of their legal rights and status? Do equivalent legal rights for women and men result in similar employment patterns? What other factors, in addition to legal rights or barriers, appear to influence the nature and extent of women's labour force participation?

This chapter will present a sociological appraisal of the place of women in contemporary Soviet society, focusing on their legal status and position in the labour force. This assessment is based on the secondary analysis of research reports and statistical evidence published during the past decade. It is also supported by first-hand observations and indepth discussions with Russian and Ukrainian women conducted in Moscow, Pyatigorsk and Kiev in the fall of 1989.[1]

THE LEGAL STATUS OF SOVIET WOMEN

the status of women is a barometer of the level of democracy of any state, an indicator of how much respect is given to human rights. (Mikhail

Gorbachev, *Welcoming Address to the World Congress of Women*, 23 June 1987)

Immediately after the Bolshevik revolution, women in the Soviet Union began to accumulate legal and constitutional guarantees which generally have exceeded those acquired by women in Western Europe and the United States. The initial post-revolutionary Constitution of 1918, for example, not only proclaimed the 'equality of all citizens', but specifically guaranteed 'the right of women to vote and hold elective office' (Bysiewicz and Shelley, 1987, p. 57). The right of Soviet women to work, and to receive equal pay for their labour, was formally established in the revised Constitution of 1936 (Tay, 1972, pp. 681–2). The equality of women and men before the law was subsequently instituted in 1977 (Bysiewicz and Shelley, 1987, p. 59).

The Constitution of 1977 broadened the scope of constitutionally mandated gender equality, to include 'all spheres of economic, state, cultural, and socio-political life' (Feldbrugge, 1979, p. 92, and Bysiewicz and Shelley, 1987, p. 59). In addition to officially affirming the general principle of women's equality, this document also endorsed specific educational and occupational means for achieving parity. According to Article 35:

> Women and men in the USSR have equal rights. The exercise of these rights is ensured by according women equal opportunities with men in receiving education and professional training, in labour, remuneration, and professional advancement. (Feldbrugge, 1979, p. 93)

On the basis of this brief review of the constitutional rights acquired by women, it does seem reasonable to claim that Soviet women in 1990 enjoy the same legal status under the constitution as Soviet men. In the words of a professional woman from Pyatigorsk: 'Officially women [in this country] have the same rights as men. We don't have a problem in this area.'

Over the past several decades, declarations of women's legal rights have frequently been paired with statements recognising women's special reproductive capacities and responsibilities for children. The 1977 Constitution, for example, not only called for women's equality, but it also recommended the creation of 'conditions enabling women to combine work with motherhood' (Feldbrugge, 1979, p. 93; Sharlet, 1979, p. 87).

Labour legislation, based on traditional views of the family roles of women, has been drafted in an effort to protect female workers, especially expectant and recent mothers. *The Fundamental Labour Law of the USSR and the Union Republics* (1970) is an exemplary model of this type of protective labour code. The law exempts working women from employment in harmful or arduous occupations. It also set limits on the conditions under which women may work at night or on overtime. In addition, this landmark legislation was responsible for establishing state-supported pregnancy and childbearing leaves and paid breaks for nursing mothers (Lapidus, 1982, pp. 299–300).

Since 1970, increasingly liberal maternity benefits have been granted to employed Soviet women. In that year, the first paid maternity leave policy was implemented. This provided state social service benefits for women for 56 days before and 56 days after the birth of a child. A new mother could also elect to extend her postpartum leave, without pay, until her child's first birthday (Lapidus, 1982, p. 299).

In 1981, the length of paid leave for mothers after childbirth was extended to one year. In 1987, the period of state-supported maternity leave was increased to 70 days before, and a year and a half after, delivery. Under both of these policies, six months of additional leave without pay was permitted. Areas of the Soviet Union with the lowest birth rates were among the first to initiate these expanded benefits (Bohr, 1989, pp. 11–12).

Through the efforts of the Soviet Women's Councils, a paid maternity leave of two years was introduced at the beginning of 1990. An optional third year of unpaid leave for mothers was also instituted. To an American or a British observer, the extent of maternity benefits available in the Soviet Union today is admirable. In contrast to the loss of income and the job insecurity frequently associated with childbearing in the United States and Britain, it is remarkable to note that a Soviet woman is legally entitled to return to her place of employment, at her former position and pay scale, at the conclusion of a maternity furlough.

It would appear that women in the Soviet Union have been granted not only legal rights, but occupational benefits which are equal to or exceed those of men. Protective labour codes and legislation, however, may undermine, as well as enhance, the rights and status of designated groups of workers.

Consider, for example, some possible negative consequences of the generous Soviet maternal leave policies. In the USSR, parental leave benefits are only available for women. Labour policies which recognise women's unique reproductive functions undoubtedly help women to combine employment with motherhood. Such policies, however, also discourage men from sharing parental responsibilities and child care. Furthermore, policies which recognise that working women, but not men, are parents may encourage the staffing of higher level and more responsible positions with men who have uninterrupted employment patterns and fewer conflicting, family responsibilities.

Under the law, Soviet women are guaranteed equal rights as citizens and equal access to employment. Protective labour practices, however, may limit and shape the pattern of women's occupational participation. Is the official egalitarian legal position of women in the USSR reflected in their position in the labour force?

WOMEN IN THE SOVIET LABOUR FORCE

An extremely high proportion of Soviet women work outside of their homes for wages. Labour analysts report that more than 90 per cent of able-bodied Soviet women are either actively employed or engaged in full-time study (Dallin, 1977, p. 385; Lapidus, 1982, p. xiv; Bysiewicz and Shelley, 1987, p. 70). The proportion of women in the labour force in the United Kingdom, the United States and the Soviet Union, by age group, is displayed in Table 8.1. With the exception of the youngest and oldest age categories, this table demonstrates that women in the Soviet Union have exceptionally high rates of labour force participation. The highest levels of employment (97 per cent) are observed among Soviet women aged 25 to 44 years. The lowest employment rates are found in women from 15 to 19 or over the age of 59. These patterns undoubtedly reflect the relatively high concentrations of students and pensioners within these age cohorts.

Since 1970, women have constituted 51 per cent of the Soviet labour force (Bohr, 1989, 12; and Lapidus, 1982, p. xv). For more than twenty years, therefore, the number of working women in the USSR has actually exceeded the number of working men. Even in the traditional, predominantly Muslim, Central Asian and Transcaucasian republics, approximately 40 per cent of the total Soviet labour supply is female. (Bohr, 1989, p. 12; Bysiewicz and Shelley, 1987, p. 71).

Work in the Soviet Union is viewed as a civic duty as well as a right. Public sentiment endorsing the value of work is supported by legislation and negative legal sanctions aimed at discouraging 'antisocial parasites'. While all able-bodied men and women are expected to engage in socially useful labour, pregnant women, women with children under the age of twelve, and 'persons engaged in household

Table 8.1   Percentage of women in the labour force in the
United Kingdom, the United States, and the
Soviet Union by age group, 1985

Age group	UK	USA	USSR
15–19	53	42	33
20–24	65	70	83
25–44	59	66	97
45–59	63	56	65
60 and over	9	14	4
Total 15 and over	45	50	61

Source: Adapted from *Compendium of Statistics and Indicators on the Situation of Women* (New York: United Nations, 1989) pp. 176–7 and 194–7.

labour' are not subject to prosecution under the antiparasite codes (Bohr, 1989, p. 12). Despite these legal exemptions, as previously shown, almost all adult Soviet women are gainfully employed.

Soviet women apparently work for a variety of compelling reasons. Surveys of workers suggest that the vast majority of working women value highly the 'economic independence, social status, and personal satisfaction' they derive from employment (Lapidus, 1982, p. xvii). While one sociologist claims that 40 per cent of all Soviet working mothers would leave their jobs if their husbands' earnings were higher, other analysts assert that 80 per cent of Soviet women would not give up their work, even if they could afford to (Bohr, 1989, p. 12; Pankratova, 1988). In the words of a Moscow physicist and mother, 'We work for the money and the joy'.

Most adult women in the USSR who are not employed are students or pensioners (Hansson and Liden, 1983, p. xi). Overall, women account for half of all Soviet students enrolled in institutes of higher education or universities (Dallin, 1977, p. 386; Sacks, 1988, p. 76). Furthermore, working women are more likely than men to have completed programmes of advanced vocational training or post-secondary education. Survey analysts report, for example, that 61 per cent of all specialists in the Soviet labour force with specialised-secondary or post-secondary education are female (Mihalisko, 1989, p. 31; Boldyreva, 1989, p. 102).

Numerically superior and competitively educated, women today constitute a significant portion of the Soviet labour force. In what sectors of the economy, if any, are women concentrated? What levels and kinds of positions do Soviet women hold?

Even a cursory examination of the distribution of women in the Soviet labour force reveals clear, sex-differentiated patterns of employment. Women constitute a high proportion of technical specialists and more than seven in ten doctors. They also make up the majority of white-collar and paraprofessional workers. Virtually all clerical workers, teachers, librarians, pharmacists, and nurses are women (Lapidus, 1982, pp. xix–xx and xxii–xxiii).

Table 8.2 Women workers and average monthly wages in Soviet economic sectors with highest proportions of employed women, 1986–7

Economic sector	Number of women employed (a)	Women as % of labour force (b)	Average monthly wage (c)
Credit and state insurance	589 860	87%	191
Trade, public catering	8 298 400	82%	156
Public education	7 552 500	75%	154
Public health	•5 564 700	81%	135
Culture	1 022 000	73%	119
Overall national	60 054 000	51%	195

Sources: (a) *The USSR in Figures for 1986.* (Moscow: Central Statistical Board of the USSR, 1987) pp. 172–5. (b) Derived from *The National Economy of the USSR for 1987* (Moscow: State Committee of the USSR on Statistics, 1988) pp. 366–7. (c) Agerage monthly wages in roubles. A. P. Pollard, *USSR Facts and Figures Annual,* vol. 13 (1989) pp. 473–4.

Although some women in the Soviet Union work in the same jobs and settings as men, the majority of women workers are employed in sex-segregated occupations or female dominated spheres of the economy (Sacks, 1988, p. 82). Fifty-seven per cent of all Soviet working women are concentrated within just five of the sixteen designated employment sectors. An analysis of the labour market sectors with the highest proportion of employed women is presented in Table 8.2. This table shows that more than four out of five employees in the spheres of trade and public catering, public health, and credit and state insurance are female. Women also account for approximately three-quarters of all workers engaged in the domains of public education and culture. If women and men customarily perform different jobs but receive comparable wages, a labour market segregated horizontally by sex could, economically, at least, be considered egalitarian. However, a national economy which is vertically differentiated by sex is always inequitable. What is the relative position of men and women in the Soviet labour force? Is the value of work performed by women comparable to the value of the work of men?

Although there is no evidence of different pay scales for men and women who perform the same jobs within a given occupational sector, most women and men in the Soviet Union work in different occupations and in different spheres of the economy. The inequality inherent in a labour market horizontally divided by sex becomes clear when the relatively low wages paid to workers in female dominated spheres of the economy are revealed. The average monthly wages of workers in the five sectors of the economy with the highest concentrations of employed women are shown in Table 8.2. While an average Soviet worker in 1986 earned 195 roubles a month, workers in these overwhelmingly female sectors received an average wage of only 149 roubles. In the same year, workers in construction and transport, the two labour sectors employing the highest proportion of males, earned an average monthly paycheck of 238 roubles (Pollard, 1990, p. 473). It seems apparent that in the Soviet Union, as well as elsewhere, women's work is not valued (or paid) as much as the work of males.

The occupational training and skills of female workers compare favourably with those of male workers. Nevertheless, in most areas of the Soviet economy women are engaged in less skilled work than their male counterparts (Bysiewicz and Shelley, 1987, pp. 71–2). Furthermore, within any given occupation or workplace, women are generally located at lower levels of the occupational hierarchy than men. In agriculture, for example, women are commonly employed as unskilled manual labourers while men usually work as mechanised machine operators (Lapidus, 1982, p. xix).

Women disproportionately work in unskilled jobs in industry as well as in agriculture. Nevertheless, women in the USSR do occupy about one-quarter of all management positions (FBIS, 1989). Despite the advancement of these women, most Soviet analysts agree that 'women are less likely than men to be promoted or given higher management responsibilities' (Mihalisko, 1989, p. 31).

Women are under-represented in the upper echelons of all sectors of the labour market. Although significant numbers of women are employed in technical and professional occupations, for example, few women hold top positions in these fields. Even in medicine where women physicians outnumber men by a ratio of more than four to one, women hold only half of all top leadership posts (Bysiewicz and Shelley, 1987, p. 72). Only in fields entirely staffed by women, such as nursing, pharmacy, teaching and clerical work, is the proportion of female supervisors equal to the percentage of female workers (Lapidus, 1982, p. xxii).

It has previously been noted that women in the Soviet Union are constitutionally guaranteed equal opportunities for promotion and equal pay. Not only are females under-represented in supervisory positions, however, but they also earn lower wages, on the average, than males. Analysts estimate that the earnings of a Soviet working woman typically range between 65 to 70 per cent of the earnings of a Soviet working man (Lapidus, 1982, p. xxi; Swafford, 1978, p. 669). Undoubtedly the relative position of women in the workforce contributes to their lower average wages. The principle of equal pay for equal work clearly does not result in income equality in a labour market vertically stratified by gender.

In the USSR, it is widely acknowledged that the proportion of women declines as the level of pay and responsibility of an occupation rises (Lapidus, 1982, p. xxi). Soviet authorities and citizens consistently deny, however, that this is the result of sex discrimination. Both labour market analysts and ordinary citizens assert that Soviet women have equal employment opportunities and receive equal pay for equal work. If observed gender differences in pay and level of employment are not believed to be caused by discrimination, to what are they attributed? One explanation commonly advanced is that the lower occupational status and earnings of women are simply inadvertent consequences of women's occupational preferences. Certainly no one claims that Soviet women intentionally seek low-paying jobs. It is frequently argued, however, that woman may prefer less demanding work in order to meet their family obligations (Swafford, 1978, p. 670).

Soviet sociological surveys reveal large and pervasive differences in the number of hours employed women and men spend caring for their children and households. Three different studies, conducted between 1970 and 1987, show that women contribute an average of 18 to 21 *more* hours of work at home per week than men (Gruzdeva and Chertikhina, 1986, p. 163; Boldyreva, 1989, p. 111; Novikova, Iazykova and Iankova, 1982, p. 171). It is important to emphasize that these figures are based on studies of employed males and employed females.

Women in the USSR assume an inordinate portion of child care and housework in addition to full-time paid employment. With a combined work-load of this magnitude, it is not surprising that some Soviet women willingly accept less demanding occupational roles with relatively low wages (Novikova *et al.*, 1989, p. 94).

SUMMARY AND CONCLUSIONS

While women in the Soviet Union officially hold the same constitutional rights as men, they clearly do not enjoy equal status or comparable rewards in the labour market. Differences in the roles and responsibilities of men and women are observed in the Soviet family as well as in the economy. Women in the USSR clearly assume a heavy and inequitable share of the work of maintaining a family and household.

Assuming the responsibility for child care and housekeeping, in addition to holding a full-time job, is obviously time consuming and arduous. Long commutes on public transportation to child-care facilities and shopping for food add additional hours to a typical work day. Upon returning home, Soviet women continue the work of the second shift – cooking, cleaning, laundry, and child care – without the assistance of microwave ovens, dishwashers, clothes dryers, vacuum cleaners, or husbands (Gruzdeva and Chertikhana, 1986, p. 164).

Protective labour codes enacted to help ease women's dual employment and family burdens, unfortunately seem to inhibit their economic advancement. While Soviet women are proportionately represented in the labour market, they are under-represented in top management and leadership roles. On average, women in the Soviet Union not only hold lower ranking positions, but they also receive lower wages than men.

A woman's place in the Soviet labour force is typically a position of low to moderate rank in a sphere of the economy dominated by women. A woman's paycheck, consequently, contains, on average, 30 to 35 per cent less than a man's. If women generally earn less than men, it is more cost effective, from a purely economic perspective, for women, rather than men, to reduce their occupational goals in order to assume unpaid domestic and family roles.

The inequitable role obligations of Soviet women are reinforced, therefore, not only by protective labour laws but by the lower than average pay scales assigned to women's work. Although, it is not unreasonable to pay women who perform less skilled or less responsible work lower wages, a centralized wage policy which consistently places a lower market value on labour in sectors of the economy with high concentrations of females is inherently discriminatory. An occupational system which is horizontally segregated by sex is equitable only when earnings are based upon a gender blind evaluation of work performed in every labour force sector and occupational category.

In conclusion, this examination of the place of women in Soviet society demonstrates that the status of women is not simply determined by the level of their legal rights nor by the extent of their participation in the labour market. More specifically, the situation of contemporary Soviet women shows that constitutional guarantees of equality and full employment do not necessarily result in equality for women in the affairs of daily life. The complex causes of gender inequities need to be publicly recognised and challenged, if the position of women is to be improved.

Notes

The author visited the Soviet Union in October 1989 as one of four sociologists in a small delegation of American educators and scholars invited by the Soviet Women's Committee to examine the roles and status of women in the Union of Soviet Socialist Republics. The delegation was organised by the Citizen Ambassador Program, People to People International, Spokane, Washington, USA.

Part II

Breaking Male Definitions
of Work

9 Wives' and Husbands' Labour Market Participation and Household Resource Distribution in the Context of Middle-class Male Unemployment

Gillian Leighton

Social theorists have conceptualised the labour market as though it was primarily shaped by men. Whilst women have been included within stratification theory it still remains the case, according to traditional theorists, that they 'remain peripheral to the class system' (Giddens, 1973, p. 288). The majority of research on family, employment and unemployment reflects this position and assumes women to be dependent upon their husbands' labour market position.

That wives' involvement in paid work is shaped by husbands' labour market position is a perspective put forward by Leonard (this volume). She shows how husbands' unemployment, the benefits system and womens' primary role in domestic labour combine together to promote wives' informal participation in, particularly, the cleaning industry. However in this chapter, which explores wives' lives in the context of middle-class male unemployment, there is evidence of women having a determining influence upon their husbands' labour market position. The data suggest that proposals about the polarisation of households in and out of work (McKee and Bell, 1985; R.Pahl, 1984) and the normal pattern of male full-wage jobs and female component jobs do not hold true, and may be reversed when the wives of middle-class unemployed men are in full-wage work. For their husbands are likely to be in stop-gap or component wage work.

Using qualitative data, this chapter takes a relational perspective and challenges the traditional view. It asserts the importance of wives' paid work as an influence upon husbands' take-up of employment. The employment situation of wives is shown to affect, not only the husbands' labour market position, but also the way money is organised within the household, the domestic division of labour and marital relations. Cumulatively, the data shed doubt upon conventional class analysis.

MATERIAL AND SOCIOLOGICAL FACTORS THAT SHAPE WOMEN'S PAID WORK

There are broadly three factors that influence wives' involvement in paid work. These are wives' domestic responsibilities and the ideologies of femininity and the family wage.

It has been a matter of debate within sociology as to whether wives do paid work for the money or for the interest. For example Hunt (1968) showed that money was an overriding factor, followed by the need to escape from domestic boredom. This finding is not surprising in our society where status is closely allied to income. More recent research provides evidence that there would have been a fourfold increase in households below the poverty line if wives had not been earning (Land, 1983). We can therefore conclude that working-class wives work for money, but the case for professional wives is less clear. Wives from both classes experience interrupted work histories (Walters and Dex, this volume). They usually work part-time and occupy feminine positions in the social structure (Wainwright, 1978; Barron and Norris, 1976). The majority of part-timers are married, and mothers especially work part-time (Chapter 1). Seventy per cent of working mothers work part-time compared to 26 per cent of working women without dependent children (Leonard and Speakman, 1983).

Moreover even wives who have professional jobs are concentrated in the lower echelons of their professions. One reason for this relates to the socialisation of women and to their resultant attitudes to paid work. Wives who pursue 'professional' careers are confronted by sharper contradictions than are working-class wives. For example, the very idea of a career contradicts everyday notions of femininity. This contradiction between the role of paid work and that of wife and mother generates ambivalent attitudes within women that manifest themselves in underachievement patterns (Oakley, 1982). Further a study of 'Women in Top Jobs' showed that even women who had achieved and persisted in high level professional careers tended to sidestep confrontation with a man's world (Fogarty, Rapoport and Rapoport, 1971).

In addition, professional wives are married to men who earn a 'family wage'. They cannot readily justify their paid work in terms of financial need, even though this may be the case. This may add pressure to wives' underachievement attitudes. The 'family wage' ideology supports the view that it is the husband's responsibility to provide for wives and children. It is because of this attitude, combined with wives' low pay, that wives are relegated to the position of secondary wage earners, and their jobs regarded as being of secondary importance compared with those of their husbands.

Together, these three factors, wives' domestic responsibilities, the ideologies of femininity and the family wage, result in a complex picture. Stephen Wood describes women's orientations to paid work as complex and distinctive although flexible (cited in Marshall, 1984). The implication is that women work for instrumental reasons but, because of low pay, do not perceive themselves as breadwinners. This account of wives' structural position does not support arguments in favour of a conventional approach to class analysis.

Wives and husbands are neither totally dependent upon each other, nor independent of each other. A more relational perspective reveals that dependency shifts between wives and husbands relative to stages of the employment cycle. Much of this is hidden by the fact that women are considered to be only semi-proletarianised and when unemployed 'disappear virtually without trace back into the family' (Beechey, 1978, p. 190). Married women, when they are in paid work, earn on average 50 per cent of their male counterparts and so the logic is that their husbands are still primarily determining the household's life chances (Goldthorpe, 1983;1984).

Whatever the reason, the data are presented within a traditional framework which suggests that husbands' work patterns shape wives' labour market patterns. No account is taken of the actions and perceptions of wives. Having pointed to the processes that operate to delimit wives' workforce participation at a conceptual level, the next section reviews survey data on employment status of wives whose husbands are unemployed.

WIVES' AND HUSBANDS' LABOUR MARKET PATTERNS

As long ago as 1973, Daniel's survey of the unemployed identified the propensity for husbands and wives to move in and out of the labour market together. When husbands became unemployed there was a tendency for wives to stop their part-time work also (Daniel, 1974, p. 34). This is summarised by Hakim as follows: 'A large proportion of the unemployed have non-working wives, 60 per cent of men newly registering and about 85–90 per cent of men unemployed for one year' (Hakim, 1982a, p. 443). This could be due to joint redundancy, to wives giving up their paid work, or wives not taking up paid work. The DHSS 1978/79 study of unemployed men found that among the wives of men who were back in full-time work four months after first registering as unemployed, 40 per cent were working themselves, compared to 28 per cent of the wives of the continuously unemployed men. Hakim notes that, 'the picture is somewhat complicated by the fact that social classes or cultural factors play an important part in wives' decisions to supplement, or replace the male breadwinner role' (1982a, p. 441). The evidence is that cultural factors influence wives' paid work participation, rather than the number of dependent children.

The argument so far is that there exists a relationship between wives' and husbands' employment patterns. The longer a husband is unemployed the less likely his wife is to be in paid work. A key factor is the UK Social Security system in which husbands' benefits are reduced by wives' part-time earnings (see Leonard, this volume). There is therefore an interaction between the benefits system and cultural factors which delimits wives' participation in the labour market. With these issues in mind and from a relational perspective, qualitative data will be used to trace out the processes behind this state of affairs for middle-class wives with unemployed husbands.

METHODS

In the mid 1980s there was, as pointed out by McKee and Bell (1985) 'an embarrassing silence on the part of sociologists to unemployment and its effects upon the populace'. They provide illuminating data on the position of young married couples in the Midlands in which the working-class husband was unemployed. Similarly Morris's study (1985a) provided data on the impact of working-class husbands' redundancy on the domestic division of labour of couples living in South Wales. At this time both South Wales and the Midlands were in economic recession.

By contrast, middle-class unemployment was a new and increasing phenomenon of the 1980s. Little was known about it or the effects of unemployment upon people who lived in a region like South East England, where unemployment was much lower. In addition, the impact of husbands' unemployment on wives' lives was a new dimension in sociological research.

The data for this study are drawn from a small qualitative sample of interviewees living in South East England. A sample of male professional and executive ex-workers was drawn from 2000 names on the Professional and Executive Register. This is an employment agency that receives a grant from the government for accepting unemployed professional people on its books. Length of unemployment was not controlled for at the sample stage but wives' paid work was. The result is a sample that almost equally divides between paid and unpaid wives. Approximately half the sample had children who were living at home and dependent, that is, the parents were in receipt of child benefit. The focus of the study was on the couple rather than the family as a whole.

The thirty couples who form the basis of the study were widely dispersed geographically. Most of the families lived in isolated villages, within the 'gin and tonic' enclaves of rural commuter belts. They were in the main the 'two car made it family' who had hit a rainy day. In the past many of them had had part-time cleaning women, child care assistance and gardeners. Entertaining relatives and friends at home and weekends away were integral to their lives prior to unemployment.

The majority of wives had been to private schools, followed by further education at, for example, the Royal Academy of Music and a variety of Teacher Training Colleges. The few wives who had less formal educational qualifications were more traditional in their ideas about the wife's role. The occupations that wives either had, or had held in the past, included teaching, social work, journalism for the BBC and the *Sunday Times*, a variety of secretarial positions and posts in personnel management. The husbands had been managers in insurance, banking and various industries ranging from engineering to pharmaceuticals. Most had previously worked within the Greater London area. The sample included very long-term unemployed husbands, whose families had been evicted and therefore no longer lived in large houses. For example, one had previously been the assistant manager of an Arab Bank in London. The couple now lived in a two bedroom council flat, with the possessions that they could salvage stacked up around them, which constrained further their limited physical space.

Couples in which there were longer-term unemployed husbands, no longer had cars. This created a problem for people living in the countryside, as the local shops were expensive and buses infrequent and costly. When absolutely necessary they often borrowed cars from friends. The physical environment in which they lived was stagnant. Objects that could not be sold at a reasonable price were eventually either pawned or parted with at great emotional and financial cost. Long silences, long walks and an uneasy loneliness tended to surround their lives, lives that were devoid of dynamism. This was reflected within the interview situation when both wives and husbands used the interview as a form of companionship.

Wives and husbands were interviewed seperately. Usually the husband was interviewed first and the wife afterwards, sometimes several weeks later. Each interview lasted most of the day and sometimes included informal activities like lunch and looking at business ventures. The sixty interviews (thirty couples) were all tape recorded. This chapter is based on the first 44 core interviews (22 couples all of which were fully transcribed). During the interviews, people often cried and found difficulty talking, causing some problems in the analysis.

WIVES' INFLUENCE ON HUSBANDS' LABOUR MARKET POSITION

One of the key findings of the research was that whether wives did paid or unpaid work influenced the length of husbands' unemployment. Long-term unemployed husbands had wives who were self defined housewives and short-term unemployed husbands had wives in paid work.

Table 9.1   Wives' employment status by length of husbands' unemployment

	Husbands' unemployment in months				
Wives' employment status	0-5	6–12	13–18	19 +	Total
Full-time employed	4	6	1	1	12
Full-time housewife	0	1	0	7	8
Unemployed	0	1	1	0	2
Total	4	8	2	8	22

Table 9.1 shows that among twelve couples where wives were in paid work, four husbands had been unemployed for up to five months, and six between six to twelve months, whereas of the eight couples where the wives were full-time housewives, seven husbands had been unemployed for 19 to 22 months. There are three exceptions to the generalisation, but a closer examination of these cases showed that each had some other unusual circumstances.

Many housewives said that they would not take work that affected their husbands' benefit. Others saw it to be categorically the husbands' responsibility to find work, making statements such as, 'If he can't find work then I can't', which also became, 'If he won't find work, why should I find work?' These statements fitted the traditional world views of the self-defined housewives.

Full-time employed wives might have given up their paid work, but only two wives became unemployed at the same time as their husbands. One had given in her notice in a fit of anger and her husband had been made redundant two weeks later. The other wife worked at the same company as her husband and both were made redundant together. None of the full-time working wives had any intention of giving up their waged work, although in the context of husbands' unemployment the meaning of work had changed for them. The pressure of taking on the breadwinner role, combined with a change in the use of their earnings, temporarily altered the meaning of work for them.

An important trend after the onset of husbands' unemployment was a change in the use of wives' earnings, with a consequent change in wives' attitudes to paid work. In the following quote, the wife, a personnel officer, tells how her income had been used before her husband's unemployment and her dissatisfaction with the changes when her husband became unemployed.

Sue T: My money was meant for luxuries, it was for holidays and the children's education and new clothes or furniture, that was the sort of thing my money bought . . . it's really a second income something extra, for luxuries. After unemployment, . . . I just worked out how much it would pay for and how much else we had to find in order to continue living at a fairly minimal level. I mean we had absolutely no luxuries at all.

Husbands' unemployment also changed the experience of employment for wives.

Interviewer: Do you find it less rewarding to work now ?

Sue T: Yes, they started a sports club at work to play a game of darts, and I said that I was going out one evening to play darts. I was told I couldn't because he doesn't like me going out especially in mixed company.... I feel much more resentful of that now. I'm having to learn, to be the breadwinner, yet I'm still treated in the same way. I feel that's unfair . . . it seems I never get to the point when I'm actually free.

The interview material shows that most employed wives are resistant to taking on the role of breadwinner, but at the same time their money provides valuable space for husbands to return to the labour market. This is significant both for the survival of the unit at an economic level and for the survival of the marriage at a social level. The distinction between the situation of paid and unpaid wives generally colours the overall life experience of couples during husbands' unemployment.

Breadwinner wives make space for unemployed husbands to take stop-gap jobs, part-time consultancy work, voluntary work and to pursue experimental freelance ventures – a favourable situation compared to those husbands depending solely upon means tested benefits. In addition the statutory unemployment benefit provides husbands with pocket money and some means of independent expression, avoiding the necessity of asking their wives for money. This advantageous position, combined with the efforts of wives, returns men to the labour market relatively quickly. These 'push factors' are the result of wives' responsibilities, which have to be carried out on low resources, and their attitude to paid work. To be a breadwinner by default is not a situation wives relish (see also Fagin and Little, 1984, p. 203).

The labour market participation patterns of these formally unemployed husbands with employed wives resembles those traditionally described as female. These couples have many more options than couples dependent upon state benefit.

In contrast the implication of 'choosing' to be a housewife is to increase the probability of long-term husband unemployment. For state dependency combined with the wife's economic inactivity leads to long-term unemployment. In this way, by shoring up relationships of dependence (McIntosh, 1979), the state social security system organises both wives' and husbands' work take-up generating a wedge between those connected to paid work and those dependent upon the state.

An analysis of the way money is organised between couples reveals the importance of the conditions upon which money enters the household. It is not necessarily the case that people on state benefit have less money than couples dependent upon a wife's low wage. The data show that conditions of entry influence the way that money is organised within the household. A wife's earnings are seen to be for the shopping; husband's state benefit is used for the major bills. Because there may not be enough money both to manage and to budget the household needs adequately, whose needs are met can depend upon the source of the money.

THE ORGANISATION OF FINANCIAL RESOURCES

The organisation of money within the household is sociologically important because it enables power relationships to be traced out between wives and husbands. Access to household resources and decisions about money divide along gender lines. A discussion of the way money is organised between couples will throw light upon the processes operating: most particularly the polarisation between the situations of wives in paid work and housewives.

The case study data reaffirm the importance of a wife's full-wage work as a major determinant of the couples' life chances. Wives who become breadwinners by default are able to provide the essential family needs which in turn helps to facilitate an early return on the part of their husbands to the labour market.

In contrast, full-time housewives are doubly oppressed by husbands' unemployment. They do not have any direct access to financial resources and it is their job to make ends meet on very diminished household assets due to their husbands' long-term unemployment. In addition traditional attitudes to paid employment and the domestic division of labour make them unlikely to take up paid work to combat husbands' unemployment.

This situation is given further legitimation by the Social Security system (Morris, 1990). Husbands are responsible for claiming benefits and these are reduced by wives' part-time earnings. These families are often therefore in a poverty trap which means that they are 'better off' on benefit – prolonging husbands' unemployment further (Morris, 1990). Particularly harmful is the social disconnectedness that accompanies his unemployment.

In the most acute situations wives struggle to gain control over financial resources which when finally obtained can be too late to prevent the execution of an eviction order. In sum, the data on resources between couples show that it is the wife's job to make ends meet in the context of poverty. A relational, intra-household perspec-

tive provides a more sensitive indication of disadvantage than traditional sociological and economic analysis which assumes the household to be a solidary unit of equivalence (Brannen and Wilson, 1987).
Household allocative systems have been conceptualised in a variety
of ways and different analytical levels have been identified within them
(J. Pahl, 1982, 1983, 1984, 1987, 1989; Edwards, 1981a, 1981b, 1981c;
Vogler, 1989). However, when couples are unemployed, the way that
they organise their money does not readily fit into the typologies
presented within the literature. The way money was organised prior to
husbands' unemployment is presented first to provide a processual
picture.

The Organisation of Money before Husbands' Unemployment

Most previous research has been on working-class couples (Gray,
1979; Pahl, 1982, 1983, 1984, 1987, 1989) whereas this study looked
at middle-class couples located in South East England.

Both the pooling system and the independent system were very
popular: 41 per cent used each of these two systems (Table 9.2). This
contrasts with Vogler (1989, p. 8) who found that only 2 per cent of
her sample used the independent system. Of the thirteen couples where
the wives held paid work before their husbands became unemployed,
nine used the independent management system and four couples used
the pooling system. Of the nine full-time housewives, five used the
husband management system and four the pooling system.

Wives' paid work is an important factor influencing the type of
system a couple adopt, and who has control of the finances. The

Table 9.2   Allocative system prior to husbands' unemployment

System	Wife and husband in paid work	Husband only in paid work	Total
Whole wage	0	0	0
Spheres of responsibility – husband management	0	4	4
Pooling	4	5	9
Independent	9	0	9
Total	13	9	22

sample was further analysed by who controlled the money entering the household, the management of finances in terms of paying bills, and daily budgeting such as shopping. Earning money gave working wives more self-expression within the home and, conversely, housewives were relatively more deferential. The findings divide sharply between couples depending on whether the wife is in paid employment.

The allocative systems, once set up, were resistant to change, even as a result of husband's unemployment. Eventually some couples were forced by external factors to change their system, which fits in with Vogler's finding (1989) that husbands' employment status was important. Paid wives did not change their system as much as housewives with very long-term unemployed husbands. The following discussion of money organisation during husbands' unemployment emphasises the polarisation of the experience of paid and unpaid wives. This was particularly important for the well-being of the family.

Money Management when Husbands are Unemployed

Two of the thirteen wives who had been in paid work became unemployed at the same time as their husbands. Of the remaining eleven, six continued to use the independent control system, but with some transfer of management to the wife, three continued to pool, and two changed to unitary wife management (Table 9.3). Where wives were full-time housewives, four couples continued to pool, three continued with the husband management system, and two changed from husband to wife management.

Table 9.3   Allocative system during husbands' unemployment

System	*Wife in paid work**	*Wife not in paid work*	*Total*
Spheres – husband management	0	3	3
Pooling	3	4	7
Independent	6	0	6
Unitary control – wife management	2	2	4
Total	11	9	20

* The two couples where the wife became unemployed at the same time as their husband are excluded from this table.

The overall trend within the sample is towards wife management. If an analysis of the changes, including both management and budgeting, are taken into account then husbands' unemployment leads to a heavier burden of financial responsibility for wives. For example, the majority of paid wives took over the management function at the onset of husbands' unemployment.

However husbands' unemployment generates confusion for those involved and therefore the interview material must be analysed as reporting a process. Finances for many couples were in a state of flux. The more reliable material is drawn from the more coping, capable, and stable couples. It was difficult to obtain systematic data from couples who had experienced husbands' unemployment as traumatic. Indeed, disarray or breakdown of a system was a part of unemployed life. Disorganised relationships added to disorganised money; and disorganised money in turn contributed towards disorganised relationships.

Most couples do not make positive decisions about finances but tend to drift along. The couples' situation is further complicated because in order to change purposefully the way that they organise their money, they would both have had to recognise that the husband was going to remain unemployed for some time. This realisation runs against the day-to-day coping mechanisms of the couples.

The way the couple organise their money changes primarily in response to external stimuli as opposed to positive actions on the part of the wife or the husband. For example, when a couple cannot afford standing orders at the bank, they withdraw from using the bank as a way of attempting to control their money. Some couples have mortgage repayments that cannot be met or adjusted: the mortgage remains unpaid and eventually the situation is one that requires adjustments.

The adjustments are in the majority of cases the responsibility of the wife. Wives, therefore, act within conditions that are structured outside their control. This is especially true in the case of wives who are not in paid work. The following statement illustrates this position.

Interviewer: When did you sit and discuss the money?
Maggie J: We didn't, we just didn't, I didn't think that this was going to be like this for so long.

As the above statement reveals, many couples did not accept that unemployment was going to be long term. This lack of recognition in part influences whether finance systems change and it differs by gender. Wives sooner or later face up to husbands' unemployment in a way that husbands generally do not. This is typified by the following interviewee.

Irene D: I mean he still continued going out. He wanted his spending money and so on. He really went on with his life as it always had been.

This trend is accentuated within the long-term unemployed couples. Some do plan, but for the majority the assumption that there is a 'job around the corner' is a coping strategy in severe social circumstances. To reorganise the finances involves accepting husbands' unemployment. This acceptance runs against the future orientation required both for job search and to keep one's emotional self intact. Wives therefore consider it to be their responsibility to intervene, but the conditions of intervention are socially shaped and constructed by patriarchal relations.

Prior to the onset of husbands' unemployment the impression had been given that it did not matter who took responsibility for financial management within the couple. But in the context of husbands' unemployment this relatively 'relaxed' attitude was replaced by a rigid attitude that displayed gender as an overt factor of concern. Social and economic contraction is a major feature of life experience when husbands are unemployed. The majority of wives buy less food and visit the shops more frequently – with the exception of wives who live in the countryside. Economic contraction severely curtails their social interaction. In the few exceptionally low resource households wives purchase television stamps and have meters installed for gas and electricity.

This heavier burden for wives was evident at the level of management and budgeting. Housewives had a heavier burden than paid wives at both the levels of management and budgeting because money was shorter as their husbands were long-term unemployed. The earnings of employed wives allowed couples to bypass the benefits system and to remain comparatively buoyant and socially connected. This is in stark contrast to the housewives who were dependent upon husbands who claimed social security payments. This process of polarisation between paid and unpaid wives is a major feature of the sample.

To point up the processes of polarisation more sharply it is illuminating to quote from those dependent upon the state who resisted transfer of control from husband to wife. Some men see managing the money as a masculine responsibility and their identity as breadwinners and fathers can be preserved if they are in control even if the source of income is the state. Katey describes her situation:

> Katey C: He kept his cheque, then he would cash it and give me part of it. He wouldn't put it in the bank account he'd just keep it in his pocket. So one day he'd have a hundred pounds and the next day nothing.

Katey C's husband supported this perspective,

> Rod C: It would just get gobbled up if it went into the bank.

Then Katey's husband became very ill and was admitted to hospital, and in addition the bailiffs had called several times to the house. Only then did he allow her to take over the finances. Asked if she was happy with the situation, she said,

> Katey C: Yes, more secure. It doesn't go any further but at least I know where it's going.

Wives are most likely to control the finances in powerless circumstances. This kind of power may not be desirable. But as Katey C points out, to have some control over a situation is better than no control. This often does not happen until finances are very much out of control. The benefits system made it difficult for wives to gain control as shown by the following interviewee:

> Jenny E: I said why can't I have the Giro [benefit cheque], and they said, 'well unless you've got particular grounds' or something they won't pay it to women . . . unless you tell us you are separated and then we'll pay you separately.

One of the main features of long-term unemployed households is that nobody manages the finances. By contrast in short-term unemployed households, where wives are in paid work, the majority of wives take over management of the finances. Very long-term unemployed households were more likely to use the unitary control – wife management system (see also Morris and Ruane, 1989).

THE DOMESTIC DIVISION OF LABOUR

It has been well documented that husbands of employed wives help more in the home (Blood and Wolfe 1960; Young and Willmott, 1973;

R. Pahl, 1984). However, the data here show that the physical separateness externally imposed upon couples where wives are in paid work, and self-imposed by traditional housewives, were important factors explaining husbands' participation in domestic tasks.

The husbands of paid wives divided into those who supported their wives in their paid work role, performing more domestic chores during unemployment, and those who did not. This work is also free from policing because the wives are physically removed from the household while at their paid work.

By contrast, amongst the housewives, it was wives' attitudes towards their housework which influenced husbands' participation in domestic chores. The more progressive husbands in this group tried to be involved in domestic work but their wives discouraged them. Amongst the more traditional couples husbands did not involve themselves in domesticity and their wives did not expect or want them to be involved. There were strictly defined gendered spheres of interest.

If the whole sample is plotted on a continuum from progressive to traditional the couples at both extremes have corresponding world views. Interestingly, it was these couples that used segregated systems of money organisation. However, towards the centre, wives and husbands had disjunctive attitudes and these were the couples who 'pooled' their money. It is within these couples that marital relations were more turbulent.

Tensions were higher between couples where the husband did not support his wife in her paid work. Her double burden of paid work and housework were set into sharp contrast by his inactivity due to unemployment. By contrast, traditional couples were more settled. Thus both the domestic division of labour and marital relations vary according to whether the wife is in paid work or not. However, the overall level of resources was also of major significance: the highest turbulence and anxiety were in very long-term unemployed households.

Low economic resources greatly constrain people's social actions and turn them in upon the private home. In these situations separateness is a way of enduring the long hours that couples must spend together. Separating oneself off from the other was a way of keeping the peace. The forms that it took resulted in accentuation of strongly defined gendered spheres of interest. Full-time housewives tended to cling to their routines as an important coping mechanism, as the following interviewee explains,

Hazel F: You don't give the impression that you're desperate . . . what happens if people come to stay with you, you go out of your way to make things even more normal than they are anyway don't you? You have to have a bit of pride. Perhaps that's what kept me going. I don't know. Neville used to say, why bother to do all. Why don't you just forget about that, and I just used to ignore him and say this is what I do, this is my routine. This is what I am doing and I shall continue to do it. If you don't like it get outside and do something else.

The most important overall trend within the sample is the heavier involvement of wives in the domestic economy in the context of poverty than when their husbands had been in full wage work.

MARITAL RELATIONS BETWEEN THE COUPLES WHO USE THE UNITARY CONTROL SYSTEM

The four couples in the sample who had finally changed to the unitary control system, wife management, had very tense marital relations. None of them had planned their finances at the onset of unemployment. One couple had lost their house and another had theirs up for sale. The material shows that length of husbands' unemployment, low resources and tense marital relations interact. These husbands' were determined to keep hold of the purse-strings until the last minute and their defences included violence and deceit. Wives complained that their husbands drew the social security benefit. In severe situations, wives endure the financial responsibilities. Jenny's situation sums this up.

Jenny E: October, two days before I'd got to get out. The letters had been coming from the court, and we were supposed to go, both go, I didn't know. I found them afterwards. I happened to be clearing out that dresser and I found this thing and he'd done nothing. I talked to him and he said 'Oh yeh, well don't worry about it, I'll do something about it'. The following day I said, 'what are you going to do about it? and he said, 'Oh I don't know'. And then I was in such a state about it I got onto the Tavern owners down the road and they said, 'well look Jen, you've got to do something'. He said, 'it's only Monday week you've got to do something, either get onto your Dad or get onto your Aunt'. I said 'I can't get onto either of them it's no good', so he said, 'you must phone his Dad'. And his Dad didn't know anything about this, did he. So of course I broke down on the phone talking to his Dad. So he said, 'you must do something', so after a while I got up to my Aunt. She took us to the Citizen's Advice Bureau and then I went to see Braintree Council and she said I'd got to see a solicitor, and this was all happening, and when he·came back he went bananas to think that I'd do

such a thing. But everybody said, I'd just go out on the street. But he didn't like it and of course I had my half of the house sent to the solicitors and he didn't like that.
Interviewer: Have these experiences brought you closer together?
Jenny E: Well, I don't know. When I go out he says, how long are you going to be?

The above is the extreme situation of isolation, desolation and dependence upon the state. It would be difficult to emphasise more starkly the advantages of wives' paid work to all within the household.

SUMMARY

This chapter has argued for the importance of wives' paid work as a factor influencing the return of husbands to the labour market. By drawing a comparison between paid and unpaid wives, the discussion has highlighted the advantages of by-passing the benefits system. It has shown that husbands of paid wives display labour market patterns similar to those usually outlined as female.

The polarisation between couples with and without paid wives was further heightened by the way that they organised their money during unemployment. In particular the material shows a heavier involvement on the part of wives, and that this is much more onerous for the housewife who does not have direct access to money. The situation of full-time housewives was particularly oppressive because husbands continue to hold the purse-strings until the debts are too large to cope with.

The polarisation was further documented at the level of domestic labour. Physical separateness was a key factor contributing to the involvement of husbands in domestic work when wives were employed outside the home. Conversely tensions arose over domestic space, between long-term unemployed husbands and their wives who were housewives. This domestic situation, and shortage of money further compounded marital tensions generally and further polarised the contrasting experience between paid and unpaid wives when their husbands were unemployed.

The data presented show the relationship between wives' and husbands' paid work to be more complicated than surveys suggest. The importance of wives' paid work in the context of middle-class male unemployment throws further doubt upon traditional stratification theory and Parsonian models of a harmonious functioning family unit.

10 The Modern Cinderellas: Women and the Contract Cleaning Industry in Belfast

Madeleine Leonard

The dramatic post-war entry of married women into the labour force has focused attention on the factors which facilitate or limit the likelihood of married women taking up paid employment outside the home. Recent research indicates that married women's movement in and out of formal employment is strongly influenced by their husbands' employment status. In particular male unemployment often reduces the probability of a wife's employment (Daniel and Stilgoe, 1977; Layard, Piachaud and Stewart, 1978; Bradshaw, Cooke and Godfrey, 1983; Warr and Jackson, 1984, Moylan, Millar and Davies, 1984). This is partly due to the disincentives embedded in welfare benefits' legislation and leads to a polarisation between two-earner and no-earner households. By concentrating on formal employment, the research suggests that married women become, or remain, economically inactive in families where the male is unemployed. But while husbands' lack of formal employment and the gendered nature of the social security system does indeed constrain women's opportunities for paid formal employment, none the less this view neglects the possibility that women may become economically active in other ways. Women in these circumstances may seek informal work and their inability to compete for formal employment may be exploited by employers seeking to minimise labour costs and maximise flexibility by employing labour 'off the books'.

While a full examination of the benefit regulations is outside the scope of this chapter, it is important to outline the different rules applying to the short-term as opposed to the long-term unemployed, because their disincentive effect becomes more prominent, the longer a person remains unemployed. Providing he has made sufficient social security contributions when in employment, an unemployed man can claim Unemployment Benefit for twelve months. The amount of benefit he receives will vary depending on, among other things, whether his wife is employed. However, in calculating the amount of benefit due, a substantial part of the wife's income is disregarded. Once a worker has exhausted his Unemployment Benefit, he transfers to a means tested Income Support benefit and the regulations concerning his wife's income become much less generous. This means that men unemployed for under one year and therefore qualifying for Unemployment Benefit are more likely to have a wife in employment. As length of unemployment increases, and the family transfers to means-tested benefit, the woman is less likely to remain in, or continue to seek employment (Morris, 1990; Leighton, this volume). These regulations adversely affect those least able to bear the brunt of unemployment. Women married to males, out of work for over one year, with little possibility of obtaining future employment, may themselves be deterred from entering the formal labour market. Instead, such women appear to be encouraged to seek employment 'off the record'.

BACKGROUND TO THE RESEARCH

This chapter is based on data collected in a working-class housing estate in West Belfast, and is referred to by the pseudonym Newbury. In Newbury, formal employment has always been a scarce resource and demand has always exceeded supply. Numerous studies have consistently confirmed an above average unemployment rate for the area. In Field's study of Unsatisfactory Tenants (1958), 50 per cent of her sample of male householders were unemployed. In October 1970, the headmaster of the local secondary school carried out a survey into the occupational status of the fathers of the boys who attended the school and found that 47 per cent were unemployed (Doolan, 1982). Newbury also topped Boal *et al.*'s study of 97 Areas of Special Need (1974) with an unemployment rate of 33 per cent among economically active males. Doherty's study of unemployment in the Belfast urban area concluded that Newbury had the 'unfortunate distinction of being the peak unemployment area in both 1966 and 1971 with one in three of its economically active males out of work' (1977, p. 259).

Between January and July 1989, I carried out a survey of one in four households in the area. The homes were randomly selected from the Northern Ireland Housing Executive Household Register for Newbury. The refusal rate was approximately 10 per cent. In each household, the householder and their spouse (if any) were interviewed. This generated a sample size of 118 males and 128 females living in 150 households. The sample included 89 married couples and for the purposes of this chapter, I concentrate on the formal and informal work strategies of married couples in order to illustrate the strong relationship between husbands' unemployment and wives' informal employment.

EMPLOYMENT STATUS AND INFORMAL WORK

In only 24 (27 per cent) of these households was the male employed in the formal economy. The remainder were in various categories of unemployment. Seventeen (19 per cent) were retired, 15 (17 per cent) were unable to work for health reasons and qualified for Invalidity Benefit, one (1 per cent) was in prison as a result of paramilitary activities, while the reminding 32 (36 per cent) were unemployed and qualified for Income Support. The data indicated a concentration of formal work in some homes and unemployment in others. Of the 24 males in formal employment, 10 (42 per cent) had wives who also worked in the formal economy. Five (33 per cent) of the males who qualified for Invalidity Benefit and 3 (18 per cent) of the males who received a Retirement Pension also had wives in formal employment. Only two (6 per cent) unemployed males had a spouse who worked in the formal economy. One husband had only lost his job six months before the interview and as he did not qualify for Unemployment Benefit, he received Income Support. The husband complained bitterly to me about the low level of benefits he was entitled to, as a result of his wife's employment. He stated that his wife is seriously considering her occupational future in the light of his new unemployed status.

More generous allowances for spouses' earnings are accorded to men receiving Invalidity or Retirement Pensions compared to Income Support. Hence women in low paid part-time employment with husbands in these categories can often take home their earnings intact without it affecting their spouses' benefit entitlements. This means that wives with husbands in these welfare categories can continue to seek at least part-time employment in the formal economy whereas women whose husbands only qualify for Income Support face more severe restrictions on earnings and hence may have to focus their attention on informal employment.

UNEMPLOYMENT AND INFORMAL WAGE LABOURERS

Informal wage labourers are people who are employed informally or casually by others who operate in the formal economy. The employers of informal wage labourers range from individuals and small businesses to large organisations. This practice is usually included in the more general sphere of 'off the books' economic activity. The latter is an umbrella term for a wide range of practices that are unregulated, untaxed, unmeasured and not directly reflected in official statistics on the economy. Evading taxes and avoiding compliance with state regulations are the main motivations behind capitalists' and workers' decisions to engage in 'off-the-books' activities. This leads self-employed individuals, small businesses and large corporations to underdeclare their profits and overstate their expenses in an effort to achieve these ends.

Individuals in legitimate employment may engage in moonlighting, that is, they may take on additional work to provide them with extra (untaxed) income. For example, those in the service industries may receive tips and pocket these additional untaxed amounts; others may take on an entirely different job from their primary occupation, in the evenings or at the weekends and again pocket the extra income. Some individuals may be provided with opportunities to engage in extra work derived from their primary occupation. The people who engage in this latter practice range from tradesmen who take on 'homers' to academics who take on extra paid teaching or pocket untaxed income from publications or guest lectures (Mattera, 1985). All these types of economic activity are dependent on formal employment. Evading income or VAT (value added tax) is dependent on legitimate employment while those who engage in moonlighting depend on their primary occupation for basic economic security. Moreover, the activities just mentioned usually depend on the individual having some formal skills. As a result, 'off the books' economic activity covers a diverse group of people from a variety of social backgrounds and occupations.

A more easily identifiable group are informal wage labourers. These people tend to be unskilled, have no formal employment and come from specific social backgrounds. They tend to occupy the lowest rungs of the labour market and often sheer financial necessity compels them to seek informal wage employment. Women, ethnic minorities, the very young and old, and the unemployed tend to be disproportionately represented in this type of informal economic activity. Many are on welfare benefits and find it almost impossible to make these benefits stretch to meet their families' basic needs. As a result they are often open to exploitation by unscrupulous employers.

The remainder of this chapter will focus on one specific group of informal wage labourers; sixteen women who work informally as contract cleaners in Belfast. I was put in contact with five of this group through relationships formed while working in a Community School in the area. The remaining eleven women were interviewed during the survey of 150 households in the estate referred to earlier. Supplementary information on this group was gained by interviewing a representative from the Irish Trade Union Congress and the manager of one of the top five cleaning firms operating in Northern Ireland. The firm in question employs women informally from the Newbury estate. Contract cleaners represent one aspect of the growth of subcontracting.

SUBCONTRACTING

According to Mattera (1985), throughout Western European industry there has been a substantial increase in the amount of work going to subcontractors. Subcontracting refers to an arrangement whereby the overall employer pays for an agreed period of labour time, but leaves the organisation, manning and sometimes the equipping of the task to the subcontractor. Main employers gain considerable benefits from employing subcontractors. Firstly, subcontracting offers the main employer a relatively inexpensive means of determining the price for a definable area of work because rates for particular operations are widely recognised and in depressed conditions, strong competition between subcontractors for work will tend to lower the general level of prices. Secondly, subcontracting enhances employers' flexibility in dealing with fluctuating product markets. The main employer can call on or lay off labour when needed and this in turn reduces fixed costs. Thirdly, by employing subcontractors on short-term contracts, much labour legislation can be avoided. Finally, the low level of trade unionisation among subcontract workers enhances control over the labour process (Bresnen, 1985).

Subcontracting plays a major role in capital's new emphasis on flexibility in working practices. Many trade unionists believe that this notion of flexibility has been seized upon by employers seeking to achieve an intensification of the work process and manpower reductions. Callaghan (1986) argues that flexibility accentuates divisions in our society. He suggests that the strategy of some employers has been to create or strengthen the development of two-tier employment. Its key feature is the insulation of a central core of workers (deemed to be the most important to the firm's operation) from the wider labour market. The other is made up of workers who are not on standard employment contracts and who often experience inferior pay and job security and unequal access to training and promotion opportunities.

Privatisation and Subcontracting

The state itself is taking a direct hand in the process of reducing wage levels. One way this is achieved is through privatisation which, according to Rainnie (1985, p. 156), 'paves the way for competitive tendering from small firms, casting them in the role of vultures hovering around the carcass of organised labour'.

Privatisation is an umbrella term for a wide range of policies aimed at re-establishing market principles in the provision of public services. According to Pulkingham (1989, p. 397), the policy to privatise public industries and services is, in effect, both an employment and a wage policy. A range of measures to reduce wages and enable the market to operate more freely have been implemented. Employment rights have been weakened and the contracting out of public services to private firms has removed the low paid from the coverage of collectively negotiated agreements. While advocates of the contracting out of public services argue that it will result in efficiency improvements, concern is emerging that this can only be achieved by reducing staff, lowering conditions of service and instituting more flexible working arrangements. These measures are facilitated by laws which provide employers with a host of special attractions to pay very low wages. Employers can escape their obligations to pay tax and national insurance contributions, or their need to observe employment rights if they keep hours and wages below the various qualifying thresholds. As the government increasingly contracts out a range of public services, shops, offices and firms are being encouraged to contract out the more peripheral aspects of their organisations, such as the cleaning of their premises to private contract cleaning firms.

SUBCONTRACTING AND FEMALE CONTRACT CLEANERS

Subcontract cleaning firms are generally involved in competitive tendering whereby the most successful tender is also the cheapest.

Since the cleaning industry is a labour intensive one, the bulk of its expenditure relates to the payment of wages. Thus to be successful and secure a contract, the subcontractor is continually involved in attempts to increase workloads, intensify work practices and lower the wages of the cleaners he employs. According to Mitter (1986, p. 55), the effective use of a flexible and non-unionised labour force is a necessary condition for survival in the cut-throat competition among subcontractors today. Employing labour 'off the books' is one of the most effective means of keeping costs low. In the Newbury estate, attempts to do this are facilitated by the large number of unemployed men with wives who are generally excluded from the formal labour market.

Cleaning is a prime example of low paid, low status work. Most women will spend some part of their daily lives involved in cleaning duties, usually under the guise of housework. Indeed, if cleaning is carried out at home by the housewife, it is not deemed worthy enough to be called 'real work'. Cleaning only becomes work when it is removed from the boundaries of home, family and marriage. The sixteen women interviewed were aged between 25 and 61. All of the sample were married with dependent children. The spouses of the women were all unemployed and all qualified for welfare assistance. In some cases, the declaration of the women's extra income would have affected benefits' entitlements and hence went unreported.

The women worked in some of the best known shops and business concerns operating in Belfast. None of the women were directly employed by the owners of the premises in which they worked. Rather, they were all employed by subcontractors who specialise in cleaning retail and business premises. The subcontractor is employed directly by the owners and/or managers of individual office blocks and retail units. Since cleaning contracts rarely make stipulations regarding the volume, deployment, organisation or conditions of contract labour, the contractor has total freedom in these matters (Daly, 1986, p. 23).

All the women interviewed worked on average between 10 and 15 hours per week. The typical rota worked was 4–5 evenings each week, for 2–3 hours from about 6.00 pm. The women who worked in large shops had to work later on Thursday nights to accommodate late-night shopping. Typically, they began work on Thursdays between 9.00 and 9.30 pm and worked until around midnight. They were paid no extra for this disruption in their work routine. The women complained that at peak periods during the year, especially around Christmas, their workload intensified due to late night shopping or office parties. Yet again, they often received no extra payment to compensate for this, although six of the sample stated that they received a Christmas bonus of either £10 or one week's wages.

Since all but one of the contract cleaners worked in the evenings, these hours were very conducive to combining the traditional housewife role with work. Most of these female wage labourers had finished their household duties before they went out to work. Only where there were young children in the household was the husband's participation noticeable and this involved putting children to bed. In this respect, the study supports Oakley's observation (1974, p. 138) that there is a greater tendency for men to take part in child care than in housework. In only one case was there significant input from other family members in carrying out household duties. This was a cleaner who also held two other informal jobs. Indeed, she cited the delegation of her household duties to other members of her family as a major incentive in encouraging her to work outside the household. As she says:

> I usually get stuff in for the dinner the night before and one of the sons or daughters makes it. The kids also do all the housework.... There is nothing I like better than coming in to a clean house and a bit of dinner. Now don't get me wrong, it's not that I don't like cleaning, it's just it's so boring in your own house. When you do it outside it's not the same. It's not like work.

WAGE RATES AND MOTIVATIONS TO WORK INFORMALLY

Cleaning is undoubtedly a low-paid occupation. The women interviewed were paid wages far below the recognised minimum. While the concept of minimum wage is problematic, none the less it serves as a useful indicator of the average earnings of the low-paid sector in the formal economy. Coyle (1986, p. 8) states that average full-time earnings in cleaning are below the average manual wage.

Looking through the job columns in Belfast newspapers in 1989, the average wage rate for cleaners in Belfast, was around £2.80 per hour. With one exception, all the women in this sample earned approximately 53 per cent of this average formal wage. Moreover, the cleaners had to make their own way to and from their work and this involved added expense. On average the women spend around 20 per cent of their weekly wages on transport costs.

In this study, the informal wage labourers' motivations lay in instrumental considerations. Informal wage labour was rarely a deliberate choice. Renumeration was the wage labourers' single, most important concern. Most of the wage labourers interviewed simply could not manage on the benefit entitlements allocated to their families and needed whatever extra money they could get. These dire financial circumstances meant that most of them were not interested in job satisfaction. Their wages were rarely spent on luxuries but were vital to providing basic essentials for the whole family, as the following quotes illustrate:

> Look love, £12 a week mightn't mean much to you, but for me it means the difference between either have a joint for the Sunday dinner or not have a joint for the Sunday dinner. It's as simple as that.

> Well, I could never buy big things with my wages, it went on wee things like ribbons for the kid's hair, socks, knickers, you know. All those things cost a fortune you know and without my wee job I couldn't even afford these bits and pieces.

These quotes reflect the inability of the families in this study to manage on welfare benefits. Because of this incapacity to stretch benefit entitlements to meet family needs, the respondents were willing to work for extremely low wages where they could get the opportunity to work informally. These circumstances are conducive to a labour intensive industry compelled by the competitive tendering process to reduce wage costs continually in an attempt to secure future tenders.

WORKING CONDITIONS

The contract cleaners interviewed were typically involved in cleaning large shops and office blocks. They rarely had any contact with the staff employed in the building, although the women working in office blocks occasionally met workers engaged in overtime. They also had little or no contact with cleaners in other buildings. Some of the women were confined to one building while others cleaned two or more smaller buildings. The women were generally allocated specific areas to clean while more heavier cleaning such as toilet areas were usually shared on a rota basis. Their main duties included cleaning, polishing and dusting. At certain times in the year, they were expected to give their areas a more thorough overhaul.

The women either worked individually or as part of a team, depending on the size of the premises in which they were employed.

They were subject to varying degrees of supervision, again depending on the size of the premises in which they operated. If they were involved in cleaning a small shop or office, they usually saw their supervisor only once per week, on pay day. (All the women were paid in cash.) If they worked in a larger concern, the supervisor would either work alongside them or remain in the overall building. In these circumstances, the standard of their work was continually scrutinised. The supervisors were not a uniform group but came from varying backgrounds. Seven of the sample stated that their supervisor was a man. None of these men engaged in any direct cleaning work, but were described as company officials who handed out wages and inspected work. The male supervisors were generally responsible for a number of premises and travelled around from one site to another supervising workloads and dealing with administrative problems. The female supervisors had often been previously employed as contract cleaners and had gained promotion. Several of the female supervisors had their own cleaning duties but mostly they were responsible for overseeing the rest of the work, making sure it met a particular standard and allocating cleaning materials as necessary.

The scarcity of cleaning materials proved a constant source of friction between the cleaners and supervisors. No bags to put rubbish in, insufficient cloths and cleaning agents and no hot water were the most frequent complaints. This meant that some of the women could not do their jobs properly and often had to bear the brunt of office employees' complaints if the employees happened to be working overtime. This motivated one woman to bring in cleaning materials occasionally from home. Another woman brought in cleaning materials on a regular basis because she had developed a pride in her work. Other cleaners stated that when complaints were made to the supervisor, the onus was placed back on their shoulders, the supervisors usually saying that the cleaners were too extravagant with their cleaning materials. Most women received a quota of cleaning materials to last a specific time and if they ran out before the time limit, they had to resort to cleaning with ordinary water. Most women felt that these quotas were inadequate to meet the cleaning workloads allocated to them.

RECRUITMENT PRACTICES

Morris (1985b) states that the poor conditions of employment associated with the increasing use of subcontractors by large-scale

enterprises has encouraged an increase in informal means of recruitment, minimising costs to the employer and maximising co-operation
from the workforce. Morris argues that enterprises working to a
contract consequently usually offer only short-term employment.
They are less likely than large-scale bureaucratic enterprises to seek
labour through formal channels. This is due to the costs associated
with formal recruitment. The more temporary the work offered, the
more important it will be to minimise costs.

Formal employers wishing to take on labour 'off the books' may
find it necessary to rely on informal recruitment as formal procedures
could increase the risk of discovery. More importantly, manipulation
of the recruitment process enhances the docility and loyalty of the
workforce. Informal recruitment mechanisms operating through social
networks are very conducive to creating bonds of mutual trust and
obligation. As Jenkins points out (1988, p. 265), labour recruited
informally via an intermediary already employed by the organisation
can to some extent be controlled by group pressure. This is because the
employee introducing the recruit will feel responsible for ensuring their
continued good behaviour. Jenkins *et al.* (1983, p. 72) state that
recruiting by networks is an attempt to make an unknown quantity,
i.e. the potential recruit, somewhat less so. Recruiting informally can
often identify in advance and thus prevent the employment of a
potential troublemaker or layabout. Morris (1985b, p. 349) suggests
that the need to bring ties of personal obligation to bear in the
recruitment and control of the workforce will be strongest among
employers employing workers 'off the books'.

Informal Recruitment and Contract Cleaners

Pahl's (1984) study on the Isle of Sheppey uncovered polarisation
between multiple earner households and no-earner households. Access
to informal work was closely bound up with formal employment.
Thus, those without formal employment were denied access to
informal work. For the female wage labourers in the present study,
access to informal work was linked, not to those in formal employment, but to those already in informal employment. All the cleaners
interviewed were recruited through networks of friends, neighbours
and relatives already in informal employment. Localities which prove
most unattractive for the formal economy can emerge as recruiting
zones for informal workers. Formal employers can exploit the social

networks of existing informal workers to take on additional labour when needed.

This suggests more complex patterns of polarisation than simply divisions between the employed and unemployed. It indicates that polarisation may exist among unemployed households with multiple informal workers and unemployed households with no access to informal work. Five of the female wage labourers interviewed also had husbands working informally. Moreover two of the contract cleaners held more than one informal job. One of these women had also worked as a waitress for the past five years in a bar in Belfast's city centre. Her involvement with contract cleaning tended to be sporadic with her moving in and out of jobs during peak periods in her family's expenditure especially prior to Christmas. Her sister and two neighbours worked for contract cleaning firms and since the subcontractor's workload coincided with her family's increased expenditure periods, she had little difficulty in securing casual informal employment. She had been involved with contract cleaning on a sporadic basis for the past three years.

The other respondent held down three informal jobs. She cleaned a small shop in the city centre from 6.30–8.30 am every morning, Monday to Saturday. She then worked in a pork factory close to the centre of Belfast from 10.30 am–2.30 pm. Finally each evening, Monday to Friday, she worked for a contract cleaning firm cleaning a major office block in the city centre.

Five of the sixteen contract cleaners were related. Two were sisters and a sister-in-law and another two were sisters. Others interviewed stated that they had been recruited by a relative. This indicates that access to informal work may be dependent on extended kinship networks located in specific communities.

CONSEQUENCES OF INFORMAL RECRUITMENT

Some of the consequences of informal recruitment are illustrated by this research. None of the sixteen women were entitled to any form of employment protection or benefits. Thus, if one of the women was off sick or had to deal with some family crisis, she did not receive any payment for the time she took off, regardless of her length of service to the organisation. Furthermore, subcontracting firms were involved in a constant effort to fulfil contracts and make profits and this resulted in a continuous intensification of the labour process. If employees took time off work, this could put the implementation of the contract into jeopardy. These problems were averted by the women through the manipulation of social relationships within the workplace. All the women stated that when a close colleague had to take time off work, her chain of social contacts within the organisation joined together and distributed her workload between them. This typically happened among friends, neighbours and relatives, but often extended over a team of cleaners working in the same part of a building. The women usually co-operated knowing that they may need the favour returned at some future date. In the process, the women taking time off work were guaranteed their weekly wage, their employment was not placed in jeopardy (unless this was a frequent occurrence) and the smooth running of the contract was ensured.

A further consequence of recruitment on the basis of informal contacts is that it made this form of exploitative work less alienating. While all sixteen of the contract cleaners stressed that they were working primarily for instrumental purposes (i.e. they needed the money), eleven of the sample stressed the close companionship of their workmates as an added incentive. Since their workmates were also their friends, neighbours and relatives, and since family obligations prevented the women from meeting as often as they would have liked, work provided a venue for catching up on local gossip and keeping up to date with news regarding the welfare of a wider range of friends and relations than they could otherwise have managed.

The informal recruitment process also resulted in no standardised wage structure existing for informal workers in the contract cleaning industry. Rather the new cleaners were paid according to the pay of the person responsible for informally recruiting them. Each of the sixteen cleaners were recruited by informal wage labourers already employed by the cleaning firms. Thus, if the friend, neighbour or relative of a new recruit was paid £1 per hour, then she would be paid £1 per hour. Similarly, if the existing cleaner was paid £1.50 per hour, then the new recruit would be paid £1.50 per hour.

Often the wage structure was uniform within specific buildings. Thus a team of cleaners would get £1 per hour for cleaning a certain building, while another team would get £1.50 per hour for cleaning a similar building for the same subcontractor. Given the scattered nature of the contract cleaning industry, cleaners in one building had no opportunity to interact with cleaners in another building, and so these wage disparities often remained hidden. Even if women became aware through personal relationships outside work that friends, neighbours or relatives were being paid more than them for similar work, they could never be sure that they were employed by the same subcontracting firm. This latter point reflects a further aspect of the informal recruitment process. Most of the women interviewed knew very little about their employing company. Twelve of the sixteen contract cleaners had no idea who they worked for, a typical response being: 'Well, I think it's a big company from across the water'. Of the remaining four women, three knew the company they worked for by name but this was the extent of their limited knowledge. The remaining cleaner knew a certain amount about her employer and was the only one to have actually met her employer. The other fifteen had no contact with their employer. Usually the supervisor was the only company employee they knew apart from their immediate work group. The supervisor was often responsible for the hiring of new cleaners and for the day to day management of the cleaning team. New recruits were put into contact with the supervisor through existing informal workers employed by the company.

CONCLUSION

Subcontracting is a process used by formal enterprises in an attempt to reduce labour costs. It provides a visible illustration of the fusion of formal and informal economic activity. The subcontract cleaning firms referred to in this chapter are formal organisations who engage in a formal manner in competitive tendering. Once that tender is secured, informality is the keynote of their enterprises. This informality is evident at every level of their operations. Informal recruiting practices, for example, have meant that subcontractors have been able to sustain a 'reserve' army of temporary labour made up almost exclusively of women. Since these women operate outside government regulations, they do not enjoy the protection of employment and labour legislation that is extended to even the very low paid workers in the formal sector.

This situation is enhanced by welfare benefits legislation which tends to discriminate against the long-term unemployed. Because of their husbands' employment status the cleaners in this study were deterred from entering formal employment. As a result these women form a trapped section of the workforce and fall easy prey to companies seeking low paid, casual workers.

11 Women, Business and Self-Employment: A Conceptual Minefield

Sheila Allen and Carole Truman

The past decade has seen a considerable increase of interest among social scientists in the small business and self-employed sectors of the economy. Despite this, relatively little is known even at a descriptive level about the extent of women's participation. The conditions under which they become self- employed or start a small business, where they are located in the market geographically and financially, what types of establishment they run, whether they differ from other women in terms of personal characteristics and how their experiences compare to men's are all areas requiring research.

This chapter explores some of the issues raised by attempts to study small business ownership and self-employment among women. To structure the collection and analysis of relevant research data within a sociologically meaningful framework requires consideration of several, largely discrete, bodies of work including research on small business, women's labour market activities, household divisions of labour, and forms of work which fall outside employment or running a small firm. In addition account has to be taken of changes in Western economies where the restructuring of industry and the effects of recession combine with an emphasis on enterprise and entrepreneurial activity to provide the material and ideological backcloth to any assessment of women's participation in small business or self-employment.

In an area where research is so scarce, theorising women's location in terms of agency and structure can only be extremely tentative. In order to accommodate women in empirical sociology, as feminist scholars in the early 1970s demanded, considerable shifts in conceptualisations of the social world were necessary. The slow but definite recognition of gender as a salient variable in theory and empirical work has challenged much that was taken for granted among sociologists less than twenty years ago. This has influenced research in several ways so that social phenomena have been reconceptualised by sociologists. For instance, 'work' now includes paid and unpaid

activities and the concept recognises that as these activities are not
carried out exclusively in the public, formal, arena, household divisions
of labour are integral to an understanding of occupational and market
divisions (Gallie, 1988; Pahl, 1988).

While it would be rash to argue that it is widely appreciated that
gender involves more than including women and treating women's
concerns seriously, there has been some movement affecting mainstream theorising. The debates, notably around gender and class, and
to a lesser extent around gender and ethnicity, have raised crucial
questions about the salience of class and ethnocentrism for conceptualising and researching gender inequalities (Allen, 1987; Crompton
and Mann, 1986; Ramazanoglu, 1989; Stacey, 1986). These debates are
ongoing evidence that in sociology at least, 'gender as a focus of
academic interest has become of considerable importance' (University
Grants Committee, 1989). However, it would be misleading to assume
from this that researchers in all or most areas of sociological interest,
including self-employment and small business activity, demonstrate an
awareness of the significance of gender.

The relatively scant attention that mainstream sociology has paid to
self-employment and small business, though understandable in terms
of the development both of the discipline and capitalist societies, has
created a substantial gap in terms of theorising these areas. There are
notable exceptions particularly in relation to class theories and the
location of the petite bourgeoisie at different stages of capitalist
development. Scase (1982) identifies three approaches; the first in
which the *petite bourgeoisie* is 'regarded as "separate" and "removed" from the two major classes of capitalist society', the second
in which it is seen as 'part and parcel of an emerging "post-industrial"
or "service" class structure' and the third which interprets it 'as a
legacy of an earlier pre-capitalist form of production'. He argues that:

> the persistence of the petty bourgeoisie cannot solely be explained . . . as a
> legacy of an earlier pre-capitalist form of production. Furthermore, it
> cannot simply be regarded as 'marginal' or 'outside' the capital accumula-
> tion process. On the contrary, it persists because of its material and
> ideological functions within contemporary capitalism. Consequently, there
> is a need for more attention to be devoted to the *empirical processes*
> whereby the petty bourgeoisie is reproduced under the conditions of present
> day capitalism. (pp. 160–1, *emphasis added*).

In the context of the 1990s where it is claimed not only that
economic change incorporates processes which reproduce small scale

enterprise, but also that these processes are central to the regeneration of economic prosperity for individuals and communities, an understanding of the gender dimensions of self- employment and small business is crucial.

In this chapter we discuss whether women's self-employment and business activity are to be analysed simply as a variant within the small firms sector or in terms of women's work and their position in the labour market more generally. We examine the statistical data on which estimates of self-employment are based and from which claims of increased growth are made. We also assess the extent to which the assumptions underlying research on the small business sector are appropriate for explaining women's participation. We draw on both extensive literature on women and the labour market, which has relevance for our understanding of women's experiences, and on our own on-going research on women and men who have their own business or who are thinking about setting up on their own.

RESEARCH INTO THE SMALL FIRMS SECTOR AND WOMEN'S 'WORK'

There has been a tendency for social scientists to focus research and analysis on firms with high capital investment and large work forces. This focus was thought to be justified both because of the relative proportions of those engaged in this sector compared to those in self-employment and small business, and because of the significance of large enterprises in dominant theories of capitalist development. Consequently most studies in industrial sociology, organisational behaviour and economics have concentrated on this sector, although as Miller (1975) pointed out 'The small business sector as a whole ... is large and strong in most capitalist nations.' There has always been literature on the small firm sector, but much of this earlier work was ignored in the 1980s.

Given the political emphasis in the UK on the 'enterprise culture', some argue it is necessary for studies of small firms to become more central to the analysis of economic life (Curran and Burrows, 1989). It has also been argued that because so little attention was paid to self-employment until the late 1980s, debates have been informed more by ideology than by empirical research (Hakim, 1988b). There can be little doubt that ideology played a significant part in much of the 1980s literature, not least in defining the parameters selected for empirical research. One of the most remarkable dimensions is the adoption of language, either explicitly male or apparently gender neutral, which in reality reflects the actual or assumed lifestyles of men. Almost without exception research and discussion on small firms and self-employment has taken it for granted that businesses are started, owned and run by men. Phrases such as 'men like themselves', 'he is inclined', 'he buttresses', 'a man with his own tools' are pervasive.

There is, however, a small and growing literature on women small business owners and self-employed women (Carter *et al.*, 1988; Cromie and Hayes, 1988; Curran and Burrows, 1988; Goffee and Scase, 1985, 1987; Halpern, 1989; Watkins and Watkins, 1984). This literature recognises that in some small businesses and in some self-employment, women are the social actors. However, it has not so far taken on board the theoretical challenges, the debates on methodology or the empirical studies of work, household and gender relations referred to earlier.

Most of the small business research to date has focused on manufacturing enterprises although '. . . manufacturing firms are a minority group, however they are counted' (Hakim, 1989, p. 30). It has been suggested that in view of the decline of manufacturing and the growth of the service sector a disproportionate amount of attention has been paid to the former at the expense of the latter (Curran and Burrows, 1989). This is particularly problematic since women are more likely to be found in the service sector of small business activity.

Hakim (1988b) claims that debates on industrial re- structuring, especially those relating to workforce flexibility, have tended to assume part-time employment as the most important alternative for women and self-employment for men. And her analyses of several data sources have led to the claim that 'overall 70 per cent [of small firms] are run by men, 30 per cent by women – very much in line with the pattern found among the self-employed nationally. . .' (Hakim, 1989, p. 34).' However, she points out that 'quite a few' of the very smallest businesses are excluded even in those surveys with the best coverage of the sector. Without more comprehensive data on very small enterprises such statements about differential gender participation remain unsubstantiated.

As discussions of industrial restructuring continue, whether focused on the manufacturing or the service sector, it is essential that women are fully integrated into empirical research rather than 'added on' as a variation to the 'normal', that is the male, framework. This will only happen if methodologies are adopted whereby researchers actively seek to investigate women's participation (see Poland, this volume). A failure to do this will lead to the replication of old patterns of classification which can do no more than reproduce distorted or biased descriptions and explanations that fail to recognise women's participation in the sector (Allen and Truman, 1988; 1989).

From studies of women in paid employment it is safe to assume that many women's working patterns differ from those of men (Beechey and Perkins, 1987; Dex, 1987; Hunt, 1988; Martin and Roberts, 1984). Adult men are expected to engage in full- time, regular paid work until retirement unless unemployed or incapacitated. A commitment to paid work to provide for their own and their dependants' material existence is part of the normative definition of being adult and male. In contrast, adult women, specifically those who are married or living with a male partner, are expected to give priority to the servicing of husband, partner, children, and the sick, handicapped and elderly. Their paid work is seen as secondary and contingent and they are assumed to be economically dependant.

Martin and Roberts (1984) clearly demonstrate that despite women's work patterns differing from those of men, women, like men, are permanently attached to the labour market throughout most of their lives. They did not specifically address self-employment, but their evidence suggests that this should be seen as one variant of women's permanent attachment to the labour force.

The context in which many, if not the majority of women enter self-employment will differ markedly from that of men. For although women are active in the labour market, few men take an active role in unpaid domestic labour. Self-employment will be only one aspect of the total work carried out by women. Studies of self-employment which fail to incorporate an awareness of women's disadvantaged position in the formal labour market give a myopic representation of women's involvement in the small firms sector (Goffee and Scase, 1985; Watkins and Watkins, 1984). For example, it is argued that women set up in business without a background of achievement, in contrast to men who are usually better prepared through training or previous experience (Watkins and Watkins, 1984). Women, it is said, take more risks when becoming self-employed. This conclusion can only be drawn if particular assumptions are made about self-employment and women's lives. Achievement is narrowly defined in terms of formal education and training and positions previously held in labour market hierarchies. Experience in managing a household and balancing a family budget are seen as neither achievement nor preparation in spite of the time and resource management involved. The notion of risk cannot be assessed in isolation. Feminist research on women and small business points to the lack of opportunity for women – in particular, those who are black or from ethnic minorities – in the formal labour market which means that self-employment is the only or last possibility of earning a living (Morokvasic-Muller, 1988). Self-employment may prove to be a very positive experience, but in many cases cannot be isolated from the lack of choice which precipitated the decision to undertake it. Epstein (1989) describes how women may not only be 'pushed' into self-employment out of necessity, but may also experience a 'pull' towards it when they face sexist barriers which block their opportunities in employment. In either case, the decision to enter self-employment is a response to the conditions of the labour market rather than a free choice.

It is therefore not possible to assume for women that 'there is a strong streak of individualism amongst the self-employed whereas workers choosing conventional employee jobs tend to hold collectivist values' (Hakim, 1988b, p. 433). Such statements require empirical investigation for they imply forms of employment status are a matter of choice. Moreover, the research of Bechhofer and his colleagues on male shopkeepers shows that most are aware of the disadvantages of being self-employed, to the extent that they would readily abandon their enterprises in favour of the security of being an employee if they had a choice (Bechhofer *et al.*, 1974).

An understanding of women's entry into small business and self-employment can only be gained in the context of their position in the formal labour market and how this articulates with other forms of work including unpaid domestic labour (Allen and Wolkowitz, 1987a; 1987b; Allen, 1989; Allen and Truman, 1988; 1989).

OCCUPATIONAL SEGREGATION

The division of labour which leads to women undertaking both paid and unpaid work forms part of broader patterns of gender segregation. Occupational segregation in the labour market has both horizontal and vertical components (Hakim, 1979). Horizontal segregation in the labour market means that women do different jobs from men and are found in different occupational groupings. This has implications for the rates of remuneration received by men and women in paid employment. Differences between the wage rates of men and women in different occupations cannot be explained in terms of skill or training (Treiman and Hartmann, 1981), yet remain a prevalent feature of labour market segmentation. An analysis of the General Household Survey (GHS) suggests that existing patterns of occupational segregation are being replicated in self-employment (Curran and Burrows, 1988, p. 56). It has been demonstrated that women's enterprise need not be confined to 'traditional female sectors' (Hertz, 1986; Cannon *et al.*, 1988), but there is no evidence so far which suggests that self-employment in itself provides women with an escape route from the lower paid, lower status occupations where the majority are found.

Considerable theoretical debate has been devoted to the causes of gender segregation in paid work, and the extent to which it results from rational free choice or from structural constraints on women (Walby, 1988). Our study of women in the small firms sector is designed to examine the choices and structures that women face when going into business on their own. Are the choices and constraints surrounding self-employment a continuation of those found in all women's paid work? Alternatively, does the small firms sector introduce additional criteria which need to be incorporated into existing theories of gender segregation? Research into both the small firms sector and women's paid work has so far failed to provide answers to these questions.

The overall structuring of gender segregation analysed in terms of the interconnections between patriarchy and capitalism leads to an expectation that existing patterns of occupational segregation will be repeated in the area of small business. The prospects for women will remain limited. They will be confined to business activity where their skills are unrecognised and their rewards low. It is argued that an attraction of the service sector compared to manufacturing is that little or even no capital investment is required in order to begin trading. The service sector may thus be an option open to women who have no access to capital assets in their own right and who experience discriminatory practices when they try to raise capital from financial institutions (Halpern, 1989). However, capital in terms of time and know-how are also needed and the differences between women and men with regard to these requires exploration. If access to the service sector is relatively open then the markets for the services are more easily saturated. Consequently even original business ideas can be copied making those dependent on the service sector for their living vulnerable. Such vulnerability is not gender specific *per se*.

The causes and characteristics of small business success or failure may differ for men and women. In so far as they are trading within the same markets, comparisons can be made which isolate market factors from causes which arise from gender relations. Such comparisons are only possible if the research methods allow both men and women to give their own accounts rather than encapsulating the characteristics of business success or failure in pre-defined categories (Smith, 1988). The failure of a small business is more likely to be recorded and the owner's change of economic status recognised if it is owned by a man than if it is owned by a woman. Thus, where women have a male partner the gendering of economic relations is such that when, for whatever reason, they cease to trade they may become economically dependent. The business failure may go unrecorded and the women's economic status as unemployed remain hidden. The domestic relationships between men and women and the interconnections between these relationships and their economic activity are intrinsic to how they organise themselves in self-employment and small business.

STATISTICAL ESTIMATES AND PROBLEMS

Women appear to be under-represented in the small enterprise sector compared with their participation in the economy as a whole. General Household Survey data show that women as employees accounted for 44 per cent of the work-force during the period 1979–84. Over the same period, women in small enterprises were consistently out-numbered three to one by men (Curran and Burrows, 1988). The adequacy of official statistics as a basis upon which to quantify women's involvement as paid employees or in self-employment has been questioned by researchers for several years. There are reports of an increase of 70 per cent between 1981 and 1987 in the number of women recorded as being self-employed either full-time or part- time (*Employment Gazette*, 1988). However, this may give a distorted picture unless account is taken of the base-line from which these official figures start. In the mid 1980s, there were only 714 000 women in Britain recorded in this sector (*Employment Gazette*, 1988; Halpern, 1989).

The unreliability of official statistics as an indicator of the number of self-employed women was highlighted by a European survey which focused on a representative sample of 17 000 women who did not have the conventional status of employee (EEC, 1987). The numbers of women who ran their own business or worked independently were found to be far greater than those recorded in official Eurostat surveys of the work-force. Eurostat estimates are based on statistics gathered regularly by member governments and are dependent upon survey methods, classifications and definitions similar to those of the General Household Survey and New Earnings Survey in the UK. Such sources estimate that there are 3 200 000 self-employed women in the EEC. When women were asked broader questions relating to their sources of income, a total of 4 395 000 were estimated to be self-employed. and a further 8 185 000 women were estimated to be non-salaried but working in their partner's businesses (EEC, 1987). The methods used therefore lead to great differences in the number of women who are counted as self-employed.

The participation (and economic contribution) of some 10 million in the EEC is made visible in the survey of women officially designated as non-employed. This alone indicates the need for research which adopts more adequate methods of data collection. Making women visible statistically is only one task. Making sense of official statistical records is another. This involves pointing out their inadequacies as databases and developing ways of conceptualising and researching work activities which do justice to the complexities in which they are embedded (see Poland, this volume). The bias towards official under-recording raises questions about the claims of growth in women's self-employment over the past decade. Compared with data on men in this sector, the data on women's participation remain poorly categorised and meagre. Our understanding of self-employment among men is limited, so it is hardly surprising that the state of the art in researching women's self-employment is largely sciolistic.

A greater recognition that the understanding of the small firms sector and self-employment in general is hindered by the paucity of official statistics now exists (Curran and Burrows, 1988, 1989; Hakim, 1988b). The number of people included in estimates of the self-employed varies considerably according to the definitions used. For example, the Labour Force Survey operates with criteria based on respondents' self-definitions. However, individuals are also asked about their status for Income Tax and National Insurance purposes and those who are salaried directors in their own firm are reclassified. They are thus excluded as small-scale entrepreneurs, even though they may, in effect, be self-employed. This reclassification affects both men and women, but as Casey and Creigh (1988) point out, regulations result in 30 per cent fewer women being classed as self-employed by the Inland Revenue than appear in the LFS statistics. Similarly statistics based on National Insurance contributions are likely to underestimate the number of self-employed women in two ways. Those who do not pay full contributions, a diminishing but not insignificant number of married women, are excluded, as are those who earn less than the threshold for paying National Insurance contributions (£48 per week in 1990). While the latter group includes both men and women, it is reasonable to assume that women are disproportionately affected. Using other definitions of self-employment, Casey and Creigh (1988) have estimated that the total number of people counted as self-employed could be nearly 40 per cent greater, 14.6 per cent of the work-force.

Our understanding of the nature of women's work leads us to agree with Casey and Creigh's suggestion that findings about self-employment and the characteristics of those involved are likely to be very dependent on the criteria adopted.

However, care needs to be taken to avoid expanding this category to include all manner of work activity, other than direct, regulated employment. For while, on the one hand, much self-employment and small business activity may be unrecorded particularly where women are concerned, on the other hand note must be taken of the substantial changes in the conditions of work and employment relations which have affected large sectors of the labour force. Through legislative change the role of the state in Britain has been crucial in fragmenting the labour process and at a more general level it has been argued that the new growth in self-employment and small business is a by-product of the overall strategies of international capital (Gerry, 1985; Offe, 1985; Purcell *et al.*, 1986). From this perspective many of the new self-employed and those setting up their own business are disguised wage workers, contract labour tied into large capital, sub-contracting for work they previously did as direct employees. These ambiguities of status are not confined to women and it cannot be supposed that improving statistical recording will of itself clarify them. Distinctions have been drawn between forms of self-employment, drawing on research on small firms and casualised work (Allen and Wolkowitz, 1987a; Fevre, 1986; Scase, 1989).

SELF-EMPLOYMENT IN WOMEN'S LIVES

The construction of work as separate from home has been shown to be conceptually misleading, as has the construction as non- working of those not employed in the external labour market. It is not necessary to rehearse the arguments which lay behind the conceptual shifts or detail the extensive research literature by which the concepts of work and home have been clarified. The considerable attention given to how paid and unpaid work interact has made little or no impact on how the domestic sphere is constructed in small business research. The male business owner is commonly assumed to receive emotional and practical support for his business activities from female kin. particularly his wife. Different assumptions are made for women.

> For male entrepreneurs, priorities are clearly defined in terms of their business and family and business roles do not conflict as the wife takes responsibility for the organisation and running of the home. Women entrepreneurs on the other hand, find themselves trying to balance the combined roles of organiser of home life and business person; a situation that often induces both stress and guilt. . . family support, particularly from a spouse is crucial to success. (O'Connor and Ruddle, 1988, p. 24)

Not all businessmen have spouses and research comparing those with access to unpaid domestic help and family labour more generally to those without would establish the extent to which these different situations affect business activity. The world of the female business owner, however, is likely to contain more competing and conflicting demands than that of her male counterpart. Women's personal circumstances have been found in one piece of research to be a great influence on their decisions about work:

> enterprises were frequently established to fulfil personal goals and needs. When these changed, businesses changed accordingly. Changes in personal ambitions and circumstances had a more direct effect on the nature and goals of the firm than has been identified in studies of male owned businesses. (Cannon *et al.*, 1988, p. 69)

If this finding is confirmed in further research, it carries implications for what may be termed 'success' in women's businesses (Allen and Truman, 1988). And similarly, the end of a period of business activity by women may not necessarily be considered 'business failures' in the commonly accepted sense, but a response to opportunities or constraints resulting from changes in their personal and domestic circumstances. Such matters will remain speculative until research into business activity is designed to take account of differences and similarities between men and women.

The importance of the life course on women's lives has been highlighted in much research on women (see for example, Allatt *et al.*, 1987). The stages of the life course deserve more attention in our understanding of women's participation in self-employment and the small firms sector. The different life-cycle stages of women's lives have both spatial and temporal implications for their business activity and may also affect men in ways yet unresearched. The presence of pre-school age children, for instance, may place different restrictions on a woman in comparison to those with older children or with no children. The only option open to women with very young children may be to undertake paid work from or at home. This may take many forms, including disguised waged work, self-employment or running a home-based business. As children grow up, so limitations and opportunities for employment, self-employment and business activity may change. Caring for elderly, sick or disabled people imposes different responsibilities and constraints which fall largely on women. There remains much to discover about how self-employment interacts with other commitments at different stages in the life course. We cannot treat women as a homogeneous group any more than men. From what is known about women's work, however, their engagement in self-employment and business activity is likely to show considerable differences from that of men.

Taking an example from our research may illustrate some of the foregoing discussion more graphically. A middle-class woman (in terms of background, education and spouse's status) working from home as a graphic designer is self-employed both legally and by self-definition. She uses the services of a child-minder and also employs a cleaner (both women). Clearly, she is self-employed, but what of the status of the child-minder and the cleaner? They are undertaking work that the graphic designer would normally be expected to carry out herself for no financial reward. They make it possible for her to engage in remunerative self-employment. Are they employees or sub-contracted labour? If they are employees, is the graphic designer to be classed as running a small business with employees rather than a sole trader? Alternatively, are the child-minder and the cleaner to be considered as self-employed in their own right? If so, are all three women to be seen as running inter-dependent businesses? If the child-minder and the cleaner have dependants who are in turn cared for by others who are paid for their services, are they self-employed with employees or contractors of sub-contracted labour? If they do not pay those who provide care, how are they and the carers to be categorised? Would the same difficulties arise if the graphic designer were a man who pays for the services of a child-minder, a house cleaner and a window cleaner to enable him to carry out his business activity? If his wife or domestic partner cared for his/their children and cleaned the house would these questions be raised or the situation simply taken for granted by researchers?

It is necessary to ask such questions about self-employed men as well as women if we are to develop clearer understandings about how gender affects self-employment and business activity in terms of differential participation and the conditions and constructions which differentiate men from women.

This chapter has emphasised the need to obtain greater knowledge about female-run small businesses. The extent to which self-employment among women is influenced by their position in the labour market raises important conceptual issues about what is meant by women's work and the relationship between paid and unpaid work. Detailed research is required to explore these concepts both in terms of what being self-employed means to women and how women's self-employment fits into our understanding of the labour market. This can only be done if gender is introduced into research on male as well as female business activity and self-employment.

Notes

We acknowledge with thanks financial support from the Leverhulme Trust which is enabling us to carry out the research on Women in Business Enterprise.

12 Trading Relationships: Home Selling and Petty Enterprise in Women's Lives

Fiona Poland

The idea of a culture of enterprise conjures up a population of free-floating, innovative sole traders and small businesses tirelessly launching new goods into circulation in ever-newer markets. However, this chapter draws attention to some types and aspects of enterprise so close to home and constitutive of everyday life that they can be seen to be neither free-floating nor independent of people's ordinary knowledge. Yet only some participants in these processes are in a position to exploit such activities to build up more conventionally recognisable 'businesses'. This holds particular implications for present re-evaluations of womens' work as enabling but not controlling what comes to be seen as successful enterprise.

Recent dramatic increases in numbers of those officially self-employed in the UK (Hakim, 1988b) encourages the impression of a burgeoning enterprise culture of small firms. However, analyses of trends in flexible employment (Pollert, 1988) highlight how much apparent new employment is merely either recategorised work, franchised or sub-contracted with less security, or casualised waged labour presented as self-employment (Allen and Wolkowitz, 1987a).

So what of the possibilities extolled in popular magazines of 'turning a hobby into a job'? These involve using non-commercially acquired skills to market a product or a service. Enterprise here implies new choices to systematically commodify work to be marketed. Commodification and marketing may be usefully seen as only two in a range of socially available options for expending time and energy – set within a framework of socio-economic factors which make certain choices less practicable for some. It is argued in this chapter that the constraints operating on many women within the totality of their social obligations limit their choices to less commodifiable or visible expenditure and exchange.

An essential aspect of what informal selling buys and sells is women's enterprise in and responsibility for managing time and relationships, deploying situational knowledge of their work across formal, informal and domestic employment. This can be related to anthropological insights into entrepreneur activity which links the domains of social and economic activity. These have received further attention in more recent debates about trends in the informal economy (Henry, 1981).

Douglas and Isherwood have analysed the price of socially and economically valuable information in terms of investments in and means of controlling one's own time. They observe: 'Anyone with influence and status would be a fool to get enmeshed with high frequency responsibilities' (Douglas and Isherwood, 1979, p. 120). They emphasise the incompatibility of the periodicities of household work with making oneself available for high-status and non-local gatherings to exchange specialised information and contacts. Such occasions, underpinned by a high scale of expenditure on a wide range of resources, guarantee social and spatial mobility. Where an individual, often a man, is successful in guaranteeing such an expenditure of time, it is often a cost borne by other people's, often women's, acceptance of constraints on their time established within exchanges where most are unable to trade upwards into profit, commodity accumulation and 'lifestyle enhancement'.

This chapter explores ways in which groups of women in the town of Rochdale have engaged in various kinds of petty selling and exchange, how they have engaged aspects of their work and relationships, and how they are constrained in the degree of further 'successful commodification'.

LOCATING 'SELLING': AN ETHNOGRAPHY IN ROCHDALE

In two years' study for the ESRC-funded Social Change and Economic Life Initiative (SCELI)[1] on the topic of changes in 'work', the Manchester team[2] in Rochdale focused on how the resources and 'service conditions' of women's work may make it more or less visible. This took as one starting- point the feminist approach of Dorothy Smith (1987, p. 162) that 'what is observable does not appear as the work of individuals and not all work and practices of individuals may become observable', nor is such work seen as attracting generally-exchangeable value.

The research did not define work as 'employment' nor even as 'paid work', but as 'obligated time' (Wadel, 1979). This has the advantage of bringing to view the servicing element involved in selling, while linking to insights deriving from anthropological concerns with the negotiation and effects of such obligations across diverse dimensions of everyday life.

Such a stance queries recent sociological approaches to the 'new culture' of UK self-employment, which too easily assumes the normality and individuality of stereotypical 'one man band' businesses in either ownership or activity. Rather than accepting given conceptual frameworks, we need, as Smith (1987) suggests, to retrace from the actualities of lives what comes to be constructed as visible or abstractly conceptual. Otherwise we may miss many of the kinds of enterprise and relationship management which ground all work. There may be links between various types of work that women do on their own account as self-employment, homework or care work. Some examples of informal selling undertaken by particular groups of women in Rochdale include: party plans, mail order 'clubs' and local traders' 'clubs' and dealings in one-off lots and end-of-line goods from local factories.

My ethnographic work in Rochdale began with shops. They offered me easy access to formally-defined settings combining paid and unpaid work, and formal and informally-organised activity. As I looked more closely at different kinds of selling I saw them less as sets of activities tied to particular work settings than as work processes that spanned physical and conceptual boundaries, in common with much womens' work (e.g. Poland and Stanley, 1989).

Although ethnographic work was limited to only some Rochdale neighbourhoods, it provides data on informal selling which could not be obtained from surveys. For example even in the SCELI time-budget diaries such activities rarely surfaced beyond general mentions of 'work' (without specifying 'petty selling in the workplace') or 'chatting' (unless respondents undertook a highly visible selling event such as a party plan). Unless selling work was someone's only employment, it would be unlikely to figure in formal work history survey data. It will have evaded other surveys like the National Homeworking Survey, findings of which contradict notions of widespread casualised home-based work (Hakim, 1987; 1988a). Participant observation is more sensitive to data on the shifting and interlinked social processes that underlie the existence and uses of petty enterprise.

The pattern of informal work in Rochdale is structured and resourced in relation to local manufacturing and national distribution. Sassen-Koob (1987) highlights increasing polarisation in global urban labour markets and distribution systems through which different class mass markets are now supplied; the middle-class through central distribution organisations distinct from working-class access to goods through various small-scale, informal outlets. The relationships of trust on which these latter rely are underpinned by particular local knowledge and work circumstances.

Common ways for working-class women to 'make a bit of extra' at home include those traditional standbys of child care, sewing, cleaning, knitting and cooking. They occupy complex continua between 'paid' and 'unpaid' work and 'leisure' (Pahl, 1984). They fit in with the kinds of work described in this chapter in that they sometimes constitute 'employment' in the sense that people's time and energies or some fraction of them are being bought. This is often through involvement in complexes of exchange, but not necessarily for profit, rarely for accumulation, more likely for use value and in ways that defy any easy official discernment and undoubtedly evade most legal responsibilities. How they are drawn on and discharged forms part of the background activity which supports the 'selling' work discussed in this chapter.

'Clubs' are a long-established and widely-used working-class means of inter-household informal saving and paying, usually through one person taking responsibility for collecting and depositing money for a particular purpose, e.g. annual holiday expenses or trips, or a particular type of good, e.g. Christmas hampers. Commercial catalogue selling has successfully exploited such traditional cooperation. Ethnographic observation and analysis is especially useful in uncovering what, other than goods, is bought and sold by different parties to exchanges.

There are parallels between ways in which anyone may use their relationships to accomplish their work, the particular, localised aspects of how these women did so and the characteristics attributed to 'entrepreneurs'. However, in the setting of the street which I came to know best over the study, I was made aware that women might be doing apparently similar activities but within very different contexts of reciprocity. An everyday activity such as running a mail-order catalogue 'club' might serve for: money-making; money saving; selling 'on one's own account' or 'for someone else'; 'something to do' with or for a friend, for the activity itself as a pastime or a token of that friendship or returning a favour. The women might make money for national companies through such activities but it is often difficult to say how far they are employed. The degree of 'money-making' or 'commodification' and 'profit', in time as well as money, derived from any one relational transaction is situationally determined. It may seem 'less commercial' to buy Tupperware at a party in a friend's house than in a shop, but constraining aspects of social relations shape such sales. Indeed the suppliers of party- plan goods count on participants' feelings of having to buy something in return for the hospitality.

These women make their everyday agendas work for them, using aspects of sociability as a resource in initiating and closing sales. However their scope to build on them is limited by their lack of access to other resources, especially mobility. The 'petty-selling' avenue is time-consuming but their time- organisation is a means of resourcing this type of work. In common with what is often written about 'home-working' (e.g. Hakim, 1988a) it offers some freedom to organise work according to one's own circumstances. This may manifest itself as a freedom to refine the route by which one is exploited within the overall process of producing one's own survival (Redclift, 1988).

Until the 1960s, more working-class Rochdale married women than today 'stayed at home'. Many undoubtedly did some kinds of informal work for money – mending, cleaning, washing, shopwork. My data from older women rarely mentioned selling, unlike that from younger women. Since the 1950s local industry has increasingly offered (not especially secure or well-paid) work in distribution, warehousing, and manufacture of various cheap 'ready-mades' for the home. Some of these – seconds, ends-of-lines, discounted goods to workers, 'knocked-off' items – have found their way to local workers, many of whom are able to use their informal contacts to make sales. Many already take part in savings, catalogue and other 'clubs'.

In a group of nine houses at the end of a small working-class terraced street I encountered the following mix of full-time and part-time employment, unofficial and voluntary trading. Gans (1962), pre-dating contemporary consumption debates, pinpoints how particular life-stages pattern social and economic sharing. The householders described here were mostly in their twenties and thirties with young families, high commitments and relatively low earnings.

Some Householders in a Rochdale Street

House A: Couple in early thirties. Both employed at the same local factory: Mrs A. (Maggie) as a cleaner and Mr A. on the production line. She runs two small savings clubs for holidays with workmates and her neighbours. Her mother, employed in another local factory, runs several savings clubs for workmates and family friends, and sells for Brenda's soft furnishings round discussed in detail below.

House B: Couple in twenties. Both work in a local factory: Mrs B. in the offices with her mother, Mr B. on the production line. Mrs B. occasionally buys seasonal bulk loads of, for example, Christmas toys and sells them at work and to neighbouring friends.

House C: Couple in thirties: Mr C. is a carpet fitter, Mrs C. looks after their two children, is a keen churchgoer (Baptist) and does voluntary work with Third World groups. She takes bookings for his work. She often hosts Church meetings and fund-raising groups in her house. These include selling parties for Christian Third World trading groups. She plans to continue selling when she takes part-time employment.

House D: Couple in twenties with baby. She works in a bank and runs one catalogue club at work and in the locality.

House E: Couple in thirties with a school-age daughter. Mrs E. has a part-time job at Marks & Spencer and, with her sister who lives nearby, sells sandwiches in local offices and factories. They start making them at 5.30 a.m. in her kitchen. Her sister, a single parent, also does fortune telling and works in cafés.

House F: Couple in thirties. He is a warehouseman. She works part-time as a cleaner, childminder and in a town centre shop. She ran two catalogue clubs five years ago but got into debt with them, ending in a court case. She does a range of informal selling – ready-made curtains for a woman she knew from a pub where she had worked, clothes from an Asian contact made when she home-sewed, pictures from a local club acquaintance, and Christmas cards for a woman who runs a corner general shop. However, she says she cannot drive and cannot do any of this on any scale. Most of her employment has been occasional and in small businesses: shops, cafés and workshops. She herself uses several 'clubs' to save for:

> Holidays: with a neighbour who pays her share into this club as payment for Mrs F's childminding.
> Personal savings: with a neighbour's mother
> Christmas alcohol hamper: with a market stallholder
> Christmas sweet hamper: with another market stallholder
> Pop concert trip for the family: with a neighbour
> Christmas meat hamper: with a market butcher
> Electric gifts for children: with an electrical goods shop

She also uses what she calls 'not personal' clubs – Telebank, hire-purchase of video and 'instant catalogue' services such as Littlewoods Department Stores.

House G: Couple in early thirties with two school-age children. Mr G. is a garage mechanic who also does car 'foreigners' at home. She manages a small caterer's including weekend and evening work, yet also finds time to run clubs for trips away and Christmas goods and fits in a few hours in a corner video shop. She hosts make-up parties.

House H: Couple in fifties. Mrs H. runs a small stationery shop and has local contacts who occasionally sell for her at work and among friends especially at Christmas.

House I: Elderly couple, now retired with daughter, Ms I. Ms I is an independent contractor in her thirties who owns her own articulated truck tractor unit. She had worked for a company fleet which encouraged drivers to buy their trucks through their wages on hire-purchase, giving them a couple of years 'driving for themselves'. Then she set up on her own with a new truck and a bank loan. She did no other work, except some spare time charity fund-raising.

This is not a complete list of local work activity, but the information obtained over six months. The five common 'self-employment' means of earning I encountered in the neighbourhood all indicate how different womens' official and unofficial work may be interlinked within the constraints of obligated time. They interweave with women's domestic work, resourcing the performance of such tasks over the formal–informal divide.

Sewing-alterations: were often done by older women using their own domestic machines, on family clothing and for local women selling small lots of soft furnishing.

Child care: rarely as a formally-registered childminder. It was mostly treated as a favour or 'a few hours paid here and there' to be fitted in with other types of patchy part-time work.

Cleaning agencies: now demand more 'flexibility' from employees who are bearing more of the costs of the work themselves to appear more 'self-employed' (see Chapter 10). Some older women reported losing work to younger women with access to phones and cars. They now work in a more isolated, fractured way than the pairs/groups often working together within particular establishments. Many work three split-shift segments over a day spreading their work over fourteen hours, travelling back and forth on public transport, unpaid, between their formally- acknowledged workplaces and home. They often enter premises when no one else works there, so lacking access to workplaces where they could trade off contacts – unlike the petty traders discussed in more detail below.

Party-plans: for example promoting Pippa Dee family clothing or Tupperware. These are often hosted by women in full or part-time jobs and depend for custom on female workmates with independent money. The goods are relatively expensive compared with market or supermarket prices. The hostess lays on coffee and perhaps food. So she needs a house with space and furniture, without feeling that the standard of décor will 'show her up'. The hostess makes a percentage, although often not in cash, only if purchases top a particular level. Rewards are often pitched as 'treats' for themselves or the kids, often from another catalogue provided by the party-plan firm. A full-time woman organiser talks to attenders about hosting parties. People pay by instalment schemes with the hostess/agent having to chase payments. There are similar arrangements for many other businesses such as make-up, sex-aids and sexy underwear.

Other forms of informal selling: include occasional and opportunistic selling on behalf of friends and acquaintances rather than the more formally-organised networks of national firms' representatives.

This latter type of 'self-employment' is the focus of analysis in the remainder of this chapter.

COMMODIFYING SOCIAL RELATIONSHIPS

Features of settings which affect 'how much one's time is worth' and the values mobilised to assess that worth within particular activities (Nelson, 1988) constrain the degree of possible 'commodification' from one's social relationships. Mrs F. is in precarious financial circumstances yet she often does selling work 'as a favour for people' and chooses not to get paid. Other forms of local and personalised social capital are more immediately useful to her than fixing a money-price on her time: access to other peoples' time or information (perhaps about jobs), or a higher evaluation of her social standing. Precisely because the market price of her time is worth relatively less than that of women in better paid employment there is more than simple enjoyment to be gained from being 'socially available'.

The high level of social activity undertaken by many middle-class women 'for the household' (Douglas and Isherwood, 1979) suggests that the values obtained through this work are not substitutable by a simple money-exchange. Building a reputation can enable trading on a 'good name'. Relationships of trust are based on personal information establishing personal qualities of reliability derived from real and constraining social knowledge. Such knowledge is formally acknowledged and used in some situations by managers (Harris, Lee and Morris, 1985). Mrs F. knows that she can make or mar her 'trusting' relationships and her hard-won social credit by how she handles her finances. She can herself use such social constraints as a 'budgeting device' within her participation in trading clubs.

Such exchanges can open up social contacts through paid work and realise multiple purposes within the same contact, according to its interpretation as being between 'friends', 'neighbours', 'workmates' or 'clients'. This extends themes raised by Pahl (1984) about how employment can generate further opportunities for remunerative work, and the difficulty of distinguishing between 'work' and 'leisure' or 'socialising'. This is a more complex view of the factors that relate home–workplace gender divisions (Osterud, 1988) to women's active work in 'bringing home into employment' (Westwood, 1984) than seeing domestic commitments only as undermining womens' activity in formal workplaces. It is not obvious which work and workplace, home or employment, should be women's priority.

Anthropologists have examined how some exchange relations may enable women to 'get their work done' (e.g. Sharma, 1980) but the resources and products of such relations may not necessarily be further exchanged for more general and highly valued goods or services. Although more care-work in the UK is now commodified and so can earn money, such employment is not only badly paid but also the avenues of socially-evaluated experience which it opens up are limited (Abrams, 1978). Mrs F., and some of her friends, had found such jobs useful in expanding their circle of social contacts within a particular range of class-linked reciprocities (Willmott, 1987). However, the potential uses to them of such contacts was limited by the particularities of caring relationships and the realisation that care-work did not constitute a formalised career route (Hakim, 1982b). Such restrictions on the evaluated relevance of women's waged as well as unwaged work experience, have operated in many historical forms (Middleton, 1988), as women have borne the brunt of providing flexible support to 'breadwinners' (MacKintosh, 1988).

COMMODIFYING WORK RELATIONSHIPS: THE SOFT FURNISHINGS ROUND

I encountered several women with factory jobs who brought in one-off loads such as tights or biscuits to the shopfloor. They often obtained goods through intermediaries, each getting a percentage commission. This sub-section presents more detailed case material about a woman supplying informal shop-floor sellers ('sellers-for') to build up her own more formal business.

Maggie (House A) was a 'seller-for' Brenda who delivered various soft furnishings to her house after Maggie had obtained orders. Maggie's husband gave her a lift (in his employer's van) to her factory where she had a place to hide the goods. 'If you got a lot of people doing it they (factory management) would put a stop to it. But they'd usually be all right if you didn't set them up on your machine.'

Brenda had taken evening class typing and bookkeeping qualifications, encouraged by one of her employers, Jimmy Smith. His firm had a mill in Rochdale making bedding material. He would spend the mornings in the factory and the afternoons in the Manchester offices and warehouse. He started one of the earliest 1950s UK mail-order businesses in ready-made soft furnishings. Brenda was secretary to this and other smaller firms in the same building.

She began selling for the firm informally, first to her mother, then to friends. The firm supplied different ready-made soft furnishings to order. The firm tried sending pattern books out to boarding houses and then to market stallholders without success. Brenda ended up as its biggest customer and made it take off. The idea caught on with women then going out to work, at a time of growing interest in Do-It-Yourself and home decoration, as employed women had less time to do that sort of sewing at home themselves.

Brenda's contacts responded because they already trusted her, knew they were getting something a bit different but did not feel that she would 'do' them. The prices seemed fair for the domestic time they would save themselves. Unlike goods which were ready-made, customers could look at pattern books, with time to choose materials and sizes, but without feeling under pressure to buy.

Brenda had 'sellers-for' in several factories. Although they were only doing for her what she was doing for Mr Smith, they could not obtain the goods directly themselves. They rarely had transport and had little spare cash. They got the orders for Brenda and collected her money. Their commission gave them 'a bit of extra'. Maggie used it to pay for the whole family's holiday. Her husband also sold through his maintenance job, driving to different sites and taking the pattern books with him, but Maggie organised his payments collection. Brenda's other sellers, like Maggie, would also sell at home to neighbours.

Brenda's access to transport was vital. She started out with a scooter and use of the Smith van, then she bought her own. By the late 1970s she had over fifty women selling for her. Brenda commented:

> The amazing thing was there was almost no trouble about getting the money. After a while I realised that most women who bought like this paid up with no problems – particularly since they were often buying in work, on pay-day so they didn't have much excuse not to pay at the time the stuff came in. So when one woman who sold for me said that she was having trouble getting her customers to pay her I knew it wasn't them it was her. She'd probably been dipping. It ended up going to court and she was going to pay back by the week, but she just left her job where the court deducted her pay in instalments and she ended up disappearing altogether.

Here, the success of Brenda's work traded on her own and other womens' knowledge and management of their relationships in different settings.

TRADING ON PERSONAL KNOWLEDGE

Recent approaches to economics (e.g. Hirschman, 1988) have begun to address the role of social ties such as trust in structuring 'market exchange' (Hart, 1988), in relation to transaction costs, limited information and the distribution of returns. The exchanges described here bring together the personal and impersonal in market exchange (Dalton, 1968).

The selling activities mentioned in this chapter epitomise womens' management of fragmented features of their work in time, task and place. Such work represents a lack of 'ownership' of the work of selling. It is typically undertaken by the lower-paid (for parallels in Ghana, see Hart, 1978), exploiting whatever resources for enterprise come to hand. However, it is important to note that most of these women were additionally employed at least part-time, or did other work which allowed them extra-household means to resource such selling.

Another connection exists between this level of informal selling and 'savings clubs' as forms of collective budgeting and home management. The women mentioned here share a culture of understanding of what knowledge and responsibilities are needed to resource the performance of their work (Kapferer, 1976). Their paid employment is seen in the context of their household work (West, 1982) at a particular phase of life and resources. Goods which sold well on the soft furnishings round did not take off with the market sellers in the 1960s. The notion of choosing such goods on the spot was new. Women did not generally know about 'ready-mades' as something to ask for on the market and preferred privacy to discuss it in a setting without overt sales pressure.

The advantage of Brenda's network over the market stalls or the mail-order contact with boarding houses was in tapping into particular sets of relationships in which a degree of trust had been generated. Such trust was not founded on ignorance or blind dependence but through personal knowledge and features of the settings which acted as constraints on 'unreliability' on the part of sellers and buyers. Brenda and her 'sellers-for' shared an understanding of what would constitute 'a good deal' (Prus, 1985), further structured by the labour market and local resources (Mitchell, 1969). The 'sellers-for' could use their even more local understandings of their home and paid work circumstances to decide how to carry out their work for suppliers like Brenda. Their time and the knowledge gained in relationships are used as buffers between the 'less personally concerned' large manufacturer and 'less reliable' customers whose unreliabilities the 'sellers-for' make good.

TRADING ON TIME ORGANISATION

The relative lack of mobility in work and access to transport shared by 'sellers-for' and customers helps to create a market for household goods sold in a way which is seen to save money or time for customers while 'making a little extra' for the sellers (Mingione, 1988).

Different places of employment provide distinctive premises. Because the work of the sellers is complementary with the rhythms of their existing work and contacts (and trades on this complementarity) it is not immediately visible. This lack of visibility itself contributes to getting their petty selling done in workplaces without attracting unwelcome notice from the official owners and managers of those workplaces. It is one type of employees' use of their employment conditions for themselves (Stark, 1988), a variation on shopfloor 'making out' (Burawoy, 1988), but one which cannot be seen as a 'fiddle' or 'taking away' from employers.

The lack of demarcation between 'work' and 'leisure'; 'selling' and 'doing a favour'; 'employing' and 'doing a favour' takes the commercial edge off the selling relationship, with an implied bargain of trust, reliability and accountability consistent with other relationships. To meet all the obligations implied by these relationships makes further and unlimited demands on the time of 'sellers-for' and the seller-suppliers like Brenda, but encourages custom (Prus, 1987).

Within less affluent communities, there is a swift 'market saturation point' for new goods. Most of my contacts found they had to change 'party plans' or goods by using their networks to find other things to sell. This happened most quickly on poorer council estates where there was widespread unemployment and where I frequently encountered debt and 'dipping' problems.

The women I knew best were not so badly-off, most just managing to buy their own terraced houses. Both the 'club' and the 'selling' networks generally leave out 'unreliables', setting limits on their own liabilities. Assessing 'unreliability' is based partly on local knowledge of family lifestyles in the management of everyday business. This links into the findings of Reid as early as 1934 and emphasised by Douglas and Isherwood (1979), that women manage household finances on a notion of 'normal consumption' which helps to maintain the household's standing and integration into local networks. However, this makes it difficult to set aside quickly commitments to spend on childrens' presents, Christmas hospitality or holidays.

Petty trading, in common with many women's activities, relies on a mixture of business with pleasure and leisure. I attended festive selling parties held at Workingmen's Clubs organised by larger-scale women sellers offering clothes seconds and ends-of-lines. These sometimes attracted 200 women arriving in groups of neighbours and families.

Those further up the selling hierarchy, like Brenda (who was better off than most of my contacts), have other resources such as transport, more professional qualifications, higher pay, contacts and access to other work settings. These enable them to obtain a more even supply of resources, placing a different structure on their use of their time.

Indeed, it was this wider social and spatial spreading of their energies that made women like Brenda generally less accessible to me. Ms I., the trucker, had what would be more clearly recognised as 'a proper business' and because of the nature of her work I rarely encountered her in the neighbourhood. Men in jobs giving access to transport are similarly in a position to double up on the work they do (as Maggie's husband did), but they built different types of networks using other work and resources than those most likely to be available for women to draw on.

CONCLUSION

The characteristics of the local economy in Rochdale have allowed for a convenient circulation of various cheap household goods, particularly made-up textile goods, paper goods and food, through petty sellers. The various types of national Avon-type direct selling and mail order which attract women as club agents (Cockburn (1977) mentions 300 000 selling for Freeman's) also offer the advantage (to the buyer) of providing access to credit and the advantage (to the business) of 'externalising' its collection and delegating the messy and often frustrating work of contact.

The work conditions discussed in this chapter illustrate less frequently considered aspects of various types of self-employment and agency which involve women in bearing more of the time costs of providing employment.

Although petty selling draws on womens' relationships, ambiguities surrounding this work mean it can be seen as contributing to resourcing and reconstituting the trust and mutual knowledge in those relationships – intimately relating economy and culture (Kapferer, 1987). The new easy availability of UK credit, including the possibility of mail-ordering 'financial services', bypasses not only high street shops, banks and lenders, but also the social restrictions and mutual budgeting which operate within the kinds of relationships described here.

This chapter has drawn some parallels between stereotypical enterprise and the ways in which our everyday life processes trade on a stock of time, knowledge of relationships and local work practices which span disparate settings. The feminist perspective on which I have relied seeks to demystify the elevation of male-oriented entrepreneurial skills and the cult of the individual go-getter, and link them to those

mundane and constraining social processes through which many
women accomplish their work.

Notes

1. The ESRC-funded Social Change and Economic Life Initiative (SCELI)
    linked activities of six research teams working in six UK towns. In each
    location, surveys were undertaken of employers, of work histories and
    work attitudes of 1000 individuals, and a household survey of 300
    households.
    Rochdale – as a northern English former textile town with the highest
    proportion of employed married women in the early 1900s – was studied
    by linked teams from Manchester and Lancaster Universities. The author
    was a member of the Manchester team which built datasets from the
    individual and household surveys, and carried out an ethnography
    focused on the relationship between formal, informal and domestic
    everyday life and work. A smaller-scale non-SCELI study of Asian
    households was funded through Manchester University Research Sup-
    port to cover the latter issues for the Asian community.
2. The Manchester researchers involved at different times and in different
    parts of the Rochdale studies were Liz Stanley, Bogusia Temple, Fiona
    Poland, Salma Ahmad and Jane Haggis. I am indebted to Monica Curran
    for her ethnographic help, detailed discussion and insights around selling
    and womens' enterprise.

Bibliography

ABRAMS, P. (ed.) (1978) *Work, Urbanism and Inequality*, London: Weidenfeld & Nicolson.

ACKER, J. (1989), 'The Problem with Patriarchy', *Sociology*, vol. 23(2), pp. 235–40.

ALLATT, P., KEIL, T., BRYMAN, A. and BYTHEWAY, B. (1987) *Women and the Life Cycle – Transitions and Turning Points*, Basingstoke: Macmillan.

ALLEN, S. (1987) 'Gender, Race and Class in the 1980s', in C. Husband (ed.), *Race in Britain* London: Hutchinson, Second edition.

ALLEN, S. (1989) 'Flexibility and Working Time: A Gendered Approach', in J. Buber Agassi and S. Heycock (eds), *The Redesign of Working Time: Promise or Threat?*, Berlin: Sigma.

ALLEN, S. and TRUMAN, C. (1988) 'Women's Work and "Success" in Women's Business', Paper presented to the 11th Small Firms Policy and Research Conference, Cardiff.

ALLEN, S. and TRUMAN, C. (1989) 'Prospects for Women's Business and Self Employment in the Year 2000', Paper presented to Conference on the Small Business in the Year 2000, Kingston Polytechnic.

ALLEN, S. and WOLKOWITZ, C. (1987a) *Homeworking: Myths and Realities*, London: Macmillan.

ALLEN, S. and WOLKOWITZ, C. (1987b) 'Women's Working Time', Paper presented to the Third Interdisciplinary Congress on Women, Trinity College, Dublin, July.

ARBER, S., DALE, A. and GILBERT, G. N. (1986) 'The limitations of existing social class classifications for women', in A. Jacoby (ed.) *The Measurement of Social Class*, London: Social Research Association

ARBER, S. and GINN, J. (forthcoming) *Gender and Later Life: A Sociological Analysis of Resources and Constraints*, London: Sage.

AUSTRIN, T. and BEYNON, H. (n.d.) 'Masters and Servants. Paternalism and its legacy on the Durham coalfield: 1800–1872', Working Paper, Department of Sociology and Social Policy, University of Durham.

BARRON, R. D. and NORRIS, G. M. (1976) 'Sexual Division and the Dual Labour Market', in D. Leonard Barker and S. Allen (eds), *Dependence and Exploitation in Work and Marriage*, London: Longman.

BECHHOFER, F., ELLIOTT, B., RUSHFORTH, M. and BLAND, R. (1974) 'The Petits Bourgeois in the Class Structure: the case of small shopkeepers', in F. Parkin (ed.), *The Social Analysis of the Class Structure*, London: Tavistock, pp. 103–28.

BEECHEY, V. (1978) 'Critical Analysis of Some Sociological Theories of Women's Work', in A. Kuhn, and A. M. Wolpe (eds), *Feminism and Materialism*, London: Routledge & Kegan Paul.

BEECHEY, V. (1987) *Unequal Work*, London: Verso.

BEECHEY, V. (1989) 'Women's employment in France and Britain: some problems of comparison', *Work Employment and Society*, vol. 3, pp. 369–78.

190

BEECHEY, V. and PERKINS, T. (1987) *A Matter of Hours: Women, Part-Time Work and the Labour Market*, Cambridge: Polity.

BENOIT GUILBOT, O. (1987) 'Les structures sociales du chomage en France et en Grande-Bretagne, influences societales', *Sociologie du Travail* pp. 219–236.

BERGER, S. (1980) 'The traditional sector in France and Italy', in S. Berger and M. Piore (eds), *Dualism and Discontinuity in Industrial Societies*, Cambridge: Cambridge University Press, pp. 88–131.

BERGER, B. and BERGER, P. (1983) *The War over the Family: Capturing the Middle Ground*, London: Hutchinson.

BLATCHFORD, P., BATTLE, S. and MAYS, J. (1982) *The First Transition – Home to Pre-School*, Windsor: NFER-Nelson.

BLOOD, R. D. and WOLFE, D. M. (1960) *Husbands and Wives*, Wesport: Greenwood Press.

BOAL, F. W., DOHERTY, P., PRINGLE, D. G. (1974) *The Spatial Distribution of Some Social Problems in the Belfast Urban Area*, Belfast: Research Paper, Northern Ireland Community Relations Commission.

BOHR, A. (1989) 'Resolving the Question of Equality for Soviet Women – Again', *Report on the USSR*, vol. 1, no. 14, pp 10–16.

BOLDYREVA, T. (1989) 'You Won't Stop the Revolutionary Horse in his Tracks', *Soviet Sociology*, vol. 28, no. 5, pp 102–18.

BOULTON, M. (1983) *On Being A Mother*, London: Tavistock Press.

BOWDEN, P. J. (1970) 'Newton Aycliffe: the politics of new town development', in J. C. Dewdney (ed.), *Durham County and City with Teesside*, Durham: British Association, pp.454–63.

BOWLBY, J. (1951) 'Maternal care and mental health', *Bulletin of the World Health Organisation*, vol. 3, pp. 355–534.

BRADLEY, H. (1989) *Men's Work, Women's Work*, Cambridge: Polity.

BRADSHAW, J., COOKE, K. and GODFREY, C. (1983) 'The Impact of Unemployment on the Living Standards of Families', *Journal of Social Policy*, vol. 12, no. 4, pp. 433–52.

BRANNEN, J. (1987) *Taking Maternity Leave: The Employment Decisions of Women With Young Children*, TCRU Working and Occasional Papers No. 7, London: Thomas Coram Research Unit.

BRANNEN, J. and MOSS, P. (1988) *New Mothers at Work: Employment and Childcare*, London: Unwin Hyman.

BRANNEN, J. and MOSS, P. (1990) *Managing Mothers: Dual Earner Households after Maternity Leave*, London: Unwin Hyman.

BRANNEN, J. and WILSON, G. (eds) (1987) *Give and Take in Families: Studies in Resource Distribution*, London: Allen & Unwin.

BRESNEN, M. (1985) 'The Flexibility of Recruitment in the Construction Industry: Formalisation or Re-Casualisation', *Sociology*, vol. 19, pp 108–24.

BRINTON, M. C. (1988) 'The social-institutional bases of gender stratification: Japan as an illustrative case', *American Journal of Sociology*, vol. 94, pp. 300–34.

BRYMAN, A. (1988) *Quantity and Quality in Social Research*, London: Unwin Hyman.

BURAWOY, M. (1988) 'Thirty Years of Making Out', in Pahl R. E. (ed.), *On Work*, Oxford: Basil Blackwell.

BURGOYNE, J. (1987) 'The Family in Crisis: Material Happiness', *New Society*, 10 April, pp. 12–14.

BYSIEWICZ, S. and SHELLEY, L. (1987) 'Women in the Soviet Economy: Proclamations and Practice', in O. Ioffe and M. Janis (eds), *Soviet Law and Economy*, Dordrecht: Martinus Nijhoff, pp. 57–78

CALDER, A. (1971) *The People's War. Britain 1939–1945*, London: Panther (first published by Jonathan Cape, 1969).

CALLAGHAN, B (1986) 'Flexibility: A UK Trade Union Response', *Social and Labour Bulletin*, No 2, Geneva: ILO.

CANNON, T., CARTER, S., ROSA, P., BADDON, L. and McCLURE, R. (1988) *Female Entrepreneurship*, Stirling: Scottish Enterprise Foundation.

CARTER, S., CANNON, T., BADDON, L. and McCLURE, R. (1988) *Female Entrepreneurship*, Stirling: Scottish Enterprise Foundation.

CASEY, B. and CREIGH, S. (1988) 'Self Employment in Britain: its Definition in the Labour Force Survey, in Tax and Social Security Law and in Labour Law', *Work Employment and Society*, vol. 2, no. 3, pp. 381–92.

CENSUS 1931 (1934) *Census of England and Wales: Industry Tables*, 1931, London: HMSO.

CENSUS 1951 (1958) *Census 1951, England and Wales, General Report*, London: HMSO.

CENTRE D'ÉTUDE DES REVENUES ET DES COÛTS (CERC) (1985), *Mères de Famille: coûts et revenues de l'activité professionelle*, Paris.

CHAFETZ, J. (1989) 'Gender Equality: Toward a Theory of Change', in R. Wallace (ed.), *Feminism and Sociological Theory*, Newbury Park: Sage.

CHERLIN, A. and WALTERS, P.B. (1981) 'Trends in United States Men's and Women's Sex-Role Attitudes: 1972 to 1978', *American Sociological Review*, vol. 46, pp. 453–60.

CHODOROW, N. (1978) *The Reproduction of Mothering: Psychoanalysis and the Sociology of Gender*, Berkeley: University of California Press.

COCKBURN, C. (1977) *The Local State*, London: Pluto Press.

COCKBURN, C. (1988) 'The Gendering of Jobs: Workplace Relations and the Reproduction of Sex Segregation', in S. Walby (ed.), *Gender Segregation at Work*, Milton Keynes, Open University Press.

CONDOR, S. (1986) 'Sex Role Beliefs and Traditional Women: Feminist and Intergroup Perspectives', in S. Wilkinson (ed.), *Feminist Social Psychology*, Milton Keynes: Open University Press.

COULSON, M. *et al.*(1975) 'The Housewife and Her Labour Under Capitalism: A critique', *New Left Review*, 89.

COUSINS, J.M. and BROWN, R.K. (1970) 'Shipbuilding (in the North East)', in J.C. Dewdney (ed.), *Durham County and City with Teesside*, Durham: British Association, pp. 313–29.

COYLE, A (1986) 'Going Private: The Implications of Privatisation for Women's Work', *Feminist Review*, vol. 21, pp. 5–25.

CROMIE, S. and HAYES, J. (1988) 'Towards a Typology of Female Entrepreneurs', *Sociological Review*, vol. 36, pp. 87–113.

CROMPTON, R. (1989), 'Class Theory and Gender', in *British Journal of Sociology*, vol. 40, no. 4, pp. 565–87.

CROMPTON, R. and MANN, M. (eds), (1986) *Gender and Stratification*, Cambridge: Polity Press.

CROMPTON, R and SANDERSON, K. (1990) *Gendered Jobs and Social Change*, London: Unwin Hyman.

CURRAN, J. and BURROWS, R. (1988) *Enterprise in Britain: A National Profile of Small Business Owners and the Self Employed*, London: Small Business Research Trust.

CURRAN, J. and BURROWS, R. (1989) 'Sociological Research on Service Sector Small Businesses: some Conceptual Considerations', *Work, Employment and Society*, vol. 3, no.4, December, pp. 527–40.

DALE, A. (1987) 'Occupational Inequality, Gender and the Life Cycle', *Work, Employment and Society*, vol. 1, no. 3, pp. 326–51.

DALE, A. and GLOVER, J. (1990) *An Analysis of Women's Employment Patterns in the UK, France and the USA: the Value of Survey Based Comparisons*, Research Paper No. 75, London: Department of Employment.

DALLIN, A. (1977) 'Conclusion', in D. Atkinson, A. Dallin and G.W. Lapidus (eds), *Women in Russia*, Stanford: Stanford University Press, pp. 385–98.

DALTON, G. (1968) 'Economic theory and primitive society', in E. E. LeClair and H. K. Schneider (eds), *Economic Anthropology*, New York: Holt Rinehart and Winston.

DALY, M (1986) *The Hidden Workers*, Dublin: Employment Equality Agency.

DANIEL, W.W. (1974) *A National Survey of the Unemployed*, London: P.E.P. Broadsheet Nos 5 and 6.

DANIEL, W.W., STILGOE, E. (1977) *Where Are They Now?*, London: Political and Economic Planning.

DEL BOCA, D. (1988), 'Women in a Changing Workplace, the Case of Italy', in J. Jenson *et al.* (ed.), *Feminisation of the Labour Force, Paradoxes and Promises*, Cambridge: Polity Press.

DELPHY, C. (1977) 'The Main Enemy: a Materialist Analysis of Women's Oppression', *Explorations in Feminism*, 3, WRCC.

DEPARTMENT OF EMPLOYMENT (1971) *British Labour Statistics. Historical Abstract 1886–1968*, London: HMSO.

DEX, S. (1984) *Women's Work Histories: An Analysis of the Women and Employment Survey*, Department of Employment Research Paper no. 46, London: HMSO.

DEX, S. (1985) *The Sexual Division of Work*, Brighton: Wheatsheaf.

DEX, S. (1987) *Women's Occupational Mobility: a Lifetime Perspective*, London: Macmillan.

DEX, S. (1988) *Women's Attitudes Towards Work*, London: Macmillan.

DEX, S. and SHAW, L. (1986) *British and American Women at Work*, London: Macmillan.

DEX, S. and WALTERS, P. (1989) 'Women's Occupational Status in Britain, France and USA: Explaining the Difference', *Industrial Relations Journal*, vol. 20, no. 3, pp. 203–12.

DEX, S. and WALTERS, P. (1990) 'Franco-British Comparisons of Women's Labour Supply and the Effects of Socio-Economic Policies', paper to EMRU Seminar, London.

DEX, S., WALTERS, P. and ALDEN, D. (1988) 'French and British Women's Employment Comparisons', Report submitted to Department of Employment, January 1988.

DOHERTY, P. (1977) 'A Geography of Unemployment in the Belfast Urban Area', unpublished PhD Thesis, Belfast: Queen's University.

DOOLAN, L (1982) 'Elements of the Sacred and Dramatic in Some Belfast Urban Enclaves', unpublished PhD Thesis, Belfast: Queen's University.

DOUGLAS, M. and ISHERWOOD, B. (1979) *The World of Goods*, London: Allen Lane.

DOWD, N. (1986) 'Maternity Leave: Taking Sex Differences into Account', *Fordham Law Review*, 54(5), 699–765.

EDWARDS, M. (1981a) 'Financial Arrangements Made by Husbands and Wives: Findings of a Survey', *Australian and New Zealand Journal of Sociology*, vol. 18, no. 3.

EDWARDS, M. (1981b) 'Financial Arrangements within Families', Australia, Research Report for National Women's Advisory Council, Canberra.

EDWARDS, M. (1981c) 'Financial Arrangements within Families', *Social Security Journal*, December, pp. 1–16.

EEC (1987) *Non-Salaried Working Women in Europe: Women Running Their Own Businesses or Working Independently – Women Involved in Their Husband's Professional Activity*, Brussels: Commission of the European Communities.

Employment Gazette (1988) 'Labour Force Survey – Preliminary Results', March, p. 147.

Employment Gazette, (1989) 'Women and Training: the Second Decade', December.

ENNIS, F. and ROBERTS, I. (1987) '"The Time of their Lives?" Female Workers in North East Shipbuilding, 1939–45', in A. Potts (ed.), *Shipbuilders and Engineers. Essays on Labour in the Shipbuilding and Engineering Industries of the North East*, Newcastle upon Tyne: North East Labour History Society, pp. 42–74.

EOC (1989) *From Policy to Practice: An Equal Opportunities Strategy for the 1990s*, Manchester: Equal Opportunities Commission.

EPSTEIN, T. (1989) 'Female Entrepreneurs and their Multiple Roles', Paper presented to the conference, *Women Entrepreneurs*, University of Bradford, March–April.

EUROSTAT (1987), *Employment and Unemployment* Luxembourg: Eurostat.

EUROSTAT (1989) *Labour Force Sample Survey, 1987*, Luxembourg: Eurostat.

EVETTS, J. (1988) 'Managing Childcare and Work Responsibilities', *Sociological Review*, vol. 36, pp. 503–31.

FAGIN, L. and LITTLE, M. (1984) *The Forsaken Families*, London: Penguin.

FELDBRUGGE, F. J. M. (ed.), (1979) *The Constitutions of the USSR and the Union Republics: Analysis, Texts, Reports*, Aphen aan den Rijn: Sijthoff and Noordhoff.

FEVRE, R. (1986) 'Contract Work in the Recession', in K. Purcell, S. Wood, A. Waton and S. Allen (eds), *The Changing Experience of Employment: Restructuring and Recession*, London: Macmillan.

FIELD, D. (1958) *A Report on Unsatisfactory Tenants*, Belfast: Belfast Council for Social Welfare.

FIELDING, N. and FIELDING, J. (1986) *Linking Data*, Qualitative Research Network Series 4, London: Sage.

FLETCHER, R. (1966) *The Family and Marriage in Britain; an Analysis and Moral Assessment*, Harmondsworth: Penguin.

FOGARTY, M.P. (1971) *Sex, Career and Family, including an International Review of Women's Roles*, London: Political and Economic Planning.

FOGARTY, M.P., RAPOPORT, R. and RAPOPORT, R.N. (1971) *Sex, Career and Family*, London: George Allen & Unwin.

FOREIGN BROADCAST INFORMATION SERVICE (1989) 'Ryshkov meets Women's International Press Club', *Moscow Television Service in Russian*, 9 March, pp. 30–3.

GALLIE, D. (ed.) (1988) *Employment in Britain*, Oxford: Basil Blackwell.

GANS, H. (1962) *People and Plans*, Harmondsworth: Pelican.

GERRY, C. (1985) 'The Working Class and Small Enterprises in the U.K. Recession', in N. Redclift and E. Mingione (eds), *Beyond Employment*, Oxford: Basil Blackwell.

GERSON, K. (1985) *Hard Choices: How Women Decide About Work, Career and Motherhood*, Berkeley: University of California Press.

GIDDENS, A. (1973) *The Class Structure of Advanced Societies*, London: Hutchinson.

GINN, J. and ARBER, S. (1991) 'Gender, class and income inequality in later life', *British Journal of Sociology*, vol. 42, no. 3, pp. 369–96.

GOFFEE, R. and SCASE, R. (1985) *Women in Charge: the Experience of Female Entrepreneurs*, London: George Allen & Unwin.

GOFFEE, R. and SCASE, R. (1987) *Entrepreneurship in Europe*, London: Croom Helm.

GOLDTHORPE, J. (1983) 'Women and Class Analysis: In Defence of the Conventional View', *Sociology*, vol. 17, pp. 466–88.

GOLDTHORPE, J. (1984) 'Women and Class Analysis: A Reply to the Replies', *Sociology*, vol. 18, pp. 491–9.

GORDON, T. (1990) *Feminist Mothers*, London: Macmillan.

GOVE, W.R. (1972) 'The Relationship Between Sex Roles, Mental Illness, and Marital Status', *Social Forces*, vol. 52, pp. 34–44.

GRAY, A. (1979) 'The Working Class Family as an Economic Unit', in C.C. Harris (ed.), *The Sociology of the Family*, Sociological Review Monograph University of Keele, No. 28, pp. 186–213.

GREATER LONDON COUNCIL (1986) *The Benefits for Employers of Providing Child Care Assistance*, London: GLC.

GRUZDEVA, E.V. and CHERTIKHINA, E.S. (1986) 'Soviet Women: Problems of Work and Daily Life', in M. Yanowitz (ed.), *The Social Structure of the USSR*, Armonk, New York: M.E. Sharpe, pp.150–69.

Guardian (1990) 'Signs of the Fathers', Angela Phillips, 20 March.

HAGE, J., GARNIER, M.A. and FULLER, B. (1988) 'The Active State, Investment in Human Capital and Economic Growth: France 1825–1975', *American Sociological Review*, vol. 53, pp. 824–37.

HAKIM, C. (1979) *Occupational Segregation*, Department of Employment Research Paper no. 9, London.

HAKIM, C. (1982a) 'The Social Consequences of High Unemployment', *Journal of Social Policy*, vol. 2, no. 4, pp. 433–67.

HAKIM, C. (1982b) 'Occupational Segregation: a Comparative Study of the Degree and Pattern of Differentiation between Men's and Women's work in

Britain, the United States and Other Countries', Research Paper No. 9, London: Dept. of Employment.

HAKIM, C. (1987) 'Home-based Work in Britain: a Report on the 1981 National Homework Survey and the DE Research Programme in Homework', London: Dept. of Employment.

HAKIM, C. (1988a) 'Homeworking in Britain', in R.E. Pahl, *On Work*, Oxford: Basil Blackwell.

HAKIM, C. (1988b) 'Self Employment in Britain: a Review of Recent Trends and Current Issues', *Work, Employment and Society*, vol. 2, no.4, December, pp. 421–50.

HAKIM, C. (1989) 'Identifying Fast Growth in Small Firms', *Employment Gazette*, January, London.

HALLDEN, G. (1988) *Parental Belief Systems and Time: Parents' Reflections on Development and Childrearing*, Research Bulletin No. 13, The Institute of Education, University of Stockholm.

HALPERN, M. (1989) *Business Creation by Women: Motivations, Situations and Perspectives*, Brussels: Commission of the European Communities.

HAMMERSLEY, M. and ATKINSON, P. (1983) *Ethnography: Principles in Practice*, London: Tavistock Publications.

HANSSON, C. and LIDEN, K. (1983) *Moscow Women*, New York: Pantheon Books.

HARRIS, M. (1981) *America Now: The Anthropology of a Changing Culture*, New York: Touchstone.

HARRIS, C.C., LEE, R.M., MORRIS, L. (1985) 'Redundancy in Steel: Labour Market Behaviour, Local Social Networks and Domestic Organisation', in B. Roberts, R. Finnegan, D. Gallie (eds), *New Approaches to Economic Life*, Manchester: Manchester University Press.

HART, K. (1978) 'The Economic Basis of Tallensi Social History in the Early Twentieth Century', in G. Dalton (ed.), *Research in Economic Anthropology*, Greenwich, Conn: JAI Press.

HART, K. (1988) 'Kinship, Contract and Trust: the Economic Organization of Migrants in an African City Slum', in D. Gambetta (ed.), *Trust: Making and Breaking Cooperative Relations*, New York: Basil Blackwell.

HARTMANN, H.I. (1979), 'Capitalism, patriarchy and job segregation by sex', in Z.R. Eisenstein (ed.), *Capitalist Patriarchy*, Monthly Review Press, New York.

HAYSTEAD, J., HOWARTH, V. and STRACHAN, A. (1980) *Pre-school Education and Care*, Edinburgh: Hodder & Stoughton.

HENRY, S. (ed.) (1981) *Can I have it in Cash?*, London: Astragal Books

HERTZ, L (1986) *The Business Amazons: the Most Successful Women in Business*, London: Methuen.

HIRSCHMAN, A.O. (1988) 'Rival Interpretations of Market Society: Civilizing, Destructive or Feeble?', in G. Dalton (ed.), *Journal of Economic Literature*, vol. 20, pp. 1463–84.

HORNBY, W. (1958) *Factories and Plant*, London: HMSO and Longmans, Green.

HOWE, E. (1988) Introductory Address to Business in the Community's Initiative on Women's Economic Development, County Hall, Preston, 24 November 1988.

HUNT, A. S. (1968) *Survey of Women's Employment*, London: HMSO.
HUNT, A. (ed.) (1988) *Women and Paid Work – Issues of Equality*, London: Macmillan.
HURSTFIELD, J. (1987) *Part-timers under Pressure – paying the price of flexibility*, London, Low Pay Unit.
HUWS, U. (1984) *The New Homeworkers: New Technology and the Changing Location of White Collar Work*, London, Low Pay Unit.
HUWS, U., HURSTFIELD, J. and HOLTMAAT, R. (1990) *What Price Flexibility? The Casualisation of Women's Employment*, London, Low Pay Unit.
INMAN, P. (1957) *Labour in the Munitions Industries*, London: HMSO and Longmans, Green.
JENKINS, R (1988) 'Discrimination and Equal Employment', in D. Gallie (ed.), *Employment in Britain*, Oxford: Blackwell.
JENKINS, R., BRYMAN, A., FORD, J. F., KEIL, T. and BEARDS-WORTH, A. (1983) 'Information in the Labour Market: The Impact of the Recession', *Sociology*, vol. 17, no. 2, pp 260–8.
JENSON, J. (1986) 'Gender and Reproduction: or Babies and the State', *Studies in Political Economy*, vol. 20, pp. 9–46.
JENSON, J. (1988) 'The Limits of "and the" Discourse: French Women as Marginal Workers', in J. Jenson, E. Hagen and C. Reddy (eds), *Feminisation of the Labour Force*, Cambridge: Polity, pp. 155–72.
JENSON, J., HAGEN, E. and REDDY, C. (eds) (1988), *Feminisation of the Labour Force, Paradoxes and Promises*, Cambridge: Polity Press.
JEPHCOTT, P., with Seear, N., and Smith, J. (1962) *Married Women Working* London: Allen & Unwin.
JOSHI, H. (1984) '*Women's Participation in Paid Work: A Further Analysis of the Women and Employment Survey* Department of Employment Research Paper No 46, London: HMSO.
JOSHI, H. (1987) 'The Cost of Caring', in C. Glendinning and J. Miller (eds), *Women and Poverty in Britain*, Brighton, Sussex: Harvester Press.
JOSHI, H. and OWEN, S. (1987) 'How Long is a Piece of Elastic? The Measurement of Female Activity Rates in British Censuses, 1951–1981', *Cambridge Journal of Economics*, 11.
KAPFERER, B. (ed.) (1976) *Transaction and Meaning*, Philadelphia: Institute for the Study of Human Issues.
KAPFERER, B. (1987) 'The Anthropology of Max Gluckman', in B. Kapferer (ed.), *Power, Process and Transformation: Essays in the Memory of Max Gluckman, Social Analysis: Journal of Cultural and Social Practices*, Special Issue Series No. 22, pp. 3–21.
LAND, H. (1983) 'Poverty and Gender: The Distribution of Resources within the Family', in M. Brown (ed.), *The Structure of Disadvantage*, London: Heinmann.
LAND, H. (1986) 'The Unwelcome Impact of Social Policies on Women in the Labour Market', Paper given to the Conference on Work and Politics: the Feminisation of the Labour Force, Harvard University Center for European Studies.
LANE, C. (1989) *Management and Labour in Europe: the Industrial Enterprise in Germany, Britain and France*, Aldershot: Edward Elger.

LAPIDUS, G. W. (ed.), (1982) *Women, Work and Family in the Soviet Union*, London: M.E. Sharpe.

LAWSON, A. (1989) *Adultery: An Analysis of Love and Betrayal*, Oxford: Basil Blackwell.

LAYARD, R., PIACHAUD, D. and STEWART, M. (1978) *The Causes of Poverty*, London: HMSO.

LEONARD, D. and SPEAKMAN, M. A. (1983) *Changing Experience of Women*, Open University Press, Units 9–16.

LOPATA, H. Z., MILLER, C. and BARNEWOLT, D. (1986) *City Women in America*, New York: Praeger.

LUKER, K. (1984) *Abortion and the Politics of Motherhood*, Berkley: University of California Press.

M.S.S.P.S. (1989) *Documents statistiques: Activité de la protection maternelle et infantile au cours de l'année 1987*, Paris: Service des Statistiques des Etudes et des Systèmes d'Information, No. 68.

MACKINTOSH, M. (1988) 'Domestic labour and the household', in R.E. Pahl (ed.), *On Work*, Oxford: Basil Blackwell.

MARSDEN, D. (1987), 'Collective Bargaining and Industrial Adjustment in Britain, France, Italy and West Germany', in F. Duchene and G. Shepherd (eds), *Managing Industrial Change in Europe*, London: Frances Pinter.

MARSDEN, D. (1989), 'Institutions and Labour Mobility: Occupational Internal Labour Markets in Britain, France, Italy and West Germany', in R. Binnetta and C. Dell Aringa (eds), *Markets, Institutions and Cooperation*, London: Macmillan.

MARSHALL, G. (1984) 'On the Sociology of Women's Unemployment, its Neglect and Significance', *Sociological Review*, vol. 32, no. 2, pp. 235–9.

MARTIN, J. and ROBERTS, C. (1984) *Women and Employment: A Lifetime Perspective*, The Report of the 1980 DE/OPCS Women and Employment Survey, London: HMSO.

MARWICK, A. (1968) *Britain in the Century of Total War. War, Peace and Social Change*, London: The Bodley Head.

MARWICK, A. (1974) *War and Social Change in the Twentieth Century*, London: Macmillan.

MASON, K., CZAJKA, J. and ARBER, S. (1976) 'Change in Women's Sex-Role Attitudes 1964–1974', *American Sociological Review*, vol. 41, pp. 573–96.

MASON, K. and YU-HSIA LU (1988) 'Attitudes Towards Women's Familial Roles: Changes in the United States 1977–1985', *Gender and Society*, vol. 2, pp. 39–57.

MATTERA, P. (1985) *Off The Books*, London: Pluto.

McINTOSH, M. (1979) 'The Welfare State and the Needs of the Dependent Family', in S. Burman (ed.), *Fit Work for Women*, London: Croom Helm, pp. 153–72.

McKEE, L. and BELL, C. (1985) 'Marital and Family Relations in Times of Male Unemployment', in B. Roberts, R. Finnegan and D. Gallie (eds), *New Approaches to Economic Life*, Manchester: Manchester University Press.

MIDDLETON, C. (1988) 'The Familiar Fate of the *Famulae*: Gender Divisions in the History of Wage Labour', in R. E. Pahl (ed.), *On Work*, Oxford: Basil Blackwell.

MIHALISKO, K. (1989) 'Women Workers and Perestroika in the Ukraine and Belorussia – a Problematic Relationship Unfolds', *Report on the USSR*, vol. 2, no. 15, pp. 30–3.

MILLER, S. M. (1975) 'Notes on Neo Capitalism', *Theory and Society*, vol. 2.

MINCER, J. (1985) 'Intercountry Comparisons of Labour Force Trends and of Related Developments: an Overview', *Journal of Labour Economics*, vol 3, no. 1, part 2, pp. S1–S32.

MINGIONE, E. (1988) 'Work and Informal Activities in Urban Southern Italy', in R. E. Pahl (ed.), *On Work*, Oxford: Basil Blackwell.

MINISTRY OF LABOUR (1943) *Women in Shipbuilding*, London: Ministry of Labour and National Service.

MITCHELL, J. (1969) *Social Networks in Urban Situations: Analysis of Personal Relationships in Central African Towns*, New York: Humanities Press.

MITTER, S (1986) 'Industrial Restructuring and Manufacturing Homework: Immigrant Women in the UK Clothing Industry', *Capital and Class*, vol. 27, pp 37–81.

MOROKVASIC-MULLER, M. (1988) *Minority and Immigrant Women in Self-Employment and Business in France, Great Britain, Italy, Portugal and the BRD*, Paris: Centre National de la Recherche Scientifique.

MORRIS, L. (1985a) 'Redundancy and Patterns of Household Finances', *Sociological Review*, vol. 32, pp. 492–533.

MORRIS, L. (1985b) 'Local Social Networks and Domestic Organisation', *Sociological Review*, vol. 33, pp 327–342.

MORRIS, L. (1990) *The Workings of the Household*, Cambridge: Polity Press.

MORRIS, L. D. and RUANE, S. (1989) *Household Finance Management and the Labour Market*, Aldershot: Gower.

MOSS, P. (1988) *Childcare and Equality of Opportunity: Consolidated Report to the European Commission, Final version*, Brussels: Commission of the European Communities, Directorate-General Employment, Social Affairs and Education.

MOYLAN, S., MILLAR, J. and DAVIES, R. (1984) *For Richer, For Poorer? DHSS Cohort Study of Unemployed Men*, London: HMSO.

NELSON, M. K. (1988) 'Providing Family Day Care: an Analysis of Home-based Work', *Social Problems*, vol. 35, no.1, pp. 78–94.

Newsweek (1986) 'Feminism's Identity Crisis', 31 March, pp. 58–9.

NOVIKOVA, E. E., IAZYKOVA, N. S. and IANKOVA, Z. A. (1982) 'Women's Work and the Family', in G. W. Lapidus (ed.), *Women, Work and Family*, Armonk, New York: M. E. Sharpe, pp. 165–90.

NOVIKOVA, E. E., MILOVA, O. L. and ZALIUBOVSKAIA, E. V. (1989) 'Modern Women at Work and at Home: A Sociopsychological Study', *Soviet Sociology*, vol. 28, no. 5, pp. 87–101.

O'CONNOR, J. and RUDDLE, H. (1988) *Growing Concerns: A Study of Growth Oriented Women Entrepreneurs*, Dublin: Industrial Development Authority.

OAKLEY, A (1974) *The Sociology of Housework*, Oxford: Martin Robertson.

OAKLEY, A. (1982) *Subject Women*, Glasgow: Fontana Paperbacks.

OFFE, C. (1985) *Disorganised Capitalism: Contemporary Transformations of Work and Politics*, Cambridge: Polity Press.

OPCS (1989) *General Household Survey 1986*, London: HMSO, Table 6.24.
OPPENHEIMER, V. (1982) *Work and the Family: A Study in Social Demography*, New York: Academic Press.
OSTERUD, N. (1988) 'Gender Relations in the Process of Capitalist Industrialization: towards a Bifocal Perspective', *Society for the Study of Labour History Bulletin*, vol. 54, no. 10, pp. 12.
PAHL, J. (1982) 'Patterns of Money Management within Marriage', *Journal of Social Policy*, vol. 9, no. 3, pp. 313–35.
PAHL, J. (1983) 'The Allocation of Money and the Structuring of Inequality within Marriage', *Sociological Review*, vol. 31, no. 2, pp. 237–62.
PAHL, J. (1984) 'The Allocation of Money within the Household', in M. Freeman (ed.), *The State, the Law and the Family*, London: Tavistock Publications , pp. 36–50.
PAHL, J. (1987) 'Earning, Sharing, Spending: Married couples and their Money', in G. Parker and R. Walker (eds), *Money Matters*, London: Sage.
PAHL, J. (1989) *Money and Marriage*, London: Macmillan.
PAHL, R. (1984) *Divisions of Labour*, Oxford: Blackwell.
PAHL, R. E. (ed.) (1988) *On Work*, Oxford: Basil Blackwell.
PANKRATOVA, M. (1988) 'The Angry Woman Wants Change'. Interview by Natalya Kraminova, *Moscow News*, 19 June.
PARKER, H.M.D. (1957) *Manpower. A Study of Wartime Policy and Administration*, London: HMSO and Longmans, Green.
PAUKERT, L. (1984) *The Employment and Unemployment of Women in OECD Countries*, Paris: OECD.
PHILIPSON, G. (1988) *Aycliffe and Peterlee New Towns 1946–1988*, Cambridge: Publications for Companies.
POLAND, F. and STANLEY, L. (1989) 'Doing Feminist Ethnography in Rochdale', *Studies in Sexual Politics*, No. 24, Manchester University Sociology Department.
POLLARD, A. P. (1990) *USSR Facts and Figures Annual*, vol. 13, Gulf Breeze, Florida: Academic International Press.
POLLERT, A. (1988) 'Dismantling Flexibility', *Capital and Class*, no. 34, pp. 42–76.
PRUS, R. (1985) 'Price-setting as Social Activity: Defining Price, Value and Profit in the Marketplace', *Urban Life*, vol. 14, no. 1, pp. 54–94.
PRUS, R. (1987) 'Developing Loyalty: Fostering Purchasing Relationships in the Marketplace', *Urban Life*, vol. 15, nos 3 and 4, pp. 331–66.
PULKINGHAM, J (1989) 'From Public Provision to Privatisation: The Crisis in Welfare Reassessed', *Sociology*, vol. 23, no. 3, pp 387–407.
PURCELL, K., WOOD, S., WATON, A., and ALLEN, S. (eds) (1986) *The Changing Experience of Employment: Restructuring and Recession*, London: Macmillan.
RADLOFF, L. (1975) 'Sex Differences in Depression', *Sex Roles*, vol. 1, no. 3, pp. 249–65.
RAINNIE, R (1985) 'Small Firms, Big Problems: The Political Economy of Small Businesses', *Capital and Class*, vol. 25, pp. 140–68.
RAMAZANOGLU, C. (1989) *Feminism and the Contradictions of Oppression*, London: Routledge.

RAPOPORT, R. and RAPOPORT, R. (1976) *Dual Career Families Re-Examined*, Oxford: Martin Robertson.

RAPOPORT, R. and RAPOPORT, R. (eds) (1978) *Working Couples*, London: Routledge & Kegan Paul.

REDCLIFT, N. (1988) 'Gender, accumulation and the labour process', in R. E. Pahl (ed.), *On Work*, Oxford: Basil Blackwell.

REID, M. G. (1934) *Economics of Household Production*, New York: Wiley.

ROSE, P. (1985) *Parallel Lives: Five Victorian Marriages*, Harmondsworth: Penguin.

RUBERY, J. (ed.) (1988), *Women and Recession*, London: Routledge & Kegan Paul.

RUGGIE, M. (1988), 'Gender, Work and Social Progress: Some Consequences of Interest Aggregation in Sweden', in J. Jenson *et al.*, *Feminisation of the Labour Force*, Cambridge: Polity.

SACKS, M. P. (1988) 'Women, Work and Family in the Soviet Union', in M. P. Sacks and J. G. Pankhurst (eds), *Understanding Soviet Society*, Boston: Unwin Hyman, pp. 71–96.

SASSEN-KOOB, S. (1987) 'Growth and Informalization at the Core: a Preliminary Report on New York City', in J. Feagin and M. P. Smith (eds), *The Capitalist City*, London: Basil Blackwell.

SCASE, R. (1982) 'The Petty Bourgeoisie and Modern Capitalism: a Consideration of Recent Theories', in A. Giddens and G. Mackenzie (eds), *Social Class and the Division of Labour*, Cambridge: Cambridge University Press.

SCASE, R. (ed.) (1989) *Industrial Societies: Crisis and Division in Western Capitalism and State Socialism*, London: Unwin Hyman.

SCHUTZE, Y. (1988) 'The Good Mother: The History of the Normative Model "Mother-Love"', in K. Eckberg and P. E. Mjaavatn (eds), *Growing into a Modern World*. Proceedings of an International Disciplinary Conference on the Life and Development of Children in Modern Society, vol. 1, Trondheim, Norway.

SCOTT, J. (1991) 'Women and the Family', in R. Jowell, S. Witherspoon and L. Brook (eds), *British Social Attitudes: the 7th Report*, Aldershot: Gower.

SECOMBE, W. (1974) 'The Housewife and Her Labour Under Capitalism', *New Left Review*, vol. 83.

SHARLET, R. (1979) *The New Soviet Constitution of 1977: Analysis and Text*, Brunswick: King's Court Communications.

SHARMA, U. (1980) *Women, Work and Property in North-West India*, London: Tavistock.

SIEBER, S. (1974) 'Towards a Theory of Role Accumulations', *American Sociological Review*, vol. 39, pp. 567–78.

SILTANEN, J. (1986) 'Domestic Responsibilities and the Structuring of Employment', in R. Crompton and M. Mann (eds), *Gender and Stratification*, Cambridge: Polity Press.

SILTANEN, J. (1990) 'Social Change and the Measurement of Occupational Segregation by Sex: an Assessment of the Sex Ratio Index', *Work, Employment and Society*, vol. 4, pp. 1–29.

SMITH, D. (1987) *The Everyday World as Problematic*, Northeastern University Press.

SMITH, D. (1988) *The Everyday World as Problematic*, Milton Keynes: Open University Press.
SMITH, P. (1978) 'Domestic Labour and Marx's Theory of Value', in A. Kuhn and A. Wolpe (eds), *Feminism and Materialism*, London: Routledge & Kegan Paul.
STACEY, M. (1986) 'Gender and Stratification', in R. Crompton and M. Mann (eds), *Gender and Stratification*, Cambridge: Polity Press.
STARK, D. (1988) 'Rethinking Internal Labour Markets: New Insights from a Comparative Perspective', in R. E. Pahl (ed.), *On Work*, Oxford: Basil Blackwell.
SUMMERFIELD, P. (1984) *Women Workers in the Second World War: Production and Patriarchy in Conflict*, London: Routledge.
SUMMERFIELD, P. (1989) *Women Workers in the Second World War*, London: Routledge, 2nd edition.
SWAFFORD, M. (1978) 'Sex Differences in Soviet Earnings', *American Sociological Review*, vol. 43, no. 5, pp 657–73.
TAY, A. E. (1972) 'The Status of Women in the Soviet Union', *American Journal of Comparative Law*, vol. 20, no. 4, pp. 662–92.
THOITS, P. (1983) 'Multiple Identities and Psychological Well-Being', *American Sociological Review*, vol. 48, pp. 174–87.
TILLY, L. A. and SCOTT J. W. (1987) *Women, Work and the Family*, London: Methuen, 2nd edition.
TRADES UNION CONGRESS (1985) *Report of the Annual TUC*, London: TUC.
TRAINING AGENCY (1989) *Labour Market Quarterly Report*, November, Sheffield: Employment Department: The Training Agency.
TREIMAN, D. and HARTMANN, H. (eds), (1981) *Women, Work and Wages: Equal Pay For Jobs of Equal Value*, Washington, DC: National Academy Press.
TRUMAN, C. (1986) *Overcoming the Career Break, A Positive Approach*, Sheffield: The Training Agency.
UNIVERSITY GRANTS COMMITTEE (1989) *Report of the Review Committee on Sociology*, London: UGC.
URWIN, C. (1985) 'Constructing Motherhood: the Persuasion of Normal Development', in C. Steedman, C. Urwin and V. Walkerdine (eds), *Language, Gender and Childhood* London: Routledge & Kegan Paul.
VOGLER, C. (1989) 'Labour Market Change and Patterns of Financial Allocation within Households', SCELI Working Paper No. 12, ESRC.
WADEL, C. (1979) 'The Hidden Work of Everyday Life', in S. Wallman (ed.), *The Social Anthropology of Work*, London: BSA and Academic Press.
WAINWRIGHT, H. (1978) 'Women and the Domestic Division of Labour', in P. Abrams (ed.), *Work, Urbanism and Inequality*, London: Weidenfeld & Nicolson.
WALBY, S. (1986) *Patriarchy at Work: Patriarchal and Capitalist Relations in Employment*, Cambridge: Polity.
WALBY, S. (ed.) (1988) *Gender Segregation at Work*, Milton Keynes: Open University Press.
WALBY, S. (1990), *Theorising Patriarchy*, Oxford: Basil Blackwell.

WALBY, S. and BAGGULEY, P. (1990) 'Sex Segregation in Local Labour Markets', *Work, Employment and Society*, vol. 4, pp. 59–81.

WARR, P. and JACKSON, P. (1984) 'Men without Jobs: Some Correlates of Age and Length of Unemployment', *Journal of Occupational Psychology*, vol. 57, pp. 77–85.

WATERS, M. (1989), 'Patriarchy and Virarchy: an Exploration and Reconstruction of Concepts of Masculine Domination', *Sociology*, vol. 23, no. 2, pp. 193–211.

WATKINS, J. and WATKINS, D. (1984) 'The Female Entrepreneur: Background and Determinants of Business Choice – Some British Data', *International Small Business Journal*, vol. 2, no.4, pp. 21–31.

WEST, C. (1982) 'Why Can't a Woman be More Like a Man?', *Work and Occupations*, vol. 9, no. 1, pp. 5–29.

WESTWOOD, S. (1984) *All Day Every Day*, London: Pluto Press.

WILLMOTT, P. (1987) *Friendship Networks and Social Support*, London: Policy Studies Institute.

WITHERSPOON, S. (1988) 'Interim Report: A Woman's Work', in R. Jowell, S. Witherspoon and L. Brook (eds), *British Social Attitudes: the 5th Report*, Aldershot: Gower.

YOUNG, M. and WILLMOTT, P. (1973) *The Symmetrical Family*, Harmondsworth: Penguin.

Author Index

Subject Index

Note: All references are to working women in Britain unless otherwise specified.

achievement, *see under* occupation/
   occupational
age, 3, 4, 93
   Britain and France, 71–2, 76
   Britain, Soviet Union and US, 122
Aycliffe, *see* munitions work

Belfast, 12, 148–61
   unemployment rate, 149, 150
   see also contract cleaners
benefits, *see* child/children; social
   security benefits
breadwinner
   male ideology, 66
   women as, 137–8
British Social Attitudes Surveys, 40
business ownership, 162–74
   see also enterprise

career-break schemes, 110–15
   and demographic change, 104–17
   part-time, flexible and job
     sharing, 111, 112–13
   re-entry and retainer schemes, 111,
     114–15
   value of, 116–17
   working from home, 111, 113–14
   workplace nurseries, 111–12
carers, 8
   and dependent population, 106,
     107, 116, 166, 173
child care, 100
   British and US, 47
   childminders, 56, 84, 85;
     France, 100
   division of labour, 64–5
   educational value, 55

and employment patterns, 84–5, 87
facilities, 3, 56; employers, 2,
   111–12; France, 73–4, 78;
   state, 56
financing, 6, 61, 62
France, 9–10, 84–6, 87, 100
male help, 38, 101
and part-time work, 9
as petty enterprise, 181
policies, 109
relatives, 100–1
United States, 9
usage of, 85
in wartime, 20
and working from home, 114
workplace, 111–12
child/children, 1
   age of: and earnings, 7; and
     employment, 3, 4
   benefit, Britain and France, 101–2
   and downward mobility, 4
   and full-time work, 6
   maternal employment as harmful
     to, 43–5, 46–9, 50, 51, 52
   and mother relationship, 59–60,
     68–9
   see also child care; mothers/
     motherhood
class
   as divisive, 1, 2
   earnings by, 5, 7
   and gendered social policies, 10
   part-time workers by, 5
   see also occupation/occupational
clubs and petty enterprise, 177, 178,
   179, 180, 186, 187, 188
community
   and change, 34

United States, 9
see also employment; feminisation;
  labour; paid work; work

gender roles, 1, 8–9
  attitudes, 8; Britain and USA, 36–
    53; egalitarian, 39, 40–1, 43–
    50, 52; housewives, 49–50, 52;
    and part-time work, 51; and
    women's employment, 49–50
  changes, 38
  and dual earner households, 54
  egalitarian, 38–40
  ideology, 8, 10
  inequalities, 1
  and shipbuilding, 27
  traditional, 38–40; and part-time
    work, 40
General Household Survey (1985–6),
  analysis, 3–4, 5, 7, 168, 169, 170
General Social Survey (US), 39, 42
Germany, 55
glasnost, see Soviet Union
guilt, 60, 68, 172

happiness and work, 44, 45, 48, 50
  and family, 44, 45, 48, 50, 51
home
  selling, 175–88
  working from, 111, 113–14
household, financial management, 58
  and middle-class male
    unemployment, 131–47
housewife/housewives
  as fulfilling, 43, 44, 48, 50, 52, 80
  gender-role attitudes, 49–50, 52
  and unemployed men, 143
human capital theory, 82–3, 87

ideology
  family life, 36, 38, 60
  family wage, 133
  femininity, 132
  gender, 1, 8, 10; and war, 20; in
    workplace, 58
  of male breadwinner, 60, 64, 66
  marriage, 60, 66–7
  motherhood, 1, 8, 9, 59, 60
  and social policies, 8–11

income, household
  attitudes to female contribution,
    44, 48, 49, 50, 51
  and unemployed women, 81
  wives', 60–4; as secondary, 133
  see also money; wages
independence, 33
  and work, 43, 44, 48, 50
inequality
  domestic, 9, 64–8, 70
  gender, 1, 163
  and gender-role attitudes, 36
  and gendered policies, 102
  labour market, 1
  in paid work, 8
  and patriarchy, 90
  Soviet, 124–5, 126, 127
  wages, 5, 167–8; and part-time
    work, 6; and war work, 21
infant mortality, and maternal
  employment, 79
informal work, 11, 13, 148, 150
  motivation for, 155–6
  recruitment, 157–9; consequences
    of, 159–61
  selling, 177–82
  see also contract cleaners;
    enterprise, small
International Social Survey
  Programme (ISSP), 41
Italy, 103

job satisfaction, war work, 24, 25, 26,
  27
  munitions, 30, 31–2
  shipbuilding, 34
job sharing, 111, 113

labour force
  marginalisation, 90, 106
  percentage of women, 3, 89
  profile of wartime, 19
  women in Soviet, 121–6
  see also employment; feminisation;
    work
Labour Force Survey, 72, 91, 97, 170
legislation, 56
  and fragmentation of labour, 171
  maternity, 2, 56, 100